Victorian Literature and Film Adaptation

VICTORIAN
LITERATURE
AND
FILM
ADAPTATION

EDITED BY
ABIGAIL BURNHAM BLOOM
AND MARY SANDERS POLLOCK

CAMBRIA
PRESS

Amherst, New York

Requests for permission should be directed to:
permissions@cambriapress.com, or mailed to:
Cambria Press
20 Northpointe Parkway, Suite 188
Amherst, NY 14228

Library of Congress Cataloging-in-Publication Data

Victorian literature and film adaptation / edited by Abigail Burnham Bloom
and Mary Sanders Pollock.
p. cm.
Includes bibliographical references and index.
Includes filmographies.
ISBN 978-1-60497-786-8
1. Film adaptations—History and criticism. 2. English literature—19th
century—History and criticism. 3. English literature—Film adaptations.
4. Motion pictures and literature. I. Bloom, Abigail Burnham.
II. Pollock, Mary Sanders, 1948-

PN1997.85.V45 2011
791.43'6—dc23

2011040692

In memory of Carter Colwell, who loved movies
—M. S. P.
Deland, Florida

TABLE OF CONTENTS

ACKNOWLEDGMENTS

I am indebted to the administration of Stetson University, especially Provost Elizabeth Paul and Dean of Arts and Sciences Grady Ballenger, for financial support of this project. I thank my department chair, Thomas J. Farrell, for his consistent and active engagement with my scholarship; my colleagues Emily Mieras and Yves Antoine Clemmen for our ongoing discussions of films and film courses; and my students, whose enthusiasm for the movies has inspired me. Finally, I am deeply grateful for the attentive and skillful technical services provided by Cathy Burke and Ann Burlin.

—M. S. P.

VICTORIAN
LITERATURE
AND
FILM
ADAPTATION

Introduction

REFRAMING THE VICTORIANS

Thomas Leitch

Victorian Literature and Film Adaptation is only the most recent in
a long line of such volumes as *The English Novel and the Movies*,
The Classic Novel from Page to Screen, *Victorian Afterlife*, and *Film/
Literature/Heritage*—not to mention associated entries such as *The
Classic American Novel and the Movies*, *Eighteenth-Century Fiction on
Screen*, and *Henry James Goes to the Movies*. Such a weighty book-
shelf suggests not only an enduring interest in adaptation but also a more
specific focus on cinematic treatments of Victorian novels. So powerful
is the attraction of this subject, in fact, that Simone Murray has com-
plained about the predominance in adaptation studies of films based
on "the nineteenth-century and Modernist Anglophone literary canon"
and urged for greater attention to adaptations of "contemporary *literary
fiction*" instead (7).

The reasons for the emphasis on Victorian adaptations date to the
days of silent film, whose obvious roots in Victorian fiction go beyond
the often stilted dialogue and expository intertitles of early adaptations

and the obligatory sequences such as the malevolent threat, the eleventh-hour rescue, and the happy-ending fadeout. Numberless commentators on silent adaptations have noted the similarity between two touchstones of novelistic and cinematic mimesis. In his 1897 preface to *The Nigger of the "Narcissus,"* Joseph Conrad wrote, "My task which I am trying to achieve is, by the power of the written word, to make you hear, to make you feel—it is, before all, to make you *see!*" (3: x). Sixteen years later, D. W. Griffith echoed Conrad: "The task I'm trying to achieve is above all to make you see" (qtd. in Jacobs, 119). Movies and novels, as commentators from George Bluestone to Brian McFarlane have argued, share the primary charge of helping their audience envision imaginary worlds.

Ever since synchronized sound upended the representational conventions that were established by silent films, "[m]ainstream cinema has owed much of its popularity to representational tendencies it shares with the nineteenth-century English novel" (McFarlane, viii). These affinities stem from early cinema's "more or less blatant appropriation of the themes and content of the nineteenth-century bourgeois novel" (Cohen, 4). Silent films borrowed their themes, tropes, and conventions from neither modernist classics nor novels of the American renaissance but from realistic, bourgeois nineteenth-century English novels such as *Pride and Prejudice*, *Middlemarch*, and *Barchester Towers*. According to Sergei Eisenstein, they were especially indebted to the work of Charles Dickens, which "bore the same relation to [his readers] that the film bears to the same strata in our time" (206).

More recent critics have questioned or refined the allegedly Dickensian foundations of cinema. Keith Cohen announces that the analogy Eisenstein draws between Dickens's and Griffith's use of specific details in novelistic or cinematic montage "has always seemed weak to me" (4). Rick Altman claims more generally that the figure of Dickens provided "a spuriously pivotal function in discussions about the relation between the cinema and the novel" (330). Kamilla Elliott attacks historical models that assume "not simply that the nineteenth-century novel influenced western film, but that in some sense it *became* film, while the modern novel evolved in a different direction" (3). Tom Gunning, proposing a very different narrative of cinema's origins, contends that many early films were based on "an aesthetic of astonishment" whose audience "does not get lost in a fictional world and its drama, but remains aware of the act of looking, the excitement of curiosity and its fulfillment" (736, 743).

Gunning's "cinema of attractions" (742), which emphasizes the carnival appeal of powerful individual images and sequences over sustained narrative, goes a long way toward explaining why, despite the alleged influence of the nineteenth-century English novel on early film, there is no silent *Barchester Towers*, no silent *Middlemarch*, and no silent *Pride and Prejudice*. Early cinema drew on Victorian fiction very selectively. The Internet Movie Database (http://www.imdb.com) lists seventy-nine silent adaptations of Charles Dickens (from the 1897 *Death of Nancy Sikes* to fourteen other adaptations of *Oliver Twist*), sixteen of George Eliot (including six of *Silas Marner*), seven of William Makepeace Thackeray (four of *Vanity Fair*), four of Thomas Hardy (two of *Tess of the D'Urbervilles*), one of George Meredith (*Diana of the Crossways*), and none of Anthony Trollope. Not one of these writers' novels was adapted as often by silent filmmakers as *East Lynne*, which was filmed sixteen times between 1902 and 1925. And, none of these authors could match the cumulative record of Sir Arthur Conan Doyle, who leads the field with eighty silent adaptations, seventy-five of them chronicling the adventures of Sherlock Holmes.

The forms and themes of Victorian novels certainly had a pronounced impact on early cinema. But the case of Dickens suggests that their most immediate contributions were quite different from the ones Eisenstein assumes. Victorian novels provided attractions, to use Gunning's term, that could be readily excerpted for anthology films such as *Tense Moments with Great Authors* (1922). *Tense Moments* includes four scenes from Dickens along with episodes from Thackeray, George du Maurier, Victor Hugo, Alphonse Daudet, and Mrs. Henry Wood (*East Lynne*, of course). It also features strong, larger-than-life figures such as Becky Sharp and Sherlock Holmes, pathetic victims such as Nancy Sikes and Tiny Tim, and the sentimentally moralizing melodrama that has long been associated with Dickens's Christmas books and recreated by Griffith. Once *The Birth of a Nation* (1915) and *Intolerance* (1916) had shown how epic social canvases could be integrated with telling details presented in expressive close-up, other filmmakers soon followed Griffith's path. However, many of the top-grossing Hollywood films in the decade that followed—*20,000 Leagues under the Sea* (1916), *The Ten Commandments* (1923), *The Covered Wagon* (1923), and *Ben-Hur: A Tale of the Christ* (1925)—emphasize spectacular attractions over psychological penetration or social analysis. Of the most successful films of the period, only *The Four Horsemen of the Apocalypse* (1921), *The Big Parade* (1925), and Griffith's own *Way Down East* (1920) follow anything like a neo-Victorian trajectory.

The arrival of synchronized sound and the quest of producers such as David O. Selznick for the cachet and the market appeal that were offered by literary sources produced adaptations of *David Copperfield* (1935) and *Pride and Prejudice* (1940) alongside *Dracula* (1931) and *Dr. Jekyll and Mr. Hyde* (1931). After these developments, the aesthetic of the dialogue-driven synch-sound feature merged more closely with that of the bourgeois realism of the nineteenth-century English novel. Even here, however, important distinctions should be made among the several legacies that nineteenth-century English novels left twentieth-century cinema. As Kamilla Elliott puts it,

> The Victorian novel looms monolithic: first, as the link pin between poetry and painting and novel and film debates; second, as film's most immediate and loudly proclaimed parent; third, as a particularly problematic, anachronistic locus of cinematic novel analogies; and fourth, as a body of literature offering multiple adaptations of single novels. (7)

Most earlier collections on the subject, focusing on this last legacy—a repository of specific stories such as *Frankenstein, A Christmas Carol,* and the adventures of Sherlock Holmes as widely adapted texts—share the project announced by Erica Sheen: to "take the question of fidelity as their primary critical point of reference" (2). How closely, they ask, do (or can, or should) cinematic adaptations recreate either particular textual features or general effects produced by the literary texts they are adapting?

Even to pose this question involves several foundational assumptions. First, as Laura Carroll puts it in the chapter she has coauthored in the present volume, adaptation is "a fundamentally binary textual system, involving a book and a film pair standing in a simple and commonsensical relation of an original and a copy" (p. 227). Second, despite Bluestone's oft-quoted warning that "[i]t is as fruitless to say that film A is better or worse than novel B as it is to pronounce Wright's Johnson's Wax Building better or worse than Tchaikowsky's *Swan Lake*" (5–6), it is reasonable to assume that there are common terms for comparing stories that are presented in modes as different as books and movies. Third, "The rhetoric of fiction is simply not the rhetoric of film, and it's in finding analogous strategies whereby the one achieves the effects of the other that the greatest challenge of adaptation lies" (Boyum, 81). Fourth, only "a structurally constrained model of analogy" in which "films locate analogous, already complete signs in their own lexicons that approximate literary signs" (Elliott, 4) can account for the otherwise unaccountable ability of movies to provide visual (or audiovisual) equivalents of novels. Finally, the books, whether because they are literature or because they are original, provide standards for judging the relative success or failure of their adaptations.

The history of adaptation studies since McFarlane wrote *Novel to Film* has been a story of increasingly sustained assaults on these assumptions. Imelda Whelehan contends that films' ability to beget their own literary offspring in the form of novelizations has "destabilize[d] the tendency to believe that the origin text is of primary importance" (3). Dianne F. Sadoff and John Kucich assemble a collection designed "to historicize postmodern rewritings of Victorian culture" in order "to begin a discussion of postmodernism's privileging of the Victorian as its historical 'other'" (xi). Sarah Cardwell rejects comparative page-to-screen analysis in favor of "a non-comparative, 'generic' approach" whose primary context for analysis is the common features television adaptations of classic novels share with one another (77). Ginette Vincendeau collects a series of essays and reviews adopting just such a generic approach to the "museum aesthetic" of "heritage cinema" whose "concern…is to depict the past, but by celebrating rather than investigating it" (xviii). Elliott, subjecting literalized and structural analogies between avowedly verbal novels and visual films to rewardingly close critique, proposes "looking-glass analogies" as a superior alternative (209). Robert Stam, citing the ubiquity and normality of adaptation, suggests that it was "less an attempted resuscitation of an originary word than a turn in an ongoing dialectical process" (64). Linda Hutcheon, driven by a determination to broaden the field beyond novels and films to the whole range of adaptations, focuses on "the *politics* of intertextuality" that seek to explain how adaptations have been perceived and received "*as adaptations*" (xii, xiv). Simone Murray, responding to the call for "a sociology that takes into account the commercial apparatus, the audience, and the academic culture industry" (Naremore, "Introduction" 10), urges adaptation scholars to redefine their field as "a *material* phenomenon produced by a system of institutional interests and actors" seeking each to maximize their financial returns (Murray, 10).

All of these theorists take such care to distance their own work from the "interminable analyses of individual cases, comparisons between novels and their filmed versions" (Ray, 39), that the persistence of such case studies, including the ones in this volume, seems remarkable. What value does a volume such as this one, whose contributors share precisely the English-studies background that is regarded with such suspicion by recent theories of adaptation, have in the current, presumably more enlightened, climate of the field? Instead of seeking to establish once and for all the textual relations between particular films and their Victorian sources—in particular, the films' success in using medium-specific devices to convey the same effects as the sources' verbal, lexical, and literary devices—they seek to provoke, develop, extend, and resolve more general questions about adaptation, intertextuality, and the continued fascination with the cultural capital that is offered by nineteenth-century English literature and literary culture.

Erica Sheen argues persuasively that classic English novels cast as long a shadow over academic writing on adaptation as they do over specific adaptations themselves because the replacement of individual authors by filmmakers as the producers of socially powerful discourse "effaces the presence of the intellectual in the production system" (7). In a calculated response, "the return of the adapted text to its literary origin reinforces a link [between authors and their works] that the literary field is now unable to maintain on its own terms" (8). This fetishizing of the author reaches a peak in heritage adaptations, but it is common to all adaptations of nineteenth-century novels because the authors who stand behind them, from Jane Austen to Joseph Conrad, are so readily available to be fetishized. Compared to earlier English writers, they benefit from biographies that are better known than those of Samuel Richardson and Laurence Sterne, are more readily assimilated to the idea of a coherent and identifiable career than those of Daniel Defoe and Henry Fielding, and are more intimately bound up with their work—or, at least, are more available for mythologizing in those terms in films such as *Finding Neverland* (2004), *Miss Potter* (2006), *Becoming Jane* (2007), and *Bright Star* (2009).

As Sheen's analysis implies, however, it is not only individual authors but also the ideal figures of the individual author and the intellectual that scholarly attention to adaptation valorizes. Thus, Victorian novelists and their novels have remained as pivotal for adaptation theorists as for filmmakers. *Tristram Shandy: A Cock and Bull Story* (2005) treats Sterne's novel as a frankly unfilmable challenge. But Victorian novels, with their well-ordered stories of rich and varied characters set against a believable social canvas, seem ripe for adaptation. At the same time, their often prodigious length, density of incident, accretion of detail, and psychological penetration all pose what one might call exemplary challenges to cinematic adaptation, particularly compared to the outrageous, one-of-a-kind challenges that are offered by the likes of *Tristram Shandy*. If Victorian culture, as Sadoff and Kucich's contributors agree, is postmodernism's designated other, and if nineteenth-century novelists, following Sheen's analysis, provide unrivaled opportunities for adaptations to valorize the fading power of the figures of the author and the intellectual, then Victorian novels are the other against which the adaptation industry has chosen to define itself.

A leading interest shared by the contributors to the present volume is expanding both the canon and the image of Victorian fiction. They extend the field by redefining the Victorian novel as including bourgeois realist English novels of the long nineteenth century, from Jane Austen and Sir Walter Scott to Joseph Conrad.

The contrasting earlier histories of Austen and Scott in adaptation studies are especially instructive. Even though Scott's works, which are as weighty as any shelf of Victorian novels, have been filmed at least sixty-three times, he has never been claimed by Victorianists and continues to be neglected by adaptation scholars. Janet Sorenson's essay on Michael Caton-Jones's 1995 film adaptation of *Rob Roy* tellingly situates it within a context of eighteenth-century costume adaptations, whose emphasis on sumptuous surfaces it "confronts" in order "to reinscribe the eighteenth century within a narrative of British national heritage" (197). Just as Scott's choice of historical subjects for his romances seems to place him outside the mainstream of nineteenth-century English fiction, Sorenson places the 1995 film adaptation of *Rob Roy* in dialogue with "the 'long' eighteenth century" (192), not the long Victorian period.

Austen has been treated quite differently. The signs of her relations to her Victorian cousins, from the outrage with which Austen scholars continue to greet MGM's Victorian-flavored *Pride and Prejudice* (1940) to the bloodthirsty rivalry between Austen and Charlotte Brontë in Michael Thomas Ford's contemporary vampire farce *Jane Bites Back*, would seem to suggest opposition rather than assimilation. But even though she shares with Scott a great, proto-Victorian subject, the rise of the English bourgeoisie, Austen's emphasis on modern manners, language, and social pressures has made her seem at once more prophetically modern—it is hard to imagine the Walter Scott equivalent of *Clueless*—and more congenial to the kind of analysis that was developed in response to the Victorians. Thus, it is eminently logical that the present volume includes two chapters on Austen adaptations

(Michael Eberle-Sinatra's reexamination of *Emma* in the light of *Clueless* and a discussion of the problems of teaching *Persuasion* and its 1995 film adaptation by Laura Carroll, Christopher Palmer, Sue Thomas, and Rebecca Waese) and one on a Conrad adaptation (Gene M. Moore's analysis of Patrice Chéreau's *Gabrielle* [2005] as an adaptation of Conrad's story "The Return").

Extending the period of Victorian fiction by pushing its temporal boundaries outward to include Austen, who died twenty years before Victoria ascended the throne, and Conrad, all of whose works through *Lord Jim* could be described as technically Victorian, is not the only way of enlarging the period's scope. Several contributors expand Victorian fiction generically as including drama and poetry. Jean-Marie Lecomte considers the ways in which Ernst Lubitsch's celebrated 1925 silent adaptation of *Lady Windermere's Fan* uses cinematic devices to compensate for the lack of Oscar Wilde's epigrammatic dialogue, not one line of which survives in Julien Josephson's screenplay. Mary Sanders Pollock's chapter on *The Sweet Hereafter* is still more adventurous in claiming Atom Egoyan's 1997 film as a Victorian adaptation. She acknowledges that Russell Banks's novel *The Sweet Hereafter* provides the film's primary source material. However, Pollock focuses on the ways in which the film is informed by Robert Browning's 1842 poem "The Pied Piper of Hamelin; A Child's Story," which one of the film's main characters is repeatedly shown reading in the edition illustrated by Kate Greenaway. The effect is not only to enlarge Victorian fiction to include narrative poetry and illustration but to indicate the importance of sources that may be remote in time, place, and genre from the novel that is listed in the film's credit sequence. In considering the sources on which the 1974 television miniseries *The Pallisers* draws, Ellen Moody casts an even wider net and discovers borrowings from several Trollope novels outside the Palliser sextet, along with echoes of George Meredith, Honoré de Balzac, Alfred Lord Tennyson, Algernon Charles Swinburne, Lord Byron, William Shakespeare, and the Bible.

A final aspect of this expansion is to redefine the nexus of Victorian fiction away from triple-decker social anatomies such as *Dombey and*

Son and *The Way We Live Now* toward more sensationalistic writers such as Mary Wollstonecraft Shelley, Robert Louis Stevenson, Bram Stoker, and Arthur Conan Doyle. The result has been not so much a shift from major to minor writers as a redefinition of "major." Instead of being major because they are long, dense, self-serious novels by prolific authors, the Victorian properties that are now most often studied for their contributions to the cinema are "*major* in the sense that they have been and remain the subject of substantial critical work" (Palmer, 6). Adaptation theorists have always been drawn to the sensationalistic side of Dickens, even though they have been reluctant to acknowledge the importance of that sensationalism in defining the legacy of Victorian fiction (Altman, 330). Like Austen's novels, *Frankenstein* has long been claimed for the Victorian period. So have Rudyard Kipling's parables and critiques of English colonialism abroad. More frankly escapist writers such as H. Rider Haggard, however, for years written out of the Victorian canon as being barely a step above what Steven Marcus calls "the other Victorians," have only recently begun to be welcomed back into the tent, along with vampire tales such as *Dracula*, detective stories such as *The Hound of the Baskervilles*, and shilling shockers such as *Strange Case of Dr. Jekyll and Mr. Hyde*. This volume adopts just such a comprehensive approach by including Thomas Leitch's chapter on Dr. Jekyll and Mr. Hyde, Tamara S. Wagner's chapter on Sherlock Holmes, and Sarah J. Heidt's chapter on *Dracula*. The result is to present a more decentered Victorian culture more deeply penetrated by the other Victorians, whose renewed prominence is largely a product of cinema's incessant reimagining of the Victorians and their legacy.

There would be little point to expanding the Victorian canon, however, if the new entries did not yield new insights. Some of these insights are textual and tactical, such as Lecomte's examination of the ways that Lubitsch's use of space in *Lady Windermere's Fan* mediates the high-brow theatrical tradition and the broader tradition of silent film comedy, both of which inform his adaptation. For Lubitsch as for Wilde, "style is all" (Lecomte, p. 60). Therefore, his goal is not to find a cinematic equivalent for every one of Wilde's notoriously unadaptable epigrams but to make his film epigrammatic in a more pervasive sense, even if his primary means of doing so involve acting, blocking, and camerawork rather than dialogue. It might be argued, of course, that in relying so heavily on techniques associated with visual exposition, Lubitsch risks the possibility that a large portion of the audience will overlook their wit (how Wilde makes his points) in the process of focusing on their exposition (what points are being made). But, as Lecomte makes clear in his analysis of Lubitsch's handling of Lady Windermere's discovery of her husband's payments to Mrs. Erlynne, Wilde's celebrated dialogue in the play is more often expository than epigrammatic itself.

Other contributors use adaptations to provoke a fresh look at their forebears. Wagner's call for a critical "re-viewing" of literary legacies (p. 206) provides a persuasive defense of reading nineteenth-century novels through twentieth- or twenty-first-century movies. Even if it were not true, as many observers have noted, that Hollywood adaptations have gone far to define and extend the influence of Victorian fiction and culture, modern readers, unable to be Victorian readers, would still be obliged to read Dickens and Hardy through modern lenses—if not those of contemporary cinema, then those of contemporary fiction or journalism.

Nothing but a superstitious deference to Austen could prevent Michael Eberle-Sinatra from asking whether, because Christian Stovitz (Justin Walker) is clearly coded as gay in *Clueless*, Frank Churchill, the false suitor of Emma Woodhouse on whom Christian is based, might be gay as well. As Eberle-Sinatra acknowledges, such an investigation is "inconclusive by nature" (p. 130) because there is no realistic possibility of uncovering hard evidence that Frank is either homosexual or heterosexual in Austen's novel. In taking off from Jill Heydt-Stevenson's influential analysis of Austen's presentation of sexual politics, however, Eberle-Sinatra not only pries open the once-forbidden topic of Frank's sexual orientation but also raises provocative questions that arise from the novel's *lack* of obvious sexual coding, which it would be fallacious to read as imposing a uniform code of unexceptionable heterosexuality throughout.

Louise McDonald also uses a film adaptation to reinterpret its nominal source, reading the mordant pessimism that characterizes Stanley

Kubrick's *Barry Lyndon* (1975) back into Thackeray's novel, in which she finds not merely a crudely satiric treatment of Barry's villainy in the broad manner of Fielding's *Jonathan Wild* but a rigorous deconstruction of Enlightenment moral positivism. The elegiac cultural critique that marks Kubrick's adaptation, she argues, is present in Thackeray's novel, but the continuities between the two have been obscured by the fact that the film focuses on an individual transgressor and the novel focuses on a dysfunctional social system. The attempt to rescue the nineteenth-century novels that have engendered apparently more adventurous film adaptations requires Eberle-Sinatra and McDonald, following Sarah Cardwell, to break with the traditional practice of reading the novels as sources to which the films owe due respect and instead treat both novels and films with equal respect.

Other contributions question more sharply the continuing value of one-one-one comparisons of novels and films in the light of the criticism many adaptation scholars have recently leveled against such studies. Different chapters announce sharply differing positions. Ellen Moody considers a wide range of influences on *The Pallisers* and acutely observes that the recent films that are most faithful to Trollope's overarching view of the relations between individual actions and social culture are not based on Trollope novels. She concludes by defending the primacy of the recognized author of eponymous source texts of films as the only basis for a practical, feasible methodology of "close comparative reading" (p. 169). Christopher Palmer, by contrast, urges that in teaching adaptations, "the literary texts are not [to be] treated simply as transparent preludes to the films" (p. 226).

Whichever positions they take on the relations between adaptations and their eponymous source texts, all of the contributors agree that one-to-one studies, even if they offer limited frameworks for everything adaptation studies might want to say, can provide focal points for more general arguments by reframing Victorian fiction and Victorian culture. They remind one as well that even the allegedly original Victorian classics have been framed—packaged and presented in many ways, but never unframed—from their first appearances. Of all the contributors,

Gene M. Moore considers the business of reframing most literally in focusing on the proscription against "making scenes" in "The Return" and *Gabrielle*. Moore observes the very different force of that proscription once the film introduces potential witnesses to those scenes, who both provide a stage audience for the characters' interior conflicts and emphasize the inherent theatricality, the incessant tendency toward self-framing, Alvan Hervey displays even when he is alone. Like Eberle-Sinatra, Moore leaves several crucial questions open. Why are the scenes in front of Chéreau's servant witnesses more embarrassing than Conrad's tête-à-têtes? Does the audience's discomfort arise more from the possibility of exposure or out of respect for the servants' sensibilities? In what ways are the servants, who are obliged to listen to the scenes without having the status or power to intervene by telling their employers what they think, figures for the audience of Chéreau's film or for films in general? Yet, Moore's analysis invites audience members to reconsider their relation to the intimate scenes that are cinema's stock in trade in ways that are more specific and nuanced than any general theory of the pleasures of cinematic voyeurism could provide.

Mary Sanders Pollock answers Laura Carroll's call for a third text (p. 227) that can destabilize the iron binary of source novel and film adaptation by directing attention away from *The Sweet Hereafter* to "The Pied Piper of Hamelin" as a formative influence on Atom Egoyan's film. Supplementing Russell Banks with Robert Browning and Kate Greenaway, his early illustrator, not only enlarges the field of sources but also redirects attention to the kinds of work the adaptation is actually doing. Instead of considering the adaptation of particular sources, Pollock focuses on the adaptation of particular techniques, such as shifting points of view, treating them as transmedial phenomena rather than the properties of any single medium. In their different ways, Carroll and Pollock demonstrate that book-to-film analyses, though they are poor masters for adaptation study, make excellent servants if they are consciously chosen and productively applied.

In addition to providing a fresh look at specific Victorian novels, the contributors suggest several ways in which adaptation study can move scholars to reconsider, reconceptualize, and reorder nineteenth-century studies. To begin with the simplest of these changes, this volume continues a tendency in recent collections to move away from organizing their contents according to the publication dates of the novels that are under adaptation. Although, as R. Barton Palmer points out, such a sequential organization "has the not inconsiderable virtue of offering literature teachers a familiar body of fiction with which to work" (4), it also inscribes those teachers as the primary audience for collections of essays on adaptation. And, by encouraging these teachers to approach adaptations in the publication sequence of their sources, it insinuates adaptations and adaptation study into historical period courses on literature as glosses on or posthumous complications in the reception of the sources themselves, which remain primary. This organizational principle, which assimilates adaptation study to literary history, persists in Robert Stam and Alessandra Raengo's *Literature and Film* (2005). The most obvious alternative, organizing a collection of adaptation case studies according to the release dates of the adaptations, as Stam and Raengo do in *A Companion to Literature and Film* (2004), simply substitutes cinema history for literary history. The present collection, following a trail that was blazed by Deborah Cartmell and Imelda Whelehan's *Adaptations: From Text to Screen, Screen to Text* but is still decidedly under construction, is organized according to the broadly different approaches its contributors take toward the process of adaptation.

Reconsidering the fiction of the long Victorian period produces a new canon shaped by adaptation. It includes not simply the novelists who are beloved of survey courses (Dickens, Thackeray, Charlotte Brontë, Emily Brontë, Elizabeth Gaskell, Eliot, Trollope, and Hardy), but also predecessors such as Austen and Mary Shelley, verse storytellers such as Browning, franchisers such as Conan Doyle, and monster-makers from Stevenson to Stoker. Clearly, these are not one's grandmother's Victorians. Such exercises in canon revision suggest that canons, whose very definition suggests eternal endurance, are always works in progress—the products of individuals and institutions that hope to project their tastes and values not only forward onto their students but also backward onto previous generations.

Not even Dickens, the central and most unexceptionable Victorian novelist, is immune to change. As Natalie Neill points out, *A Christmas Carol*, the single Victorian classic that is most often subjected to adaptation, is the perfect text to adapt repeatedly for several reasons that considerably complicate its claims to classic status. These include its susceptibility to such free adaptations as *It's a Wonderful Life* and *How the Grinch Stole Christmas!*; its status as a sure-fire holiday moneymaker, every theatrical troupe's answer to *The Nutcracker*; the importance of a resurrection and reanimation play in its own parable; its justification of generous gift giving through its own original packaging as a gift volume; its repeated readaptation by its author in hundreds of public readings; and a process of ritualizing that, far from being imposed only by later adapters, "begins in the text itself," which, "like a carol…is meant to be performed over and over again" (Neill, p. 81). Neill reminds readers that the stability of the Dickens they know and love as a classic, or revere as an unread classic, is only an illusion. The 1925 student edition of *A Tale of Two Cities* my grandmother gave me as a child, whose editorial apparatus emphasizes Dickens's sentimentality and his unmatched skill in drawing memorably comic characters, places at the head of his achievements *Oliver Twist* ("one of the greatest of Dickens' novels"; 19), *The Old Curiosity Shop* ("almost unsurpassed for its pathos and its humor"; 19), *David Copperfield* ("deserves to rank with *A Tale of Two Cities*"; 20), and *A Tale of Two Cities*. Dickens's most searching anatomies of English society are dismissed as marginal. According to the editor of the volume, *Bleak House* is "less fiction than…criticism of the English system of laws and courts" (20), *Little Dorrit* is a criticism of "the debtors' prisons and the 'red tape' of government offices" (20), *Great Expectations* is a "great romance" (21), and *Our Mutual Friend* is a "story of London life; loose in plot, but interesting in details" (21). Readers who are tempted to plume themselves on their superior insight would do well to prepare for the inevitable revaluation of particular Dickens novels and of Dickens in general that will undoubtedly make their own canonical opinions seem just as quaintly dated.

The ultimate goal of a collection of case studies like this, then, is not to present a new, improved, and definitive view of nineteenth-century English literature and literary culture but to remind one of the radical contingency of the culture that is so often proposed, for example, as an anchor or bulwark against the erosion of middle-class values in modern times. This contingency of both specific historical values and the literary tradition that has been created to enshrine them is nowhere better dramatized than in the classroom. Dennis Cutchins has recently contended that "studying literature via adaptations offers our students a better, more effective way to study literature. In fact, I would argue that studying literature through adaptations can teach students what we mean when we say 'literature'" (87). The general tendency of the essays collected in this volume, as Laura Carroll puts it, "to destabilize the tendency to see either the novel or the film as fixed in its meanings, or as having a kind of documentary authority" (p. 226), is perhaps best demonstrated in the three concluding chapters, which are devoted specifically to teaching adaptations.

As Sarah J. Heidt expresses it in her chapter on *Dracula* and its multiple adaptations, a worthy goal for adaptation studies is to overturn the hierarchy that enshrines literature over film in the classroom by inviting students to see their own analyses as adaptations of texts whose claim to original status is everywhere challenged by their demand to be rewritten. Heidt's experience teaching Stoker's novel alongside its unauthorized silent adaptation *Nosferatu* (1922) "help[ed] students become savvier readers of novelistic and cinematic texts" (Heidt, p. 199) by using the strangeness and remoteness of silent-filming techniques such as color tinting as a gateway to understanding Stoker's emphasis on "the *textual* nature of his characters' experiences" (Heidt, p. 187). This emphasis is achieved in both the novel and its film adaptation through strikingly non-naturalistic means whose defamiliarizing force encouraged figurative readings. The reading and viewing experiences Heidt's course produced subordinated linear, what-happened-next questions to interpretive, what-is-this-telling-me questions.

In the same way, Tamara S. Wagner uses the dated qualities of the film adaptations of Sherlock Holmes that resurrect Holmes and Watson to enlist them in the fight against Hitler in order to impart to her students "a heightened alertness to any such agendas" (p. 219), whether they appear in Holmes adaptations or the Holmes canon. Such an approach emphasizes not only the medium-specific features of fiction and film but also the culturally specific reading practices that different versions of the Dracula story and the Holmes franchise by turns foster and challenge. It restores the sense of nineteenth-century culture as a repository of strategies for making sense of the world for both the Victorians who lived in it and the modern students who labor to understand it. In reawakening a sense of cultural values as equipment for living for both a culture's members and its inheritors, it allows students to recognize nineteenth-century values more recent cultures have chosen to accept, transform, or reject in favor of values they find superior. It also empowers students to begin making such choices themselves and to consider critically the ways their own culture is doing so. Perhaps more importantly, it recognizes the classroom as the pivotal site where reading practices and cultural values are negotiated.

Sue Thomas's argument that working to develop "film literacies" around race, class, and empire has enabling effects in the classroom (p. 231) can readily be applied to other literacies—novelistic literacy, literary literacy, and cultural literacy—that have only in modern times begun to be identified as specific modes of literacy rather than literacy itself. Teaching literature and film, as these chapters powerfully demonstrate, does not amount to teachers merely transmitting their collective knowledge; rather, it requires them to hold their aesthetic, political, and cultural beliefs up to the challenge of constant reframings, their students' as well as their own. Just as literary and film scholars' research is dedicated to teaching each other better ways to read, so teaching has the power to sharpen scholars' own communal literacy by making them more resourceful teachers, more sensitive readers, and more adventurous framers of the texts they teach. Better reading, that is, leads to better teaching, which in turn leads to still better reading, because teaching, more than any other activity, challenges educators to reconsider, reinterpret, and challenge the authority of the very texts in whose name they teach.

BIBLIOGRAPHY

Altman, Rick. "Dickens, Griffith, and Film Theory Today." *South Atlantic Quarterly* 88.2 (1989): 321–359. Print.

Bluestone, George. *Novels into Film: The Metamorphosis of Fiction into Cinema.* Baltimore: Johns Hopkins University Press, 1957. Print.

Boyum, Joy Gould. *Double Exposure: Fiction into Film.* New York: Universe Books, 1985. Print.

Cardwell, Sarah. *Adaptation Revisited: Television and the Classic Novel.* Manchester: Manchester University Press, 2002. Print.

Cartmell, Deborah, and Imelda Whelehan. *Adaptations: From Text to Screen, Screen to Text.* New York: Routledge, 1999.

Cohen, Keith. *Film and Fiction: The Dynamics of Exchange.* New Haven: Yale University Press, 1979. Print.

Conrad, Joseph. *The Works of Joseph Conrad.* 20 volumes. London: Heinemann, 1921–1927. Print.

Cutchins, Dennis. "Why Adaptations Matter to Your Literature Students." *The Pedagogy of Adaptation.* Ed. Dennis Cutchins, Laurence Raw, and James M. Welsh. Lanham: Scarecrow Press, 2010. 87–96. Print.

Dickens, Charles. *A Tale of Two Cities.* Ed. Archibald Rutledge. New York: F. M. Ambrose, 1925. Print.

Eisenstein, Sergei. "Dickens, Griffith, and the Film Today." *Film Form: Essays in Film Theory.* Ed., trans. Jay Leyda. New York: Harcourt Brace & World, 1949. 195–255. Print.

Elliott, Kamilla. *Rethinking the Novel/Film Debate.* Cambridge: Cambridge University Press, 2003. Print.

Giddings, Robert, and Erica Sheen, eds. *The Classic Novel from Page to Screen.* Manchester: Manchester University Press, 2000. Print.

Griffin, Susan M., ed. *Henry James Goes to the Movies*. Lexington: University of Kentucky Press, 2002. Print.

Gunning, Tom. "An Aesthetic of Astonishment: Early Film and the (In) Credulous Spectator." 1989. *Film Theory and Criticism: Introductory Readings*. Ed. Leo Braudy and Marshall Cohen. 7th ed. New York: Oxford University Press, 2009. 736–750. Print.

Hutcheon, Linda. *A Theory of Adaptation*. New York: Routledge, 2006. Print.

Jacobs, Lewis. *The Rise of the American Film: A Critical History*. New York: Harcourt, Brace, 1939. Print.

Marcus, Steven. *The Other Victorians: A Study of Sexuality and Pornography in Mid-Nineteenth-Century England*. New York: Basic Books, 1966. Print.

Mayer, Robert, ed. *Eighteenth-Century Fiction on Screen*. Cambridge: Cambridge University Press, 2002. Print.

McFarlane, Brian. *Novel to Film: An Introduction to the Theory of Adaptation*. Oxford: Clarendon Press, 1996. Print.

Murray, Simone. "Materializing Adaptation Theory: The Adaptation Industry." *Literature/Film Quarterly* 36 (2008): 4–20. Print.

Naremore, James, ed. *Film Adaptation*. New Brunswick: Rutgers University Press, 2000. Print.

Naremore, James. "Introduction: Film and the Reign of Adaptation." *Film Adaptation*. Ed. James Naremore. New Brunswick: Rutgers University Press, 2000. 1–16. Print.

Palmer, R. Barton. Introduction. *Nineteenth-Century American Fiction on Screen*. Ed. R. Barton Palmer. Cambridge: Cambridge University Press, 2007. 1–8. Print.

Peary, Gerald, and Roger Shatzkin, eds. *The Classic American Novel and the Movies*. New York: Ungar, 1977. Print.

Ray, Robert B. "The Field of 'Literature and Film.'" *Film Adaptation*. Ed. James Naremore. New Brunswick: Rutgers University Press, 2000. 38–53. Print.

Sadoff, Dianne F., and John Kucich. "Introduction: Histories of the Present." *Victorian Afterlife: Postmodern Culture Rewrites the Nineteenth Century*. Ed. John Kucich and Dianne F. Sadoff. Minneapolis: University of Minnesota Press, 2000. ix–xxx. Print.

Sheen, Erica. Introduction. *The Classic Novel from Page to Screen*. Ed. Robert Giddings and Erica Sheen. Manchester: Manchester University Press, 2000. 1–13. Print.

Sorenson, Janet. "*Rob Roy*: The Other Eighteenth Century?" *Eighteenth-Century Fiction on Screen*. Ed. Robert Mayer. Cambridge: Cambridge University Press, 2002. 192–210. Print.

Stam, Robert. "The Dialogics of Adaptation." *Film Adaptation*. Ed. James Naremore. New Brunswick: Rutgers University Press, 2000. 54–76. Print.

Stam, Robert, and Alessandra Raengo. *A Companion to Literature and Film*. Malden: Blackwell, 2004. Print.

———. *Literature and Film: A Guide to the Theory and Practice of Film Adaptation*. Malden: Blackwell, 2005. Print.

Vincendeau, Ginette. Introduction. *Film/Literature/Heritage*. Ed. Ginette Vincendeau. London: British Film Institute, 2001. xi–xxvi. Print.

Whelehan, Imelda. "Adaptations: The Contemporary Dilemmas." *Adaptations: From Text to Screen, Screen to Text*. Ed. Deborah Cartmell and Imelda Whelehan. London: Routledge, 1999. 3–19. Print.

FILMOGRAPHY

Becoming Jane. Dir. Julian Jarrold. Perf. Anne Hathaway and James McAvoy. HanWay, 2007. Film.

Ben-Hur: A Tale of the Christ. Dir. Fred Niblo. Perf. Ramon Novarro and Francis X. Bushman. MGM, 1925. Film.

The Big Parade. Dir. King Vidor. Perf. John Gilbert and Renée Adorée. MGM, 1925. Film.

The Birth of a Nation. Dir. D.W. Griffith. Perf. Lillian Gish and Mae Marsh. Griffith, 1915. Film.

Bright Star. Dir. Jane Campion. Perf. Abby Cornish and Ben Whishaw. Pathé Renn, 2009. Film.

The Covered Wagon. Dir. James Cruze. Perf. James Parrott and Katherine Grant. Roach, 1923. Film.

David Copperfield. Dir. George Cukor. Perf. Freddie Bartholomew and W.C. Fields. MGM, 1935. Film.

Dr. Jekyll and Mr. Hyde. Dir. Rouben Mamoulian. Perf. Fredric March and Miriam Hopkins. Paramount, 1931. Film.

Dracula. Dir. Tod Browning. Perf. Bela Lugosi and Helen Chandler. Universal, 1931. Film.

Finding Neverland. Dir. Marc Forster. Perf. Johnny Depp and Kate Winslet. Miramax, 2004. Film.

The Four Horsemen of the Apocalypse. Dir. Rex Ingram. Perf. Rudolph Valentino and Alice Terry. Metro, 1921. Film.

Intolerance. Dir. D.W. Griffith. Perf. Mae Marsh and Robert Harron. Wark, 1916. Film.

Miss Potter. Dir. Chris Noonan. Perf. Renée Zellweger and Ewan McGregor. Phoenix/BBC, 2006. Film.

Pride and Prejudice. Dir. Robert Z. Leonard. Perf. Greer Garson and Laurence Olivier. MGM, 1940. Film.

The Ten Commandments. Dir. Cecil B. DeMille. Perf. Theodore Roberts and Charles De Roche. Paramount, 1923. Film.

Tense Moments with Great Authors. Dir. H.B. Parkinson, et al. Perf. Phyllis Neilson-Terry and Charles Garry. 1922. Film.

Tristram Shandy: A Cock and Bull Story. Dir. Michael Winterbottom. Perf. Steve Coogan and Rob Brydon. BBC, 2005. Film.

20,000 Leagues under the Sea. Dir. Stuart Paton. Perf. Dan Hanlon and Curtis Benton. Universal, 1916. Film.

Way Down East. Dir. D.W. Griffith. Perf. Lillian Gish and Richard Barthelmess. Griffith, 1920. Film.

PART I

REINTERPRETING THE VICTORIANS

ADAPTATION AND THE TECHNE OF REVISION

CHAPTER 1

JEKYLL, HYDE, JEKYLL, HYDE, JEKYLL, HYDE, JEKYLL, HYDE

FOUR MODELS OF INTERTEXTUALITY

Thomas Leitch

Whatever its claims as a work of cinematic art, *Nutty Professor II: The Klumps* boasts a genealogical table that is both clear and instructive. Peter Segal's 2000 romantic comedy is clearly a sequel to Tom Shadyac's *The Nutty Professor* (1996). These films are closely linked by their stories and their star, Eddie Murphy, who in both of them plays the digitally obese Sherman Klump and his sociopathic alter ego Buddy Love. As its credits attest, *The Nutty Professor* is "based on the [1963] motion picture by Jerry Lewis and Bill Richmond," which is based in turn on earlier film versions of Robert Louis Stevenson's 1886 story *Strange Case of Dr. Jekyll and Mr. Hyde*, most notably Rouben Mamoulian's 1931 film starring Fredric March and Victor Fleming's 1941 film starring

Spencer Tracy. Thus, Stevenson begets Mamoulian and Fleming, who beget Lewis, who begets Shadyac, who begets Segal.

Students of adaptation have proposed four different models that might be applied in understanding the intertextual relations between Stevenson's story and the other stories it has apparently begotten: a spoke, or sunburst, model that has long been prevalent in adaptation studies; a genealogical model, implied by the word "begotten"; a daisy chain model which is so closely related to the genealogical model that it might be called its offspring; and a tracer text model. Each of these models is perceptive and useful. Yet each is also limited by gaps or blind spots that are illuminated in surprising and dramatic ways by Stevenson's story and the circumstances of its composition. More than a century after its first appearance, *Strange Case of Dr. Jekyll and Mr. Hyde* continues to offer prescient wisdom about the tricky nature of the relations between alleged individuals and their alleged progeny.

The simplest of these four models of adaptation, the spoke, or sunburst, model, regards every story about Dr. Jekyll and Mr. Hyde as a more or less free adaptation of Stevenson, with the emphasis on "more or less." It often ranks specific adaptations according to how closely they follow the particulars of *Strange Case of Dr. Jekyll and Mr. Hyde* as their common source. This model sometimes figures each adaptation as a spoke attached to that common source as a central hub. But, because there is no wheel to which all of the spokes are connected at the other end, the model could more accurately be illustrated by a sunburst graphic, with Stevenson's story at its center and the films as rays that are all motivated by that center but shooting out in different directions with no common function, goal, or end. This sunburst model has held sway for more than fifty years of adaptation studies, and it is easy to see why. By subordinating each adaptation both logically and spatially to the text that marks its starting point, it confirms the primacy of what is generally called its source text or its original and implies that adaptations borrow their value from the originals that spin them off.

A leading problem with this model is the difficulty of establishing a single hub in which all adaptations have their source. Murphy's two *Nutty Professor* films owe less to Stevenson than to Jerry Lewis, who is appropriately credited as an executive producer on both of them. Murphy's films, like Lewis's, are both set in contemporary America rather than Victorian England. Both ridicule the Jekyll figure (Lewis's Julius Kelp, Murphy's Sherman Klump) whose self-induced ordeal Stevenson takes seriously, and both use their hero's divided nature as the basis for slapstick comedy rather than moral allegory. (Both, for example, give prominent roles to digitized hamsters, though the first features projectile hamsters and the second features projectile hamster droppings.) All three of these films can proceed to happy endings that are pointedly at odds with Stevenson's work, though not without precedent in the long history of Jekyll and Hyde updates stretching from Lucius Henderson's *Dr. Jekyll and Mr. Hyde* (1912), Herbert Brenon's *Dr. Jekyll and Mr. Hyde* (1913), Robert Broderick's *A Modern Jekyll and Hyde* (1913), and John S. Robertson's *Dr. Jekyll and Mr. Hyde* (1920) to the cartoons *Mighty Mouse Meets Jekyll and Hyde Cat* (1944), *Dr. Jekyll and Mr. Mouse* (1947), and *Doctor Jerkyl's Hide* (1954).

Lewis's own film borrows less from Stevenson's story, whose author and title are nowhere mentioned in its credits, than from the 1931 and 1941 film versions, though it does not mention them either. Mamoulian's film, for example, provides Lewis with the triangular relationship involving the Jekyll character, the Hyde character, and the woman they both know—a complex relationship in Mamoulian that Lewis simplifies into a sexual rivalry between Kelp and Love. The obligatory scene in which Jekyll first transforms himself into Hyde, which Stevenson covers in three paragraphs of Jekyll's first-person narrative, becomes a staple of the film adaptations of the story. Lewis's transformation scene, which combines the agonized physical torment of Fredric March in Mamoulian with some visual effects taken from Fleming, establishes in turn a new cartoonlike color scheme of bright primary hues that Murphy's two films borrow for this scene.

Even the earliest Jekyll and Hyde films depend less directly on Stevenson's story than on the dramatic adaptation Thomas Russell Sullivan made in 1887 for the stage actor Richard Mansfield. To Stevenson's virtually all-male cast, Sullivan adds three female characters: Dr. Lanyon's wife, Hyde's servant Rebecca Moor, and most important, Sir Danvers Carew's daughter Agnes, Jekyll's fiancée. The intrusion of women who are identified by their prominent functions and proper names into Stevenson's male world allows Sullivan to emphasize Hyde's lawless sexuality, most notably when he demands to speak to Agnes because "I saw her face through the window, and I *like* it.... I will make the house mine, the girl mine if I please" (Danahay and Chisholm, 56). At the same time, the new prominence of women raises questions that more recent analysts have pondered about the exclusion of them in Stevenson's repressively cloistered world, in which every man seems to be unmarried, unsexed, and uninterested in anything except his professional and personal relations with other men.

Unlike Stevenson's story, which unfolds as a mystery ending with Dr. Henry Jekyll's written account of his transformation into Hyde, "[a]ll major adapted versions of the story take place in 'real time,' that is, they obey the dictates of linear development" (Rose, 31). This linear reorganization of the story first enters with Sullivan, who retains Stevenson's emphasis on the mystery of the relation between Jekyll and Hyde until the climax of act 3 of his four-act play but dispenses with the long letter in which Jekyll provides a posthumous explanation. Virtually all later versions of the story follow Sullivan's linear structure rather than Stevenson's retrospective structure.

In many ways, in fact, Sullivan's play has been more influential in shaping later adaptations than Stevenson's story. Its power suggests that the sunburst model of adaptation, in which a single original text inspires a series of adaptations that are primarily indebted to a sole begetter, is inadequate to the adaptation history that runs from *Strange Case of Dr. Jekyll and Mr. Hyde* to *Nutty Professor II: The Klumps*. This model is implicitly endorsed by Harry M. Geduld's contention that Stevenson's story was inspired partly by the author's recollections of his youth as a "would-be debauchee" (Geduld, 4); partly by the double life of the eighteenth-century deacon William Brodie, which

Stevenson had dramatized as a teenager; and partly by a vivid dream that suggested several crucial elements in the story.

The tendency of Jekyll and Hyde adaptations to borrow features from earlier adaptations rather than from Stevenson's story and the tendency of those earlier adaptations to veil their own sources or origins in multiple, contradictory, or indeterminate narratives imply an alternative to the sunburst model of adaptation: a genealogical model in the form of a family tree. Instead of positing a central original text around which all adaptations take their place, this model, positing a line of descent within a given textual family, values both the similarities that are to be expected between successive members and the differences that are bound to crop up over an extended period of time. Accordingly, it is sensitive to the many different kinds of relations that are possible between successive incarnations of a given story. Shadyac's *The Nutty Professor*, for example, is a film-to-film remake of Lewis's *The Nutty Professor*, not an adaptation to a new mode of presentation. *Nutty Professor II* is not an adaptation of Shadyac's *The Nutty Professor* but a sequel, and Charles Lamont's *Abbott and Costello Meet Dr. Jekyll and Mr. Hyde* (1953) is a burlesque. Because the relations among different members of this family can be wildly varied, the most specific intertextual imperative that can be drawn from the resemblances among them is "be fruitful and multiply."

A genealogical model of adaptation acknowledges not only the different relations that are possible among different generations but also the many different kinds of work they may undertake. The focus on Hollywood Victorian detail in Fleming's 1941 film, for example, suggests that viewers who are looking for entertaining thrills can be better insulated from the threat represented by Hyde if Jekyll and Hyde are historically situated in a comfortably remote world. Adaptations of Stevenson's story have used it as the basis for explorations of contemporaneous cultural anxiety, analyses of historical pathology, horror-film franchises (and in the case of Abbott and Costello, a comedy franchise), and star vehicles for actors eager to show their range by playing both Jekyll and Hyde.

But this genealogical model is not without its own problems, several of them revealed by the varying accounts of how *Strange Case of Dr. Jekyll and Mr. Hyde* first came to be written. Stevenson himself wrote F. W. H. Myers that "*Jekyll* was conceived, written, rewritten, re-rewritten, and printed inside ten weeks" (Stevenson, *Letters* 5: 216). Lloyd Osbourne, the son of Stevenson's wife Fanny, maintained that Stevenson burned the first draft of the story, which was written in three days following his dream, in response to Fanny's unexpectedly critical reaction: "He had missed the point, she said; had missed the allegory; had made it merely a story—a magnificent bit of sensationalism—when it should have been a masterpiece" (Osbourne, 64; cf. Balfour, 2: 15–16). According to Osbourne, Stevenson first reacted with angry disagreement, then with a concurrence so intense that he burned the manuscript in order to put himself beyond the temptation of attempting to save any of it. He retired forthwith to produce a second, sharply revised draft in another three days. However long Stevenson may have spent in the composition of the tale Longmans published in January 1886 and whatever Fanny Stevenson's role in shaping that tale may have been, it is clear from all accounts that it represents a substantial revision of Stevenson's earlier draft, which had its own roots in several different sources.

The most celebrated of these sources is Stevenson's dream, which he describes in his 1887 essay "A Chapter on Dreams" as the work of "some Brownie, some Familiar, whom I keep locked in a back garret, while I get all the praise and he but a share (which I cannot prevent him from getting) of the pudding":

> I had long been trying to write a story on this subject, to find a body, a vehicle, for that strong sense of man's double being which must at times come in upon and overwhelm the mind of every thinking creature. I had even written one, *The Travelling Companion*, which was returned by an editor on the plea that it was a work of genius and indecent, and which I burned the other day on the ground that it was not a work of genius, and that *Jekyll* had supplanted it. Then came one of those financial fluctuations to which (with an elegant modesty) I have hitherto referred in

the third person. For two days I went about racking my brains for a plot of any sort; and on the second night I dreamed the scene at the window, and a scene afterward split in two, in which Hyde, pursued for some crime, took the powder and underwent the change in the presence of his pursuers. All the rest was made awake, and consciously, although I think I can trace in much of it the manner of my Brownies. The meaning of the tale is therefore mine, and had long pre-existed in my garden of Adonis, and tried one body after another in vain; indeed, I do most of the morality, worse luck! and my Brownies have not a rudiment of what we call a conscience. Mine, too, is the setting, mine the characters. All that was given me was the matter of three scenes, and the central idea of a voluntary change becoming involuntary. Will it be thought ungenerous, after I have been so liberally ladling out praise to my unseen collaborators, if I here toss them over, bound hand and foot, into the arena of the critics? For the business of the powders, which so many have censured, is, I am relieved to say, not mine at all but the Brownies'. (Stevenson, *Lantern-Bearers* 224–225)

As an account of the story's composition, this is as enchanting as it is illogical. Stevenson claims that the basis of the story is a universally available sense of human moral duality even though "the meaning of the tale is mine" because "I do most of the morality"; that he had to rack his brains for the incidents in which the meaning would be clothed even though he had already written an earlier story on the same subject; that he is unfairly taking authorial credit that should rightly go to his "unseen collaborators" and yet that those collaborators should get the blame for the mechanical nature of the "powders" that effected Jekyll's transformation. In short, he claims that as a dreamer of what amounts to an ur-text of his story, he both is and is not the story's author. These contradictions are further sharpened by an interview Stevenson gave a few weeks before writing "A Chapter on Dreams" in which he claimed that although "I am quite in the habit of dreaming stories…. I am never deceived by them. Even when fast asleep I know that it is I who am inventing" (qtd. in Harman, 298).

Even if "the use of dreams as a direct inspiration to storytelling is unique to Stevenson among writers" (McLynn, 255), the implications of these contradictions are sweeping. Ronald R. Thomas has argued that

> [t]he shift between the first- and third-person pronouns when Stevenson refers to himself as an author-agent in this statement, enacts his uncertainty about his control over his own texts, and it directly echoes Jekyll's inability to speak confidently about himself in the first person in his narrative. (85)

Thomas links the resulting instability to Beckett's "modernist claim that the self is not represented at the scene of writing. It is reinvented there" (73). Taken together with the tangled tale of the story's composition, this instability also provides a basis for Jacques Derrida's postmodern claim that "the entire history of the concept of structure...must be thought of as a series of substitutions of center for center, as a linked chain of determinations of the center" (279). The testimony of both the author and his tale—if it is indeed his tale—challenges the assumption that any given text or ur-text presents a center from which later adaptations radiate. Centers are always stipulated, never given.

Stevenson's story dramatizes these problems through its implicit critique of the surprisingly slippery patriarchal relationship it establishes between Jekyll and Hyde. Throughout the story, Jekyll attempts to govern his relation to Hyde by a series of masquerades and documents that position Hyde as Jekyll's son. Hyde is repeatedly described as "smaller, slighter and younger than Henry Jekyll" (Stevenson, *Strange Case* 61). More than once after Jekyll has unexpectedly and involuntarily assumed the shape of his alter ego, witnesses see Hyde wearing clothes that are much too big for him. Jekyll makes a will in Hyde's favor and gives him "full liberty and power about my house in the square" (63). Jekyll aptly remarks that although "Jekyll had more than a father's interest [in his alter ego]; Hyde had more than a son's indifference" (66). However, the relation between them is far more intimate than that of father and son— more intimate than either of them can endure. Jekyll attempts to regulate his relation to Hyde by making him his legatee, signing the check Hyde presents to the father of the girl he has trampled, and signing Hyde's letter to Lanyon begging his help in what turns out to be his transformation back to Jekyll. But, these efforts are all doomed by what William Veeder describes as the failure of Victorian patriarchy in Stevenson:

> Traditionally the obligations of patriarchs are three: to maintain the distinctions (master-servant, proper-improper) that ground patriarchy; to sustain the male ties (father-son, brother-brother) that constitute it; and to enter the wedlock (foregoing homosexuality) that perpetuates it.... What Stevenson devastatingly demonstrates is that patriarchy behaves exactly counter to its obligations. Distinctions that should be maintained are elided, so that bonds occur where divisions should obtain; and affiliations that should be sustained are sundered, so that males war with one another and refuse to wed. (109–110)

The critique of Victorian patriarchy Veeder finds implicit in Stevenson is dramatized more explicitly in Valerie Martin's 1990 novel *Mary Reilly*, which

> retell[s] the story of Dr. Jekyll and Mr. Hyde from the point of view of someone who might well have been a witness to the events, but who was invisible to the original teller—doubly invisible, for Mary Reilly is not only a woman but a servant. (Crowley, 7)

Martin's retelling makes Jekyll kind, sympathetic, and weak; Hyde both loathsome and Byronically compelling; Poole the butler fearsomely powerful in household matters; and Mary's abusive father quite as evil in his commonplace way as the prodigious Hyde. Like Veeder, Martin focuses on "the way the Jekyll/Hyde relationship is replicated throughout Jekyll's circle" (Veeder, 108). Her afterword meticulously describes the physical particulars of Mary Reilly's journals, poses straight-faced questions about possible relations between Jekyll and Hyde, and speculates inconclusively about the heroine's future before conceding "the possibility that the sad and disturbing story unfolded for us in the pages of Mary's diaries is now and always was intended to be nothing less serious than a work of fiction" (Martin, 263). Although her analysis proceeds by inventing a broader fictional context for the story, Martin's critique of patriarchy echoes Veeder's in its technique of supplementation masking as restoration. Both the critic and the novelist—and indeed the screenwriter Christopher Hampton and the director Stephen Frears, who adapted Martin's novel in their 1996 film—seek to rewrite Stevenson's tale while pretending to release the truths it represses. This is the very same procedure followed by adaptations that claim descent from a powerful father-text, as Hyde does with Jekyll, only in order to dethrone it.

In short, it would be hard to imagine a more withering attack on the patriarchal implications of the genealogical model of adaptation than Stevenson's story, from the conflicting accounts of its birth to its checkered afterlife. Fortunately, several of the problems of the patriarchal model can be avoided by a third model that substitutes a daisy chain for the more fraught image of the family tree. Although this third model does not explain how a given daisy chain—from Stevenson to Sullivan to Mamoulian to Fleming to Lewis to Shadyac to Segal, for example—is renewed or transformed by its interactions with other chains, it at least acknowledges that these transformations are normal, not exceptional or transgressive. Whether or not Stevenson's story or Sullivan's play inspired the series of London sex murders that were attributed to Jack the Ripper in 1888, "it can be said without doubt that the Jekyll and Hyde story and the Ripper case quickly became inextricably confused in the popular imagination" (Geduld, 7). As a result, in a celebrated example of a daisy chain of influence that is not necessarily a genealogy,

> elements of the Jack the Ripper case [especially the emphasis on sexual sadism against prostitutes] have been introduced into adaptations of *Dr. Jekyll and Mr. Hyde*, while aspects of the latter have left their mark on stories and films about Jack the Ripper. (Geduld, 7)

To turn to more lightsome influences, it is well known that *Abbott and Costello Meet Dr. Jekyll and Mr. Hyde* owes more to earlier generic pairings of the comedy team with Universal's franchise monsters (*Abbott*

and Costello Meet Frankenstein, 1948, etc.) than to the specifics of
Stevenson's story. The impact of *Star Wars* and *2001: A Space Odyssey*
on *Nutty Professor II*, which briefly parodies them both, is clear. And it
is obvious—except to Jerry Lewis, who has repeatedly disclaimed any
intentional resemblance—how much Lewis's portrayal of the leering
Buddy Love owes to his former partner Dean Martin.

But in finessing around the leading problem of the genealogical model—its failure to account for the patriarchal authority of the
original text—the daisy chain introduces a new problem: the fact that
a given intertextual chain has no beginning, no end, and no boundaries. Theorists such as Robert Stam who follow Mikhail Bakhtin in
speaking of "an artistic utterance" as "a 'hybrid construction'" (Stam, 9;
cf. Bakhtin, 305) would presumably welcome this development because
it promises to set intertextuality free from regulation by patriarchal
forbears by acknowledging that every text is an intertext that is borne
and inflected by myriad other texts. In breaking down the distinction
between progenitor texts and intertexts, however, this model of intertextuality threatens to dissolve the very notion of adaptation. As hard
as Linda Hutcheon works to distinguish adaptation from the network of
intertextual relationships that shape every text, her definition of adaptation as "an extended, deliberate, announced revisitation of a particular work of art" (170) is too broad to distinguish adaptation from a
wide range of other intertextual relations she considers, from repeated
musical performances and covers to sequels, prequels, and marketing
spin-offs.

Stevenson's story provides a powerful critique of the daisy chain
model in Jekyll's anguished discovery that he cannot replicate the potion
that first turned him into Hyde because "my first supply was impure,
and…it was that unknown impurity which lent efficacy to the draught"
(Stevenson, *Strange Case* 73). As Thomas observes,

> The larger point that Jekyll misses here is that he fails because any
> text is "impure" in the sense that it is never a perfect representa-
> tion of what it seeks to represent. The representation is always
> something else; it always takes on a life of its own. (79)

Because the daisy chain model defines every text as an intertext, it not only blurs the distinction between sources and adaptations but also makes it impossible to distinguish pure adaptations, which it brands as chimeras, from texts that simply resemble other texts. The resulting profusion of intertextual wildflowers may be an accurate description, but it does not make for useful categorization or analysis.

Ten years ago, Brian A. Rose proposed a fourth model for the adaptation history of Stevenson's story that combines features of the sunburst model and the genealogical model. Rose's model offers the possibility of avoiding both the uncritical anterior privileging of the sunburst model and the unacknowledged patriarchalism of the genealogical model without opening the doors to the ungovernable intertextuality of the daisy chain model. For Rose, Stevenson's story is a "tracer text," which he defines as "a story containing motifs, themes and/or images of archetypic import, which…is adopted by a culture for repeated use over a significant time" (15). The primary use of such tracer texts, as Rose explains, is their usefulness in motivating repeated dramatizations of irresolvable cultural anxieties:

> A group-text (or a body of adaptations extended over time) that has grown from a tracer has the potential of becoming a larger, reflexive body of narratological, performative and cultural elements: a culture-text. A culture-text is located between text, group-text and the popular-cultural body of images, icons and meanings that have some reference to the original. The productions of this group-text are informed by, and in turn restructure, the culture-text; thus, the evolution of the culture-text…permits the redefinition of anxiety-provoking issues. (2)

When the cultural importance of the imagery can successfully be combined with a complex of dramaturgical, formal, and market-related elements so as to make the original texts prime candidates for reformatting in multiple media and for a range of economic markets, such texts are in positions to generate bodies of culture-textual associations which grow from the process of adaptation itself (2).

There is a great deal to recommend Rose's model over its rivals. The proposition that texts are most likely to be repeatedly adapted when they speak to continuing cultural anxieties helps explain why the story of Dr. Jekyll and Mr. Hyde, like those of Frankenstein, Dracula, and Robin Hood, is not only enduring but remarkably malleable. The term "tracer text," borrowed from medical technology, is a less fraught term than "original text," which places Stevenson at the center of the textual universe instead of injecting it into a culture's bloodstream, where it works through a process of continual transformation. The relations Rose proposes among tracer texts, group-texts, and culture-texts go far to explain why texts such as *Strange Case of Dr. Jekyll and Mr. Hyde* are most useful when they are most fully dissolved.

Even so, Rose retains crucial features of both the sunburst model and the genealogical model that undermine his own model. These features follow from his foundational distinction between close adaptations, "those heavily influenced by the original's theme, locale and style," and loose adaptations, or "works adopting the essential device of the story…but including no other characters from it, nor requiring the original's locale, time or theme (5). Unlike close adaptations, which "tie the creation of the group-text to the initial reasons for appropriation of the text," loose adaptations, Rose claims,

> would be of interest in a study of Jekyll and Hyde *qua* myth of the "double," but shed little light on the manner in which a culture is using the original story, or its integrally related internal motifs, except as techniques for exploiting submarkets through the creation of various, targeted forms. (5)

For this reason, Rose's extensive analysis of Jekyll and Hyde adaptations deliberately ignores loose adaptations such as Lewis's *The Nutty Professor* or Roy Ward Baker's *Dr. Jekyll & Sister Hyde* (1971) even though such adaptations "offer evidence that the social or cultural value of a text's motifs transcend [*sic*] limited usage by dominant social discourses" (21).

Apart from depriving Rose of the chance to discuss a wide range of Jekyll/Hyde texts, this procedure raises several problems. One is the question of how important a tracer text's potential to transcend the social discourses in which it is first embedded can be when the loose adaptations that provide the best evidence of that transcendence are marginalized. A broader question concerns the specificity of location and time as an indication of the reasons for appropriating a text in the first place. Is a twenty-first-century Hollywood adaptation of the Jekyll/Hyde story better equipped to perform its task of staging cultural anxieties if it is set in Victorian London or in contemporary America? Although the Victorian setting is more faithful to Stevenson in one sense, it is less faithful in another. Stevenson was not writing about long ago and far away; he was writing a tale that was set in his own time, if not exactly in his own place. (Stevenson, who had never lived regularly in London, wrote the story while he was convalescing in Bournemouth.) Virginia Wright Wexman has argued that Mamoulian's 1931 film uses Hyde's physical ugliness, a characteristic he lacks in Stevenson, as the pivot for staging a contemporary conflict "between new business interests and new utopian aspirations held by previously disenfranchised groups" (Wexman, 285). In its strenuous attempts to recreate the setting of Victorian London, by contrast, Fleming's 1941 film, which combines Freudian imagery with period costumes and architecture, risks fetishizing its Victorian trappings and becoming a study in historical pathology rather than an exploration of contemporary cultural anxiety.

The supposition that the more Victorian the adaptation, the more closely it ties the group-text to the rationale for the enduring choice of the original text reveals an underlying circularity in Rose's argument. The reason that loose adaptations "shed little light on the manner in which a culture is using the original story, or its integrally related internal motifs" is that close adaptations are more likely to preserve the specific details of the story on the assumption that these details are indeed integrally related (Rose, 5). Loose adaptations, which by definition are less likely to preserve these details without alteration, cannot challenge that assumption precisely because their bearing on the argument is marginal.

Rose's handling of exceptions to this rule is revealing. As I have already observed, he notes that all later adaptations of Stevenson's story follow the linear structure of Sullivan's dramatic adaptation rather than Stevenson's retrospective structure. However, he does not pursue the obvious implication of this insight: because it is in Sullivan's play, not Stevenson's story, that the tale of Jekyll and Hyde receives its most influential formal presentation, his tracer text model should logically consider the play, not the story, its definitive articulation. Rose would no doubt recoil from this heretical suggestion because his analysis of close and loose adaptations ends up reinstalling what he calls the tracer text in a place that exactly corresponds to the patriarchal root of the genealogical model or the center of the sunburst model, which in his reckoning takes the form of a series of concentric circles. At the very center is "the essential device of the story" (Rose, 26), the parable about the doubleness of humankind and the danger of attempting either to indulge repressed desires or to sever oneself from them. Next comes the tracer text, then the group-text, and finally "the popular-cultural body of images, icons and meanings that have some reference to the original" (26), with the culture-text floating somewhere in the middle distance like an asteroid belt. Paradoxically, the original text's success in working as a tracer text is judged partly by the density of its culture-text and the sprawling variety of the larger, looser body of images, icons, and meanings it has spawned, even though the boldest and most adventurous of these are by definition the most marginal.

Like the sunburst and genealogical models, the tracer text model as Rose uses it cannot account for the popular appeal and influence of Lewis's movie *The Nutty Professor*, which has too little connection to Stevenson's story for Rose to take seriously, or for the prestige of Martin's novel *Mary Reilly*, which has the temerity to rewrite Stevenson instead of being content to adapt him. Its most serious inadequacy is its inability to account for the power of great adaptations such as Shakespeare's history plays to realign their originals in Plutarch and Holinshed in ways that virtually eclipse them, so that Shakespeare, unlike Sullivan, becomes the new original.

This power begins in a feature that is foregrounded in the genealogical model: the constant struggle among generations of texts to establish their supremacy by marginalizing their successors as mere adaptations or by disavowing their forbears as mere predecessors. Both of these processes are darkly prophesied in Stevenson's story, in which Jekyll comes to view Hyde as "something not only hellish but inorganic," while Hyde regards his repeated transformations of himself back to Jekyll in a "return to his subordinate station of a part instead of a person" as "temporary suicide" (Stevenson, *Strange Case* 72).

The second of these processes of abjection—in which "readable writing (or sanctioned discourse) is used to suppress a prewriting, which naturally resists suppression because it is so bound up with that which tries to deny it" (Hogle, 186)—is dramatized by adaptations such as Lewis's *The Nutty Professor*, which disavows its most obvious predecessors by failing to list Stevenson, the title of his story, or any of its earlier film versions in its credits, and by its writer/director/star's continued denial that his Buddy Love owes anything to Dean Martin. The first process, which leaves its mark on both the sunburst and the tracer text models of adaptation, is memorably dramatized in Jekyll's increasingly frantic attempts, in the closing pages of *Strange Case of Dr. Jekyll and Mr. Hyde*, to distinguish himself in his written account from his wicked double. Recalling the divisions that had characterized his behavior from an early age, he observes,

> Though so profound a double-dealer, I was in no sense a hypocrite; both sides of me were in dead earnest; I was no more myself when I laid aside restraint and plunged in shame, than when I laboured, in the eye of day, at the furtherance of knowledge or the relief of sorrow or suffering. (Stevenson, *Strange Case* 58)

At length he concludes that "man is not truly one, but truly two," and that, "of the two natures that contended in the field of my consciousness, even if I rightly could be said to be either, it was only because I was radically both" (59). Regarding Hyde's image for the first time in the mirror, Jekyll acknowledges that "[t]his, too, was myself" (61). When he comes to describe the habitual opposition between the "wholly evil" Hyde and "the old Henry Jekyll, that incongruous compound of whose reformation and improvement I had already learned to despair" (62), Jekyll speaks of both in the third person. Immediately after his first unwitting awakening as Hyde, however, he is terrified lest "the character of Edward Hyde become irrevocably mine" (65), identifying himself as Jekyll alone. He traces the last stage of his involuntary possession by Hyde to his yielding to the temptation of sinful vanity "in my own person" (69). Once Hyde's ascendancy is unmistakable, Jekyll's attempt to disavow him assumes definitive form: "He, I say—I cannot say, I" (70). Jekyll concludes his statement with the claim that "this is my true hour of death, and what is to follow concerns another than myself" (73).

Although it does not render them unusable, *Strange Case of Dr. Jekyll and Mr. Hyde* suggests that none of the four models of adaptation I have considered—the sunburst, the genealogy, the daisy chain, and the tracer text—is adequate to the complexities of intertextual relations. A model of adaptation fully informed by the fable of Jekyll and Hyde might well begin by inverting Linda Hutcheon's provocative question, "What Is *Not* an Adaptation?" (Hutcheon, 170), and assuming, along with Jekyll, that every text speaks in the voices of many texts, some of which it eagerly solicits, some of which it does its best to silence. Hence, Murphy's two *Nutty Professor* films duly record their borrowings from Lewis's film but make no mention of Stevenson's story or any of its other cinematic incarnations. And *Nutty Professor II*, which borrows so freely from Murphy's first *Nutty Professor* film in its story of Sherman Klump's impending marriage to Professor Denise Gaines (Janet Jackson), dismisses the absent Professor Carla Purty (Jada Pinkett Smith), the remarkably similar colleague Klump seemed about to bring to the altar at the end of *The Nutty Professor*, as "just a good friend."

Gérard Genette's apparently exhaustive attempt to catalog the various subclasses of "*transtextuality*," which he defines as "all that sets the text in a relationship, whether obvious or concealed, with other texts" (1), barely mentions adaptation. That underemphasis has not prevented theorists from seeking a place for adaptation within Genette's taxonomy (see especially Stam, 27–31). A primary lesson of the career of Jekyll and Hyde suggests that it might make more sense to waive the whole question of which of them to count as adaptations and substitute the term "generations." Instead of focusing retrospectively on the specious ideal of the original text that is not itself an adaptation, generation looks both backward, in terms of genealogy, and forward, in terms of production. Like Stevenson's story, which holds a critical light up to the problem of human identity by showing the ways that the self is other, the term "generation" unmasks the apparent unity of textual identity by asking how a given text is its generations and vice versa. Thomas completes his reading of Stevenson by concluding that

> [t]he self cannot be found if it is looked for in one place; it refuses to be only an "I" or a "you" or a "he" in these texts. Rather, the self exists on the boundaries between them, in the play of relational forces between father and son, doctor and patient, past and present, speaker and listener, writer and reader. (90)

This list might be completed: between generation and generation.

True, the term "generation" seems so unidiomatic ("I just saw a great generation of *Dr. Jekyll and Mr. Hyde*") that it may be impossible to use. But its very awkwardness offers a salutary reminder that there are more problems in intertextual relations than any set of analytical categories can contain. In the end, both Stevenson and Henry Jekyll would no doubt agree that whatever its promise, a model is just a model.

Bibliography

Bakhtin, Mikhail. *The Dialogic Imagination: Four Essays.* Ed. Michael Holquist. Trans. Caryl Emerson and Michael Holquist. Austin: University of Texas Press, 1981. Print.

Balfour, Graham. *The Life of Robert Louis Stevenson.* New York: Charles Scribner's Sons, 1901. Print.

Crowley, John. "The Woman Who Loved Dr. Jekyll." *New York Times Book Review* 4 February, 1990: 7. Print.

Danahay, Martin A., and Alex Chisholm, eds. *Jekyll and Hyde Dramatized: The 1887 Richard Mansfield Script and the Evolution of the Story on Stage.* Jefferson: McFarland, 2005. Print.

Derrida, Jacques. "Structure, Sign, and Play in the Discourse of the Human Sciences." *Writing and Difference.* Trans. Alan Bass: Chicago: University of Chicago Press, 1978. 278–293. Print.

Geduld, Harry M. Introduction. *The Definitive Dr. Jekyll and Mr. Hyde Companion.* New York: Garland, 1983. 3–15. Print.

Genette, Gérard. *Palimpsests: Literature in the Second Degree.* Trans. Channa Newman and Claude Doubinsky. Lincoln: University of Nebraska Press, 1997. Print.

Harman, Claire. *Myself and the Other Fellow: A Life of Robert Louis Stevenson.* New York: HarperCollins, 2005. Print.

Hogle, Jerrold E. "The Struggle for a Dichotomy: Abjection in Jekyll and His Interpreters." *Dr. Jekyll and Mr. Hyde after One Hundred Years.* Ed. William Veeder and Gordon Hirsch. Chicago: University of Chicago Press, 1988. 161–207. Print.

Hutcheon, Linda. *A Theory of Adaptation.* New York: Routledge, 2006. Print.

Martin, Valerie. *Mary Reilly.* New York: Doubleday, 1990. Print.

McLynn, Frank. *Robert Louis Stevenson: A Biography*. London: Hutchinson, 1993. Print.

Osbourne, Lloyd. *An Intimate Portrait of R.L.S.* New York: Scribner's, 1924. Print.

Rose, Brian A. *Jekyll and Hyde Adapted: Dramatizations of Cultural Anxiety*. Westport: Greenwood, 1996. Print.

Stam, Robert. "Introduction: The Theory and Practice of Adaptation." *Literature and Film: A Guide to the Theory and Practice of Film Adaptation*. Ed. Robert Stam and Alessandra Raengo. London: Blackwell, 2005. 1–52. Print.

Stam, Robert, and Alessandra Raengo, eds. *Literature and Film: A Guide to the Theory and Practice of Film Adaptation*. London: Blackwell, 2005. Print.

Stevenson, Robert Louis. *The Lantern-Bearers and Other Essays*. Ed. Jeremy Treglown. New York: Farrar Straus Giroux, 1988. Print.

———. *The Letters of Robert Louis Stevenson*. Ed. Bradford A. Booth and Ernest Mehew. 8 vols. New Haven: Yale University Press, 1994–1995. Print.

———. *Strange Case of Dr. Jekyll and Mr. Hyde*. 1886. Ed. Richard Dury. Edinburgh: Edinburgh University Press, 2004. Print.

Thomas, Ronald R. "The Strange Voices in the Strange Case: Dr. Jekyll, Mr. Hyde, and the Voices of Modern Fiction." *Dr. Jekyll and Mr. Hyde after One Hundred Years*. Ed. William Veeder and Gordon Hirsch. Chicago: University of Chicago Press, 1988. 73–93. Print.

Veeder, William. "Children of the Night: Stevenson and Patriarchy." *Dr. Jekyll and Mr. Hyde after One Hundred Years*. Ed. William Veeder and Gordon Hirsch. Chicago: University of Chicago Press, 1988. 107–160. Print.

Veeder, William, and Gordon Hirsch, eds. *Dr. Jekyll and Mr. Hyde after One Hundred Years*. Chicago: University of Chicago Press, 1988. Print.

Wexman, Virginia Wright. "Horrors of the Body: Hollywood's Discourse on Beauty and Rouben Mamoulian's *Dr. Jekyll and Mr. Hyde*." *Dr. Jekyll and Mr. Hyde after One Hundred Years*. Ed. William Veeder and Gordon Hirsch. Chicago: University of Chicago Press, 1988. 283–307. Print.

FILMOGRAPHY

2001: A Space Odyssey. Dir. Stanley Kubrick. Perf. Keir Dullea and Gary Lockwood. MGM, 1968. Film.

Abbott and Costello Meet Dr. Jekyll and Mr. Hyde. Dir. Charles Lamont. Perf. Bud Abbott and Lou Costello. Universal, 1953. Film.

Abbott and Costello Meet Frankenstein. Dir. Charles Barton. Perf. Bud Abbott and Lou Costello. Universal, 1948. Film.

Doctor Jerkyl's Hide. Dir. Friz Freleng. Warner Bros., 1954. Film.

Dr. Jekyll and Mr. Hyde. Dir. Lucius Henderson. Perf. James Cruze and Florence La Badie. Thanhouser, 1912. Film.

Dr. Jekyll and Mr. Hyde. Dir. Herbert Brenon. Perf. King Baggot and Jane Gail. Independent, 1913. Film.

Dr. Jekyll and Mr. Hyde. Dir. John S. Robertson. Perf. John Barrymore and Charles Lane. Famous Players–Lasky. 1920. Film.

Dr. Jekyll and Mr. Hyde. Dir. Rouben Mamoulian. Perf. Fredric March and Miriam Hopkins. Paramount, 1931. Film.

Dr. Jekyll and Mr. Hyde. Dir. Victor Fleming. Perf. Spencer Tracy and Ingrid Bergman. MGM, 1941. Film.

Dr. Jekyll and Mr. Mouse. Dir. William Hanna and Joseph Barbera. MGM, 1947. Film.

Dr. Jekyll & Sister Hyde. Dir. Roy Ward Baker. Perf. Ralph Bates and Martine Beswick. Hammer, 1971. Film.

Mighty Mouse Meets Jekyll and Hyde Cat. Dir. Mannie Davis. Terrytoons, 1944. DVD.

A Modern Jekyll and Hyde. Perf. Robert Broderick and Irene Boyle. Kalem, 1913. DVD.

The Nutty Professor. Dir. Jerry Lewis. Perf. Jerry Lewis and Stella Stevens. Paramount, 1963. Film.

The Nutty Professor. Dir. Tom Shadyac. Perf. Eddie Murphy and Jada Pinkett Smith. Universal, 1996. DVD.

Nutty Professor II: The Klumps. Dir. Peter Segal. Perf. Eddie Murphy and Janet Jackson. Universal, 2000. DVD.

Star Wars. Dir. George Lucas. Perf. Mark Hamill and Carrie Fisher. 20th Century–Fox, 1977. DVD.

CHAPTER 2

THE POETICS OF
SILENT FILM IN LUBITSCH'S
LADY WINDERMERE'S FAN

Jean-Marie Lecomte

Oscar Wilde's comedy of manners *Lady Windermere's Fan* relies so heavily on verbal wit and dialogue to satirize late Victorian society that turning it into a silent motion picture might seem unthinkable. But Ernst Lubitsch's eponymous film, shot in 1925, shortly before the advent of talking cinema, makes wit out of visual style. Lubitsch invented a silent language to express wit and paradox and turn a sophisticated Victorian drama into a stylish American melodrama. In addition, Lubitsch's cinematic storytelling was well attuned to an American audience who would not have cared much for the mores of a turn-of-the-century social circle or for Wilde's barbs at English hypocrisy.

The motion picture stands out as a masterpiece of adaptation. Lubitsch's style of cinematic storytelling metamorphoses the play into a bittersweet

American comedy of the Jazz Age. Lubitsch draws on Wilde's dramatic content, roles, and relationships and builds upon its central "myth," the matrix of secrecy that underlies the drama. Lubitsch's style is not an authorial sleight of hand, a mere touch, but a process of semiotic and cultural metamorphosis.

Lubitsch rewrote the dramatic text into a screen text without violating the deep structure of the original, and the changes are medium-driven. It appears contradictory to say that Lubitsch has been faithful to Wilde's play while changing it substantially. But paradoxically, Lubitsch, like the poet of *Cynara*, was faithful in his fashion (Dowson, p. 39). The substance is the medium, and therefore, transposing the play into film entails substantial changes. As Thomas Leitch suggests in his article on *Strange Case of Dr. Jekyll and Mr. Hyde* in this volume, a transformation of setting does not necessarily make an adaptation less faithful (p. 40). My argument addresses the poetics of filmmaking—how a movie is fabricated with a view to captivating a particular audience—and it enters the workshop of the craftsman to observe how he puts his building blocks together. Poetics is all about the act of re-creation or reprocessing what the artist has seen, heard, or read, not about what the artist may have done to the fictitious world or the cognitive content of the original story (whatever that illusory world may be). One simply wants to understand how Lubitsch assembled the fragments of cinema to conjure up a world that might be just as real as the empirical one.

Because narrative sequencing is integral to the poetics of film craft, it is important first to address the structural changes that Wilde's play underwent in the filming process. *Lady Windermere's Fan* is basically a "drama of Victorian marriage," in which a happily married couple is threatened by a dark secret in the shape of a female blackmailer, Mrs. Erlynne. As a "charming wicked creature" (19), Wilde's villainess functions as Lord Darlington's—and Oscar Wilde's—female *doppelgänger*. All of the ingredients of a Lubitsch film are already there: the flimsiness of love, especially love which is sanctioned by the marriage institution; transgressing but not depraved characters; and a secret. The melodramatic thrust of both the play and the film springs from what might be called the "social taboo" formula.

To put it briefly, the taboo is a dark family secret, an underground swell that creates disturbances on the surface of the body politic. Mrs. Erlynne, a disgraced socialite, returns to the circle who ostracized her. Her daughter, Lady Windermere, has been brought up to believe that her mother is dead, but Mrs. Erlynne threatens to reveal her own shameful past, and Lord Windermere buys her silence. Lubitsch whittled down the play to five main characters (the Windermeres, Lord Darlington, Lord Augustus, and Mrs. Erlynne), adding, for comic relief, stock burlesque types (the three gossips, female allegories of social sanctimony). But the main changes concern the reconstruction of the plot along a chronological storyline and the addition of two outdoor sequences.

At the beginning of Wilde's play, as Lord Darlington brazenly courts the married Lady Windermere, it is revealed that Lord Windermere has already met Mrs. Erlynne and given in to her blackmail. In contrast, in the film, Lubitsch places Mrs. Erlynne's encounter with Lord Windermere after the scene in which Darlington tries to seduce Margaret Windermere. It is in keeping with the style of silent cinema to present events in a chronological sequence (before talkies could verbally represent them within a more complex narrative structure).

The two outdoor scenes reveal Lubitsch's cinematic wit by visually representing some aspects of verbal language such as gossiping or so-called pragmatic failures, verbal and discursive misunderstandings leading to a breakdown in communication. The first of these scenes takes place at the races, a sporting event offering filmic space and vistas, where the members of high society can observe one another from various angles. There, Lubitsch's *mise en scène* emphasizes different ways of seeing. The second scene is the garden sequence, in which dramatic irony is cleverly represented in film language. (These two sequences will be revisited.)

The matrix of secrecy is also reinforced by a few significant modifications altering the characterizations of Lord Windermere and Lord Augustus. In the play, Lord Windermere insists on sending an invitation card to Mrs. Erlynne. In Lubitsch's scenario, however, Lord Windermere refuses to invite Mrs. Erlynne to his wife's birthday party, and the fallen woman tricks Lord Augustus into taking her to the reception. Further, although Wilde's text makes it clear that Mrs. Erlynne and Lord Augustus will be married, the film ends on an ambiguous note when Lord Augustus is merely shown getting into Mrs. Erlynne's car after being reprimanded by her. These variations tend to present the characters in line with the aesthetics of the Hollywood cinema of the early 1920s. Film dramatics (especially influenced by *A Woman of Paris*, the trend-setting Charlie Chaplin melodrama that was released in 1922) needed to mesh in two strains: the melodramatic and the comedic. In this light, Lord Augustus is more of a puppet in the hands of the skilful Erlynne than is his Wilde counterpart. Similarly, Lord Windermere appears to be less developed in the motion picture—more stereotypical, more bland or irresolute as a husband than Wilde's character, who comes into sharp linguistic conflict with his wife. In the Lubitschian scheme of things, men appear to yield to women in the gender struggle because they are outwitted by the women. (In Lubitsch's talking and singing films that were soon to come, however, men, by sheer verbal or tonal power, manage to tip the balance back in their favor [see Binh and Viviani].)

Lubitsch does not simply modify characters and plot points: his heterogeneous style of cinematic storytelling keeps close to the theatrical mode as he adapts the play to the filmic mode of representation. This is not to say that he shot the motion picture like a play, even though the film's technique is so subdued and low-key that the viewer could well believe herself to be watching a play. Indeed, one of the greatest achievements of Lubitsch's *Lady Windermere's Fan* is precisely the balance between these two modes. As a comedy of manners, the film belongs firmly to the stage, but in the end, there is no doubt that this is silent cinema at its peak. Thus, the overall style which gives the film its stamp as a work of adaptation takes its cue from the apparent tug-of-war between two traditions: the theatrical, or "highbrow," tradition, in which Wilde worked, and the popular tradition of Hollywood, with its taste for comic situations, pathos, sparkle, and pace. Lubitsch interlaces both modes of fiction, and he does it particularly well in his use of screen space.

Lubitsch's poetics of space involve the careful construction of space onscreen and off—and the movements of bodies throughout both kinds of space. For example, the opening long shot of a vast, high-ceilinged room reveals Lady Windermere seated at a desk, slightly off-center in the middle of the frame. The screen corresponds to a stage, and the camera takes a pro-scenic viewpoint. This establishing shot belongs to a theatrical universe. Margaret Windermere sits alone, engaged in a symbolic social activity: using cards to plan the seating arrangement of guests for a dinner party. The composition of the first shot is both ironic and metonymic. The center of the frame is occupied by the large door, with its dramatic potential of unleashing callers into the lady's private space, but the vastness of the room throws the scene into an imbalance, suggesting both emptiness and solitude, possibly within Lady Windermere's marriage as well as in her material space.

Lubitsch had already explored the defective spousal bond and a couple's guilty desire to play the adulterous game in *The Marriage Circle*, in which his language of proxemics spatially represents the forces of intimate attraction or repulsion between men and women, obviating the use of intertitle cards. In *Lady Windermere's Fan*, when Lady Windermere places Lord Darlington's card next to hers, a cut to a reaction shot reveals mixed feelings of amusement, hesitation, and vexation which seem to ripple over her somewhat nondescript face. (She finally elects not to sit next to Darlington.) The three fleeting moods suggest feelings that are at odds with one another. Her face is a space "wherein we can read strange matters," and whereas Wilde's Lady Windermere is "a fascinating puritan" (17), Lubitsch's heroine briefly evinces ambiguous feelings towards her tempter. Right from the beginning, the Hollywoodian Windermere has been "Americanized" as less strait-laced than her Victorian model.

Lubitsch's camera can freeze a shot into a striking photographic inscape (to borrow a term from Gerard Manley Hopkins). Such a shot is seen at the end of the film when Mrs. Erlynne, to save her daughter from social ruin, pretends to be Darlington's lover. She literally comes out of the closet to face the cold and disapproving stare of Darlington's male guests. The socialites stand in two symmetrical lines forming a passage as the fallen woman steps out of the door frame. The scene is backlit, so she comes out of a bright room into a shaft of light surrounded by darkness. This is a shining path or a walk of shame where she has to face the gauntlet of social anathema. The metaphorical shot obviously carries an ambivalent meaning. Mrs. Erlynne is viewed as a sacrificial victim, a social outcast on the viewer's side of the screen (the eyes of society) and a good woman on the other (off-screen) side, from where a symbolic light comes. The off-screen lighting is not to be taken as evidence of the transcendent or divine viewpoint, but as evidence of the view of the implied storyteller—a kind of metaleptic statement which, incidentally, accords with Wilde's characterization of Mrs. Erlynne. That is, the framing and lighting of this shot suggest an abstract, archetypical pattern or design whose meaning is gradually revealed as universal.

Sometimes, Lubitsch frames an inanimate object or an empty space and lets characters pop in and out of it, like a view though a window that catches a passing world—a central tenet of André Bazin's cinema aesthetics. This technique is used to comic effect in the birthday party scene, when the camera is focused on a wall painting or tapestry which fills the screen. The allegorical painting represents three robed men who appear to confer with one another over the fate of some individual who is lying on a couch. Then, the heads of the three sanctimonious women (the three gossips who earlier had criticized Mrs. Erlynne) are seen bobbing up and down at the bottom of the frame. Their inquisitive faces, cut off at the neck, craning and straining to look at the scandalous Erlynne against an allegorical backdrop, project visually a synthetic satirical comment that no wording can possibly match. This is an instance of Lubitsch's skill in making the best of both cinematic and theatrical codes.

Lubitsch's style includes showing body movements through space to express characters' relationships and suggest paradox and irony. In one particular sequence, which has no counterpart in Wilde's play, he uses body postures and movements through space to express Lord Darlington's strange declaration of love. A long shot of a vast room sets the stylized scene: there is a bench in the background and a sofa far left in the foreground, suggesting depth of field and great distance. Darlington and Margaret Windermere stand on the right of the frame, two diminutive bodies in relation to the room. They cut an odd geometrical shape as Ronald Colman's much larger silhouette leans dynamically towards May McAvoy's frail and intimidated body. The male character is shot as an active agent of both sensual initiation and sexual threat, and, at this early stage at least, the woman is confined to a helpless and passive role.

The kinesic ballet that ensues plays fast and loose with the female body. Lady Windermere crosses the whole room horizontally, right to left, to sit on the sofa, a movement signifying proxemic negation or conflict. Lord Darlington paradoxically moves slowly into depth of field and comes to sit on the bench, far in the background, adding even greater distance. A medium shot of the uneasy woman, looking off frame, is contrasted with a similar view of the devilish aristocrat, gazing in her direction and yet again dynamically leaning forward, as if ready to pounce. Yet, after being tempted verbally (signified with an intertitle card), the hunted lady moves into the background to sit near her tormentor, who bluntly tells her, "I love you." He then rises to move upstage at a leisurely pace, leaving her alone again, in a different screen plane altogether, where she slowly fades out.

This is masterful cinematic and dramatic storytelling. The young woman in Wilde's play holds her own against the insidious wit of her aesthete lover and firmly rebuffs his adulterous advances. Using screen space and body movement along various axes of direction, Lubitsch, in contrast, shows the victimization of the female body: Margaret is threatened, tempted, isolated, and, visually and metaphorically, led a dance. Furthermore, the American Margaret Windermere contrasts with Wilde's Victorian character by evincing more emotional body language towards the would-be adulterer.

Much of what Lubitsch achieves in this scene could have been shown on a stage, but Lubitsch also draws upon the resources of cinematic screen space for comic purposes. It is worth quoting the passage from the play when Lady Windermere pries her husband's checkbook open, only to discover the disturbing truth:

> Lady Windermere: ...I *will* find out. [*Opens drawer.*] No, it is some hideous mistake. [*Rises and goes C.*] Some silly scandal! He loves *me*! He loves *me*! But why should I not look? I am his wife, I have a right to look! [*Returns to bureau, takes out a book and examines it page by page, smiles and gives a sigh of relief.*] I knew it! There is not a word of truth in this stupid story. [*Puts the book back in drawer. As she does so, starts and takes another book.*] A second book—private—and locked! [*Tries to open it, but fails. Sees paper knife on bureau, and with it cuts cover from book. Begins to start at first page.*] 'Mrs. Erlynne—£600—Mrs. Erlynne—£700—Mrs. Erlynne—£400.' Oh! It is true! It is true! How horrible. [*Throws book on floor.*] (23)

This passage is faithfully rendered on the screen entirely by means of film grammar. Lubitsch makes fun of the young wife's guilty temptation, and therefore his adaptation of Lady Windermere's theatrical monologue alters the tone of the passage more than its content. The scene consists of six shots, all of them showing the woman's choreographed moves in and out of the screen, with frame borders working as transgression metaphors. First, in a long shot of her husband's office, she is shown looking gingerly at the desk drawer, an object of desire and danger, her Pandora's box. The desk will remain a magnet for her gaze throughout the scene. Then she darts offscreen. The camera cuts to her as she sits awkwardly in an armchair at the left side of the room. Another cut shows her turning her eyes towards the desk offscreen as she rises. Next, a medium shot holds the desk for quite some time and slows the editing pace. Margaret reenters the screen and comes near the desk, has a look at the drawer, and darts left offscreen again. Then, quite surprisingly, she reappears on-screen, coming from the right edge of the frame, disorientating the viewer. The scene ends on Margaret's failed attempt at wrenching the drawer open. Her effort is interrupted by the arrival of Lady Berwyck. (Later, on Windermere's return, he sees his drawer has been jammed open; thus, the actual act of jimmying the lock is elliptical.)

The edges of the frame and the contiguous off/on-screen space are here used as signs. The center area—the mystery desk—forms the forbidden space, bounded by transgression lines. The young woman is gingerly circling round some irresistible danger. Without words, Lubitsch manages to convey Margaret's inner conflict, or her inability "to resist anything but temptation" (Wilde, Act 1).

Another remarkable scene in the film occurs during the garden scene at Margaret Windermere's birthday party. Here the young wife sees Mrs. Erlynne's hand being held by a person who is hidden behind a bush (whom, in her jealous state, she assumes to be her husband). At first, the shot is static, with a frontal, pro-scenic point of view. A cut reveals the same scene, but this time, viewed from a diametrically opposed "backstage" vantage point (a sudden shift which breaks the 180-degree rule of Hollywood cinema). The hidden person is in fact Lord Augustus, Mrs. Erlynne's suitor. This detail is the cinematic equivalent of dramatic irony: a cut on simultaneous action which alters focalization allows the spectator to see what is denied to Margaret Windermere. Lubitsch never resorts to obvious cinematic effects; he is truly a master of screen space, which he segments with artfully concealed film semiotics.

Another closely related dimension of Lubitsch's semiotics is his figurative language. Discursive figures are fairly easy to identity and define in the noncinematic arts—rhetoric, drama, mime, photography, painting, and music. In film, pans, tracks, cuts, close-ups, and tilts can be used as filmic tropes or schemes. Although they are not as neatly codified as they are in other art forms, cinematic techniques of storytelling lend themselves to transfers of meaning and therefore can be interpreted figuratively. Admittedly, such hermeneutics is hazardous: the only safe way to read cinematic figures is to work at the level of individual style or film.

For example, Lubitsch is fond of close-ups on hands. What is at stake is not so much the close-up in itself as how it relates cinematically to other shots in the dynamics of screen time and space. In the opening sequence, Lord Darlington strides boldly into Lady Windermere's room; then, a medium shot shows him shaking hands with her. Lubitsch cuts to a close-up of the man's hand clasping the woman's for some time, then cuts back to the man trying to bring her hand to his lips and being rebuffed by a cold, offended stare. The close-up breaks time and space continuity and places the hand synecdoche in a different screen plane. The shot is a true foregrounding trope. Slowing screen time and magnifying screen space breaks the narrative pace and sets up a different diegetic plane. Thus, Lubitsch's close-up inserted into a series of medium shots is a trope and a stylistic variant, like a sentence which suddenly introduces a parallel topic on a semantic and narrative plane. The hands locked in a conflict are both metonymic and metaphoric; they are foregrounded subjects acting out an amorous war of attrition in which the hapless woman is a prisoner. The shot could be cut from the scene with no loss to the story, but it adds humor and style. And, for Lubitsch, as for Wilde, style is all.

Another close-up used as a stylistic variant comes shortly after the handshake scene. Lord Windermere is trying to hide Mrs. Erlynne's letter out of his wife's sight, but he cannot reach it. A close-up focuses on Lord Darlington's hand secretly helping the letter into his rival's. The foregrounding shot is more effective than any other shot would be here because the filmmaker wants the viewer to have the ironic impression that the woman is left out of the action. The hand metonym opens up another diegetic plane in which the woman has no part. A less skilful filmmaker might have shown the surreptitious gesture from a different angle and in a different shot scale; the referential content would have been the same, but the ironic effect would have been radically different.

Because it breaks the cinematic flux of Hollywood storytelling time, the close-up calls attention to itself. When Lord Augustus, the aging love-struck bachelor, pays his first visit to Mrs. Erlynne, Lubitsch elaborates on a close-up of his hand ringing her doorbell. The scene is introduced by a (rare) textual commentary: "A gentleman's relation to a lady is indicated by the manner in which he rings her doorbell." The gentleman's right hand is first shown about to push the bell button, but it hesitates and draws back. His left hand opens his waistcoat pocket and produces a small mirror which is raised offscreen and returned to its place. Then, the right hand rings the bell without hesitation. Obviously, the storytelling pace is slowed, and time expands with this focus on detail. What would have been backgrounded in the logic of Hollywood economic storytelling (the detail of ringing a bell) is here foregrounded.

The stylistic effect is humorous rather than ironic. By deautomatizing a subsidiary event in a narrative chain, the camera pokes fun at a man's subtle body language, which betrays unmanly emotion and vanity. As a visual counterpart of Wilde's witty aphorism "None of us men do look what we really are," Lubitsch's witty close-up has no rival. It takes the microscopic eye of his camera to detect what men really are.

Two types of close-ups retain one's attention. The objective close-up reproduces the filmmaker's viewpoint, and the subjective close-up represents a character's point of view. Lubitsch likes to defamiliarize shots that are viewed from a subjective perspective—not to break the illusion of reality, but to satirize. A common dramatic use of the point-of-view shot is to increase viewers' emotional involvement with a character onscreen. But Lubitsch combines point-of-view close-up shots with a mask (a literal image of looking through binoculars or a keyhole) to suggest voyeurism and introduce ironic distance between the secret focalizer and the spectator. Here again, as is the case for most of these examples, the mask in isolation is hardly significant: what matters are the focalizing shifts which happen in screen time over a given scene or sequence.

The sequence at the horse races (which is not in Wilde's play) rests on the social game of who sees whom and who is seen. Unlike Lady Windermere's birthday party, where guests come close together and are bound to socialize, the racetrack scene is the cinematic equivalent of a social register recording the current standing of an individual in high society. This particular event takes place in an open setting which allows a wider view on a larger crowd and where the watching game can be conducted with relative secrecy. A keen observer of people, Lubitsch was well aware of the bearing of setting on social behavior. He chose a day at the races to represent visually the rumors concerning Windermere's supposed kept woman and to discredit the gossip mongers.

In the race scene, the binocular mask is used as a figure of construction (a filmic scheme). Mrs. Erlynne is the focalized subject, or more accurately, perhaps, the object. She magnetizes the gazes of all the other characters except Margaret Windermere, who is oblivious of her mother's presence and the scandal centering on her. But Lubitsch prevents the film spectator from identifying with the voyeurs and therefore uses focalizing techniques to divide onlookers into voyeurs (negative) and viewers (positive). Lord Windermere, Lord Augustus, and Lord Darlington are characterized as being favorably disposed towards the lady adventurer, whereas the women, focalizing in voyeuristic shots, evince hostility towards Mrs. Erlynne, seeing her as a sexual rival.

The comical horse race sequence opens with a series of high-angle wide shots of crowds milling around the ground of the track. Then, in the only dynamic shot of the film, the camera pans down to reveal the plumed hat of Mrs. Erlynne, surrounded by a crowd of bowler hats. This hat parade is funny in itself, evoking a mating ritual among birds. As she turns to walk off-screen at the bottom right of the frame, Mrs. Erlynne magnetizes the gaze of the men around her. Next, she walks up a gangway to stand isolated against a railing. There is a wide shot of officials in a booth watching her through binoculars, and then the camera cuts to a subjective close-up of Mrs. Erlynne seen through the binocular mask. This is Lubitsch's stylish visual way of saying that the scandalous lady is the talk of the town.

The most dramatic and ironic focalizing shift comes when the focalized character becomes the focalizer. Mrs. Erlynne looks offscreen, and a matching cut shows the back of Lady Windermere's hat and the smiling faces of Lord Augustus and Lord Windermere. Mrs. Erlynne's face stiffens. The viewer assumes that one of the men is the reason for her emotional turn, because she cannot see Lady Windermere's face. Then the film cuts to a close-up of Lord Windermere, looking offscreen and freezing in shocked surprise. Mrs. Erlynne looks down demurely. Darlington notices the turmoil and smiles knowingly. But, another point-of-view close-up reveals that Mrs. Erlynne has caught sight of her daughter and is anxiously waiting for her to turn and show her face. Thereafter,

Mrs. Erlynne will revert to her role of the focalized object of gossip and be seen through masked shots, in "camera voyeur" style.

What is meaningful in Lubitsch's film is the cinematic play of viewpoints, not the mask itself or the point-of-view shot in isolation. There are three focalizing displacements, or shifts. The first concerns the mask versus nonmask point-of-view shot—the voyeur versus nonvoyeur gaze—with respective connotations of negative or positive interest. Second, there is the sudden shift when the object of the representation, which magnetizes the eyes of all observers, becomes the subjective viewer for a brief but intense moment, a filmic epiphany that is meant to affect the spectator who empathizes with Mrs. Erlynne's longing to see her daughter. Finally, there is dramatic irony in the absence of subjective shots from Lady Windermere's perspective. Unlike all the other characters, she is denied any focalizing knowledge, or filmic center of consciousness. Throughout the movie, she will stand for a victimized character until, in the ultimate sequence, she too will "see" clearly. These focalizing deviations are cinematic figures connoting satire, pathos, and irony.

Shot composition, body moves within a frame, close-ups, and shifts in viewpoint belong to the poetics of space. These aspects of filmic staging interact with the poetics of screen time such as echoes, temporal sequencing, and other details of editing. Lubitsch uses specific cinematic codes such as panning or fancy angles sparingly, shooting scenes primarily by theatrical rules. Cutting from one static shot to another (often using doors as transitions) remains his favored dramatic technique to advance the story. The motion picture is segmented in eight long building blocks (sequences, or acts), and within these sequences, scenes and shots are fairly rapidly paced and cut. Although it is theatrical, the picture is enlivened by subtle figures, or "turns."

One such figure rests on the structural and temporal device of a variation within a recurrent scene, introducing a form of echo, or a variation on a structure. Lubitsch shoots three man-meets-woman sequences with a sofa to visualize the respective roles and relationships between his male and female characters. In her first encounter with Lord Darlington, Lady Windermere is shown sitting on a sofa at the left of the frame, turning her back. Darlington comes to sit fairly close to her, leaning slightly forward. Her uneasy posture is metaphoric: she is cornered by her overzealous lover and is afraid of eye contact. Darlington looks predatory, and although he is rejected, he seems to make an impression on her. A few minutes of film time later, Lubitsch creates a contrasting echo. Lord Windermere calls on Mrs. Erlynne, who invites him to sit down. Lubitsch shows an empty sofa and cuts to the man refusing with a nod to take a seat. The sofa will remain conspicuously empty all through this sequence, while the antagonists' body postures will tell a subtly choreographed tale of strife brewing between the lady and her son-in-law. Yet another variation on the theme occurs when Lord Augustus pays his first visit to Mrs. Erlynne. Here, Lubitsch opens with a long shot of a large room with a sofa in the background in front of a brightly lit bow window. Both protagonists stand in the foreground and slowly turn to walk into the depth of field and sit down. A cut to a medium shot reveals them sitting face to face with their knees nearly touching. August offers Mrs. Erlynne a cigarette; she taps the tip on the back of her hand, wets it between her lips a couple of times, and he—metaphorically—lights her fire. In all three sequences, the symbolic sofa reads like a subtext respectively frustrating, negating, or fulfilling love or erotic attraction.

Incidentally, the sequence featuring the lovers ends in a fade-out, contrary to the sequences showing a man and a woman at odds. Fading signals a particular kind of temporal punctuation, and here, it does not merely mark the end of a sequence and a new narrative turn, it is also meant to be read figuratively. The fade represents a narrative ellipsis, an omitted scene rather than a temporal transition. Lubitsch leaves the viewer "in the dark" as to what happens next between the bachelor and the adventuress. This information is not so much cut from the sequence as left to the imagination of the spectator.

The greatest challenge confronting any filmmaker of the silent era was to create the illusion of spoken dialogue. There was an inherent absurdity in filming soundless conversation, even with the help of intertitle cards. Frequently, the characters in silent movies looked somewhat like oneiric creatures whose words were begging entrance.

Yet, in adapting Wilde's play, Lubitsch had to translate Wilde's witty, epigrammatic discourse into silent film grammar. The screenplay consists almost entirely of dialogue scenes or indoor "speech events," with hardly any actions in a narrative sense. Unimaginative dialogue representation would have killed the movie, but Lubitsch's inventive and entertaining style conveys dramatic communication on the screen.

Here is an example. During the exchange between Mrs. Erlynne and Lord Windermere as they argue over Mrs. Erlynne's invitation to Margaret's birthday party, only two written intertitle cards are needed. Lubitsch chose not to include the presequence (the entrance of the characters, greetings, topic initiating, and so on) for this scene. Instead, the conversation starts in *medias res*: a long shot of a large room shows the two speakers standing wide apart and turning their backs to each other. The *mise en scène* thus indicates dialogic distance and deadlock over an unknown topic; the aporia creates suspense as to what brought the dialogue to an angry standstill. This opening shot sets the conflictual atmosphere of the conversation and therefore translates into what is known in silent film language as the "key," the component that sets the mood and the tone as of a speech event. Here, the topical content is delayed. After the exchange, one sees Mrs. Erlynne turning around to look at Windermere and walking towards him. A matching cut on the action combined with a change in shot scale reveals her in a pleading role and him in a silent, channel-closing role, turning his back on her and gazing downward. Next, a medium shot brings out both emotional states and speaking roles, two components of the conversation related to the affective and interpersonal layer of a speech event. Again, the revelation of semantic content is delayed. Windermere walks away, and finally, the viewer is shown a title card of Mrs. Erlynne's words to Windermere: "I am desperate—if you refuse to invite me tonight—I will go to my daughter and will tell her who I am!" The scene ends with a series of shot/reverse shot scenes, which shows them angrily conversing.

Although there was no soundstage when *Lady Windermere's Fan* was shot, Lubitsch insisted on his actors' speaking their lines aloud as if they were being recorded by a microphone. As a result, some utterances can be construed from lip-reading, especially when their content is predictable from both the context and the topic. It is possible to "see" the dialogue in the scene that was just described:

> WINDERMERE: "You won't do that!"
> MRS. ERLYNNE: "Yes. [pause] I will do it!"
> [long pause]
> WINDERMERE: "All right."

Here, even the tone is discernable, not only in the use of space, timing, and intertitle cards, but also by allowing the viewers to see head movements, facial expressions, and speech itself.

In closing the interaction, Lubitsch has Mrs. Erlynne explain the purpose of her plea by means of a second continuity title: she needs social recognition to be eligible to marry Lord Augustus. The epilogue is skillful and inconclusive. The antagonists shake hands with sad, resigned faces; then the woman is left alone and forlorn on the fading screen. One does not know, at this stage, what decision the man will make.

This sequence is highly stylized and tightly structured. First, in terms of sequencing and topical coherence, the soundless dialogue tends to invert the structure of a verbal conversation and perhaps for this reason is suspenseful and entertaining. Then, shot scales are chosen to define the frames of discourse components. Finally, other codes, such as lip-reading and continuity intertitle cards, supply semantic content. Overall, it is striking how much stylized verbal discourse silent film semiotics can represent. Incidentally, attention to Lubitsch's technique also explains why verbal dialogue appeared so redundant and inept when commercial talkies invaded the silver screen after 1927.

Judging on the basis of this scene alone, by any reasonable standard, Lubitsch's filmic art is remarkable. Any film dialogue is a literary discourse, a far cry from everyday conversation. Viewers experience film dialogue as a stylistic variant of "real" talk and judge the aesthetic value of cinematic speech in part according to how much it departs from their own conversational habits; in ordinary conversation, speakers do not usually wait until the end of an exchange to expose the purpose and content of their messages. Against the grain of ordinary conversation, in the scene between Mrs. Erlynne and Lord Windermere, Lubitsch gives maximum impact to Mrs. Erlynne's desperate plea for social recognition by delaying the semantic and teleological levels of her utterances. He immediately sets the key of the exchange (what is often called the interpersonal level, or "tenor," of discourse [Halliday 117]). The intertitle cards recording speech are not allowed to split the visuals. And, the topical coherence is neatly framed by the shot scale structure of the sequence: full shots and medium shots establish situation context, attitudes, and pragmatic roles and medium close-ups establish content and purpose.

I will return, for a moment, to the play. In Wilde's last dialogue between Mrs. Erlynne and Lord Windermere, the lady comes across as a stereotypical fallen woman, placed in a subservient and begging role. Lubitsch's character is more realistic. The filmmaker often said that he wanted his film characters to behave like common people, not ideal types given to heroics. Mrs. Erlynne in the play could be interpreted as Wilde's female *doppelgänger*, an aesthete who acts as a moral litmus test for late Victorian mores, whereas in Lubitsch's film adaptation, one experiences the Americanization of Mrs. Erlynne, who turns out to be not a female dandy, but a mere woman. By hook or by crook, she must fight her way through hostile territory. This transformation is achieved perhaps to the detriment of psychological complexity, but complexity here would have stood in the way of wit.

As skillfully as any director of his time, Lubitsch demonstrates in *Lady Windermere's Fan* the varied and subtle possibilities of silent film for transposing wit and dramatic discourse into visual semiotics—and the paradox of the enterprise of adaptation. Style is the artful selection of choices that are afforded by the possibilities of the medium. But, in the very process of rendering the play, the formal characteristics of the medium force changes upon the original material. Film form plays its part in recreating dramatic matter, and adaptation should be thought of as a two-way process: choices made by the author and changes resulting from the nature of film poetics. Indeed, the artist's struggle with the limitations of the medium contributes to style, which can be understood as a compromise between the artist's intention and what can be constructed with the stubborn building blocks of art.

Short of filming an actual stage performance from a pro-scenic and unchanging viewpoint, Lubitsch could only depart from Wilde's brilliant farce from the moment he started to rewrite the play into a screenplay. This is not to say that the medium, rather than the artist, made the film, but simply to point out that no artist has a free hand. Every art form has a life of its own. Cinema does not simply mirror life; it is life made more vivid than reality—otherwise nobody would watch flickering shadows.

Bibliography

Baticle, Yveline. *Clés et codes du cinéma*. Paris: Magnard, 1973. Print.

Bazin, André. *What Is Cinema?* Trans. Hugh Gray. Berkeley: University of California, 1967. Print.

Binh, N. T., and Christian Viviani. *Lubitsch*. Paris: Editions Rivages, 1991. Print.

Bordwell, David, and Kristin Thompson. *Film Art: An Introduction*. Boston: McGraw Hill, 2008. Print.

Collet, Jean, et al. *Lectures du film*. Paris: Editions Albatros, 1973. Print.

Dowson, Ernest. *The Poems and Prose of Ernest Downson*. New York: Boni and Liveright, 1919. Print.

Elam, Keir. *The Semiotics of Theatre and Drama*. London: Methuen, 1980. Print.

Eyman, Scott. *Ernst Lubitsch: Laughter in Paradise*. Baltimore: Johns Hopkins University Press, 2000. Print.

Halliday, Michael *Language as Social Semiotics*. London: Edward Arnold, 1978.

Katz, Steven D. *Film Directing Shot by Shot: Visualizing from Concept to Screen*. Studio City: Michael Wiese Productions in Conjunction with Focal, 1991. Print.

Kracauer, Siegfried. *Theory of Film; the Redemption of Physical Reality*. New York: Oxford University Press, 1960. Print.

Metz, Christian. *Film Language: A Semiotics of the Cinema*. Chicago: University of Chicago, 1991. Print.

Montagu, Ivor. *Film World*. Harmondsworth: Penguin, 1964. Print.

Spottiswoode, Raymond. *A Grammar of the Film: An Analysis of Film Technique*. Berkeley: University of California, 1973. Print.

Van, Sijll Jennifer. *Cinematic Storytelling: The 100 Most Powerful Film Conventions Every Filmmaker Must Know*. Studio City: Michael Wiese Productions, 2005. Print.

Vidor, King. *King Vidor on Film Making*. New York: McKay, 1972. Print.

Wilde, Oscar. *Lady Windermere's Fan*. London: Penguin, 1986. Print.

FILMOGRAPHY

Lady Windermere's Fan. Dir. Ernst. Lubitsch. Perf. Ronald Colman, May McAvoy, and Bert Lytell. Warner Brothers. 1925. Film.

CHAPTER 3

ADAPTING DICKENS'S
A CHRISTMAS CAROL IN PROSE

Natalie Neill

In December of 1843, Charles Dickens published his first and most popular Christmas book, *A Christmas Carol. In Prose. Being a Ghost Story of Christmas*. Beautifully bound and containing hand-colored illustrations by *Punch* artist John Leech, it was designed specially for the emerging Christmas market. A gift book that flaunted its own commodity status, *A Christmas Carol* was fated to become among the most peddled, parodied, remade, and retailed of Dickens's works. Its swift and enduring popularity is owing to the fact that it was, from the beginning, a text that involved readers in its message by encouraging the celebration of Christmas. *A Christmas Carol* justifies through its very moral those people who would purchase and consume it. Even as it taught audiences the importance of seasonal traditions and altruistic spending, it became a "Christmas institution" (Childers, 116) and holiday product in its own right.

Less than three weeks after the publication of *A Christmas Carol*, the process of adaptation began in the form of a pirated version of the story, which appeared in issue 16 of *Parley's Illuminated Library*. Arguably the first in a long line of *Christmas Carol* knockoffs and remakes, the piracy was called "A Christmas Ghost Story. Re-Originated from the Original by Charles Dickens, Esq., and Analytically Condensed Expressly for This Work." The title reveals that far from wishing to conceal the debt to Dickens, publishers Richard Egan Lee and John Haddock sought to capitalize on the original author's celebrity. By invoking his name, they effectively advertised the work as a Dickensian product and, in this respect, their pirated abridgment anticipated countless *Christmas Carol* adaptations that followed.[1]

Dickens soon had many other imitators whose spin-off texts, without question, assisted in the canonization of *A Christmas Carol*. Long before the advent of the cinema, *A Christmas Carol* had a rich adaptation history.[2] It is a text that may be used to support Linda Hutcheon's broadly conceived theory of adaptation. In her 2006 study, Hutcheon rightly urges adaptation scholars to expand the definition of what constitutes an adaptation. Her book opens with this blunt address to the reader: "If you think adaptation can be understood by using novels and films alone, you're wrong" (xi). Undoubtedly, to limit adaptation studies to discussions of intertextual relationships between literature and film is to restrict the field; yet it is the link that Hutcheon makes between Victorian and postmodernist adaptation practices that is most germane to the topic of *Christmas Carol* adaptations. "The Victorians had a habit of adapting just about everything," she observes,

> —and in just about every possible direction; the stories of poems, novels, plays, operas, paintings, songs, dances, and *tableaux vivants* were constantly being adapted from one medium to another and then back again. We postmoderns have clearly inherited this same habit, but we have new materials at our disposal. (xi)

Victorian adaptations were manifestations of emergent mass culture. As Grahame Smith argues, the "absence of copyright protection meant that all kinds of literature were liable to be appropriated in the highly commercialized world of early Victorian entertainment" (Smith, "Dickens and Adaptation" 51). The early pirated version of *A Christmas Carol* demonstrates that the popularity and marketability of Dickens's works made them particularly attractive as source texts. Richard Kelly has remarked that many people now know *A Christmas Carol* only through the adaptations (28); in fact, this may have been the case in Victorian times as well. Dickens's story would have been familiar even to those who had not (or could not) read the book. Fred Guida, in his study on adaptations of *A Christmas Carol*, lists various precinematic adaptations, including *Christmas Carol* sheet music and magic lantern shows (39, 50–61). Shortly after the publication of the book, a flurry of stage adaptations appeared. Dickens made a point of attending the first *Christmas Carol* play, Edward Stirling's musical, *A Christmas Carol, or, Past, Present, and Future*, which premiered early in February 1844. Stirling had brought Dickens's earlier novels to the stage too, so when the author conceded, in a letter to John Forster, that the performance was "[b]etter than usual" (50), he was likely making a comparison to prior adaptations of his work. Astonishingly, before the end of February 1844, at least five more *Christmas Carol* plays were staged (Guida, 41). There can be no doubt that the culture industry that has grown up around Dickens has its origins in the author's own day.

Of the many Victorian adaptations of *A Christmas Carol*, Dickens's own lively performances of the story were perhaps the most popular. Between 1853 and his death in 1870, the author delivered hundreds of public readings. His *A Christmas Carol* readings were particularly beloved by audiences. Likely prompted by the 1852 publication of his collected Christmas books, Dickens chose *A Christmas Carol* for his first reading. He also selected the work for his final performance in 1870. When Dickens gave readings of *A Christmas Carol*, he used as his script a copy of the text which he had marked and annotated in his own hand.[3] The prompt copy reveals that Dickens abridged the text considerably for his performances. As Philip Collins explains, the author regularly added new scenes, sometimes spontaneously (Collins, Introduction xv–xvi).

Dickens's "impromptu improvements and variations" (xvi) demonstrate that he was not overly concerned with maintaining fidelity to his original work. Moreover, according to Collins, audiences did not object if Dickens was not faithful to the letter of the text; when they recognized that he was making extemporaneous additions or deviations, they were delighted.

It would seem that fidelity is not the main concern in more recent adaptations either. The development of film, radio, and television opened up new possibilities for Dickens adapters. The number of *Christmas Carol* adaptations grew exponentially in the twentieth century, and many of the "endlessly spun out versions" of Dickens's novella (Glavin, 28) use the original story merely as a point of departure. Guida's annotated filmography lists more than 140 cinematic and televisual adaptations made between 1901 and 1995. Certainly, the most canonical of the film versions—which Guida terms the "major *Carols*" (4)—are relatively faithful. Best identified by the actors who performed the part of Scrooge, these include the two 1930s adaptations featuring Seymour Hicks and Reginald Owen, respectively; the 1951 classic starring Alastair Sim (who is, for many, the quintessential Scrooge); the Albert Finney musical (1970); and the 1984 television movie with George C. Scott. More recently, Patrick Stewart, who has won awards for his one-person stage performances of *A Christmas Carol*, appeared as Scrooge in a 1999 made-for-TV adaptation. Soon thereafter, the stage musical starring Kelsey Grammer was turned into another television movie. In 2001, Simon Callow, Kate Winslet, and Nicolas Cage lent their voices to an animated adaptation directed by Jimmy Murakami. In 2009, Jim Carrey played Scrooge in a 3-D Walt Disney picture. One could add to this list countless looser adaptations. A few notable late-twentieth-century reimaginings of *A Christmas Carol* include *Mister Magoo's Christmas Carol* (1962); the 1988 modernization *Scrooged*, in which Ebenezer Scrooge becomes Frank Cross (Bill Murray), a selfish television executive; *Blackadder's Christmas Carol* (1988), a parody in which ghostly visitations cause Rowan Atkinson's Ebenezer Blackadder to *lose* his Christmas cheer; and *The Muppet Christmas Carol*

(1992), featuring Michael Caine in the miser's role and Kermit the Frog as Bob Cratchit.

The early film adaptations in particular trade on the high cultural cachet of the original text. For example, the 1951 film opens with the image of a shelf of handsome editions of Dickens's novels. A hand removes a copy of *A Christmas Carol* from among these and opens it to display the credits. In effect, the film *is* the book. At the other end of the spectrum are spin-offs that alter Dickens's story in ways that make it almost unrecognizable. Included in this category is Frank Capra's *It's a Wonderful Life* (1946), which Guida and others have identified as an adaptation of *A Christmas Carol*. Capra's movie is, in fact, based on a 1943 short story by Philip Van Doren Stern called "The Greatest Gift." In Van Doren Stern's story, a suicidal man, George Pratt, is visited on Christmas Eve by a kindly ghost who shows him that his life does have meaning. Capra's adaptation is less *Carol*-esque in that supernatural intervention comes in the form of the "angel, second class," Clarence, who earns his wings after teaching George Bailey (James Stewart) that his life has mattered and that he ought to be grateful for what he has. The film strengthens the connection to Dickens's story, however, by adding the plotline involving the miserable Old Mr. Potter (Lionel Barrymore), clearly a Scrooge-like figure, though he undergoes no transformation. Dickensian resonances would have been especially strong for early audiences, Guida notes, because Barrymore had since the mid-1930s often performed the role of Ebenezer Scrooge in radio adaptations of *A Christmas Carol* (162).

A midcentury *Christmas Carol* spin-off that goes unmentioned in Guida's list is the Dr. Seuss children's book *How the Grinch Stole Christmas!* (1957). This book was further popularized through the 1966 Christmas special directed by Chuck Jones. Although differences between the stories by Dickens and Seuss are obvious, there are points of similarity that are worth considering. Both *A Christmas Carol* and *How the Grinch Stole Christmas!* are redemption narratives that unfold over two days, Christmas Eve and Christmas Day. Both Christmas books give accounts of the integration into the community of hardened, cynical outsiders. The Grinch, like Scrooge, at first scorns holiday revelry for "his heart was two sizes too small" (3), but he embraces Christmas after learning its true meaning. Finally, both characters have memorable made-up names, which are now standard dictionary words used to denote a killjoy (OED). That actor Jim Carrey was selected for the role of Scrooge after having played the Grinch in Ron Howard's 2000 adaptation of the Seuss book suggests that the correspondences between the two characters were not lost on casting agents.

It's a Wonderful Life and *How the Grinch Stole Christmas!* are texts that would not exist had *A Christmas Carol* never been written. Now these spin-offs are Christmas traditions in their own right. Yet, there have been many far more ephemeral twentieth- and twenty-first-century *Christmas Carol* offshoots—for example, the *WKRP in Cincinnati* spoof (1980), *A Jetson Christmas Carol* (1985), and *An All Dogs Christmas Carol* (1998), to name just a few. Dickens's novella has been reworked in almost every imaginable way. In the 2003 Hallmark television movie *A Carol Christmas*, the Scrooge character is an egotistical female talk show host (Tori Spelling) and the Ghost of Christmas Present (William Shatner) "teleports" from one location to the next. In the political comedy *An American Carol* (2008), liberal documentary filmmaker Michael Malone (Kevin Farley) is visited by three ghosts who teach him to be more conservative. Such spin-offs are possible only because *A Christmas Carol* is so well known. In the latter movie, Dickens's story is merely a vehicle for right-wing satire. Its familiar structure is taken up and used by the filmmaker to serve his own purpose and agenda.

In addition to the audiovisual adaptations mentioned previously (and countless others), there have been many literary rewritings of *A Christmas Carol*. In some *Christmas Carol*-inspired books, Dickens's tale is retold from the perspective of secondary characters. Such is the case in Tom Mula's *Jacob Marley's Christmas Carol* (1995) (also an award-winning play by Mula) and Louis Bayard's *Christmas Carol* sequel *Mr. Timothy* (2003), a murder mystery which imagines Tiny Tim in his mid-twenties. Other recent sequels include *The Last Christmas of Ebenezer Scrooge* (2003) by Marvin Kaye and *Ebenezer: The Final*

Years (2008) by Donna Lee Howell. Most recent of the rewritings, in the tradition of Seth Grahame-Smith's *Pride and Prejudice and Zombies* (2009), is the mash-up novel *I Am Scrooge: A Zombie Story for Christmas*, by Adam Roberts (2009). Allen Grove has noted that as Jane Austen was concerned in *Northanger Abbey* with criticizing "readers for their indiscriminate consumption" of Gothic novels, she might very well have approved of such works as *Pride and Prejudice and Zombies* (355). Through the trope of the voracious undead, the novels by Grahame-Smith and Roberts exploit and at the same time satirize modern consumers' insatiable appetites for Austen and Dickens. Yet, this raises a question: Why has Dickens's "Ghostly little book" (as it is described in the preface to *A Christmas Carol*) in particular been so often reanimated by adapters and so eagerly and repeatedly consumed by audiences? What accounts for its longevity and adaptability?

First, it is necessary to address some of the obstacles that confront adapters of *A Christmas Carol*. One issue concerns the darkness and negativity of some scenes in the original work, which reflect the dire social conditions of 1840s England and Dickens's moral indignation over the suffering and treatment of the poor in that period. Many film versions and plays gloss over the social realities of the Hungry Forties. In order to make the end product more palatable and appealing to audiences, adapters of *A Christmas Carol* romanticize Victorian England or modernize the story, thus removing it from its historical context altogether.

Theater critic Jerome Weeks identifies several more practical challenges that the story presents to those wishing to bring it to the stage, including the problems associated with portraying the chimerical Ghost of Christmas Past and the difficulty of depicting such supernatural effects as the appearance of Marley's face in the door knocker (28). In stage adaptations, this latter effect is usually not attempted; an alternative method is employed to let the audience know that Marley has appeared to Scrooge. Yet on the whole, *A Christmas Carol* is easy to render visually due to its vivid characterizations and evocative imagery. Moreover, one must not forget that the text of *A Christmas Carol* is interspersed with actual images, Leech's color plates, which are essential to the meaning of the work. These illustrations had an appreciable influence on later incarnations of the story. Brian Desmond Hurst (the director of the 1951 adaptation) closely studied them prior to making his highly influential film. As Lester J. Keyser notes, Leech's artistic style informed the "look" of the movie (122–123). Even without the accompanying illustrations, however, Dickens's book is powerfully visual, and for this reason, it lends itself well to stage and screen adaptation. Indeed, the author's writing style has long invited comparisons to theater and film. F. Dubrez Fawcett suggests that Dickens's novels are so often made into plays because the author's mode of writing is already dramatic (1–2). Dickens's writing is also, according to a recent study by Grahame Smith, "proto-cinematic" (*Dickens and the Dream of Cinema* 58). Sergei Eisenstein makes this argument in his groundbreaking 1949 essay "Dickens, Griffith, and the Film Today," in which he asserts that such basic film editing techniques as crosscutting were derived from Dickens's storytelling methods. Thus, Eisenstein maintains, the Victorian author exerted considerable influence on the evolution of narrative cinema.

Although theater and film directors take advantage of Dickens's visual style, they must also find ways to accommodate the first-person narrator of *A Christmas Carol*—the "voice that everyone hears in their heads when they read [the book]" (Weeks, 27). Dickens's narrator is at once an authorial surrogate and a character in his own right. He addresses readers directly in a confidential and compelling manner. By the time he brings the reader to Scrooge's countinghouse on Christmas Eve with the comfortable phrase "Once upon a time" (Dickens, *A Christmas Carol* 41), the reader is hooked; he or she is "listening" attentively. The manner of narration was a key ingredient in the early success of *A Christmas Carol*, because arguably the book was written to be read aloud. In stage and film versions, the narrating voice has been handled in various ways: it has been embodied as Dickens himself and transposed to a framing narrative, relegated to voice-over, abridged, and simply eliminated. In Desmond Hurst's movie, several of the narrator's lines are given to the ghosts. Stage adaptations such as Michael Shamata's *A Christmas*

Carol—performed since 2001 by the Toronto-based Soulpepper Theatre Company—recreate the intimacy of Dickens's book by turning the narrator into a character who speaks to the audience at the beginning and end of the play. At a performance of Shamata's adaptation on December 24, 2010, the actor in this role welcomed the audience with a hearty "Merry Christmas" and then paused noticeably so that audience members could respond in kind. In this adaptation and others, breaking the fourth wall is an effective means of approximating the intimate relationship that Dickens always cultivated with his readers.

Michael M. Riley mentions a final problem associated with adapting Dickens—namely, the canonical status of the author's work. "We are drawn to the film because of its origins in Dickens," explains Riley, "yet our very interest in the original becomes the greatest obstacle to our appreciation of the offspring it has spawned" (112). The familiarity and status of *A Christmas Carol* is a problem, however, only when faithfulness is the criterion that is used to evaluate the success of a given adaptation—and it rarely is. Among scholars, fidelity has become an unfashionable critical standard. More than twenty-five years ago, in "The Discourse on Adaptations" (1984), Christopher Orr identified "fidelity criticism" as the dominant discourse in the new field of adaptation studies (73). Fidelity criticism has, since then, become the discipline's "dead horse." As has already been suggested, most adapters of *A Christmas Carol* are also willing to forego fidelity. Indeed, as many consumers of the adaptations have never read Dickens's book, they are not in a position to note similarities and differences anyway. Instead, audiences may be more likely to make comparisons among adaptations. They might, for example, judge a theatrical performance of *A Christmas Carol* against their memory of the film starring Alastair Sim. Interpretations are gauged against earlier interpretations, without reference to the original. Dickens's text challenges what Thomas Leitch, in his chapter in this collection, calls the "sunburst model" of adaptation as well as other models that posit the original text as the sole source of all adaptations. Paul Davis observes that there are two *Christmas Carols*, the actual text written by Dickens and the "culture-text" that is a fixture in the popular imagination (4). In fact, it would seem that even as the myth of *A Christmas Carol* gained cultural traction, the original text receded in importance for both adapters and audiences. Gradually, it became just one of hundreds of versions.

Weeks states that *A Christmas Carol* "regularly ranks as the most-produced play among resident theatres for a reason": "it's the annual check in the bank" (25). Given the moral of Dickens's story, it would be a sad comment indeed if the love of lucre were the only factor behind its adaptation. Yet undoubtedly, adapters of *A Christmas Carol* are guaranteed a ready-made audience consisting of admirers of the original book or adaptations of it. Of course, this is true of all adaptations of classic literary works, but because *A Christmas Carol* is a Christmas story, there is an occasion every year to resurrect and re-present it—and profit from it. Although it may seem counterintuitive, adaptations of the book are profitable precisely because there are so many of them. The story's ubiquity at Christmas time has made it an important part of the holidays. *A Christmas Carol* is now an established Christmas ritual, and its many adaptations—beginning with those of the 1840s—have been the means of ritualization.

That Dickens's story now "practically tells itself" (Weeks, 25) is an advantage, not a liability, for adapters. Collins claims that for audiences of Dickens's public performances of *A Christmas Carol*, great pleasure lay in "anticipation and recognition"; audience members burst into applause before favorite characters such as Tiny Tim were introduced (Collins, Introduction xx). As anyone who has attended a live performance of *A Christmas Carol* knows, recognition still plays a vital role: audiences react most perceptibly to those lines of dialogue which are well known and most often quoted. Scrooge's curmudgeonly behavior elicits knowing laughter. Like other fairy tales, *A Christmas Carol* holds out the promise of a happy ending: one knows from the outset that "the squeezing, wrenching, grasping, scraping, clutching, covetous older sinner!" (Dickens, *A Christmas Carol* 40) will undergo a moral transformation because one is already well versed in the story.

Catherine Waters has argued that Dickens's "Christmas Books make the season an object of representation, and simultaneously become a part of it through their commodification and consumption" (65–66). *A Christmas Carol*, more so than Dickens's other Christmas writings, is a Christmas product that lends itself to repeated consumption. It has become a traditional Christmas story because it crystallizes those secular ideas that are now most associated with the holiday: giving and receiving, goodwill toward others, joviality, togetherness, and self-improvement (the latter of which is most familiar through the tradition of New Year's resolutions). Yet these are not just themes in *A Christmas Carol*; they are also, ostensibly, the work's intended effects. Those who attended Dickens's public readings of the book did so because "it provided not merely a glorious entertainment but also a spiritual tonic," contends Collins; "they came away from it 'better' persons" ("Reception" 172). *A Christmas Carol* encourages audiences to engage, along with Scrooge, in self-evaluation. Moreover, as the story is often consumed collectively, it becomes an occasion each year for people to come together and celebrate the season, thus creating a further opportunity for the performance of its moral. In short, Dickens's tale allows the *reader* "to keep Christmas well" (Dickens, *A Christmas Carol* 125).

If *A Christmas Carol* has been ritualized through repetition, this is only what the text invites. It announces itself as a prose Christmas carol, and like a carol, it is meant to be performed over and over again. Indeed, the story has the repetitive quality of a song, fairy tale, or an oral tale. Scrooge's famous phrase, "humbug," is repeated five times over the course of the work (Dickens, *A Christmas Carol* 41, 42, 54, 59, 94). The heartless question that he puts to the charitable gentlemen ("Are there no prisons?" [44]) and his Malthusian observation that poor people had better die to "decrease the surplus population" (45) are later quoted back to him by the Ghost of Christmas Present (89, 101). Tiny Tim's "God bless us every one!" is echoed by the narrator at the close of the work (89, 125). Through these internal repetitions, Dickens ensures that stock phrases are familiar even after the first reading. In effect, the process of ritualization begins in the text itself.

The carol-like repeatability of Dickens's story was recognized by its first readers. Most strikingly, in 1844, Laman Blanchard prophesied that the work would be "heard and remembered a hundred Christmases to come" (88; qtd. in Collins, "Reception" 171). Blanchard's prediction proved to be correct. Notwithstanding the familiarity of *A Christmas Carol*, and perhaps in large measure because of it, audiences willingly return to the story again and again. Its repeatability is suggested by the dictionary definition of "Scrooge," a term that is now used to designate any miserable, avaricious person. In fact, as is well known, Ebenezer Scrooge is only grasping and ill-tempered at the beginning of Dickens's tale. Only a few pages into the book, he "tried to say 'Humbug!' but stopped at the first syllable" (Dickens, *A Christmas Carol* 59). In stave 2, Scrooge shows great sensibility: his lip trembles, he sheds a tear, and his voice catches when he goes back to the place where he was a boy (64). After seeing his former self, he wipes away another tear, and already the transformation has begun: he recalls the "boy singing a Christmas Carol at [his] door" the night before and regrets not "giving him something" (66). By the time Scrooge meets the Ghost of Christmas Present, he is eager to profit from his lessons (80). Yet "Scrooge" does not mean "one who has turned over a new leaf"; instead the word carries a negative connotation, which goes to show that one loves to forget the character's conversion, if only so that one may appreciate it anew each time one revisits the story. Indeed, what is most important about Dickens's story is not Scrooge's conversion per se but rather the reader's vicarious participation in his conversion. Arguably, the success of *A Christmas Carol* lies in its power to reaffirm, with each new stage and screen transformation, not only the value of Christmas traditions, but also the potential for transformation in every person.

ENDNOTES

I am grateful to Paul Cnudde, Jennifer Judge, and Jason Taniguchi for their feedback on versions of this chapter.

1. For a discussion of the pirated text and the Chancery suits that Dickens launched against the publishers, see Hancher.
2. Several books have been written about adaptations of *A Christmas Carol*. See, for example, Davis and Guida. Many of my examples come from Guida's book. General works on Dickens and adaptation include Fawcett and Bolton.
3. A facsimile of the public reading version of *Carol* was published in 1971. In his introduction to this fascinating document, Philip Collins discusses Dickens's alterations, his performance style, and the public's response.

BIBLIOGRAPHY

Blanchard, Laman. "Charles Dickens." *Ainsworth's Magazine: A Miscellany of Romance, General Literature, & Art* 5 (Jan. 1844): 84–88. Print.

Bolton, H. Philip. *Dickens Dramatized.* London: Mansell, 1987. Print.

Childers, Joseph W. "So, This is Christmas." *Contemporary Dickens.* Ed. Eileen Gillooly and Deirdre David. Columbus: Ohio State University Press, 2009. 113–130. Print.

A Christmas Carol. Dir. Michael Shamata. Perf. Joseph Ziegler, John Jarvis, Oliver Dennis, and Matthew Edison. Young Centre for the Performing Arts, Toronto. 24 Dec. 2010. Performance.

Collins, Philip. Introduction. *A Christmas Carol: The Public Reading Version. A Facsimile of the Author's Prompt-Copy.* Ed. Philip Collins. New York: New York Public Library, 1971. ix–xxiii. Print.

———. "The Reception and Status of the *Carol.*" *The Dickensian* 89.3 (1993): 170–176. Print.

Davis, Paul. *The Lives and Times of Ebenezer Scrooge.* New Haven: Yale University Press, 1990. Print.

Dickens, Charles. *A Christmas Carol.* Ed. Richard Kelly. Peterborough, Ontario: Broadview, 2003. Print.

———. "To John Forster." 21 Feb. 1844. *The Letters of Charles Dickens.* Vol. 4. Ed. Kathleen Tillotson. Oxford: Clarendon, 1977. 49–50. Print.

Eisenstein, Sergei. "Dickens, Griffith, and the Film Today." *Film Form: Essays in Film Theory.* Ed. and trans. Jay Leyda. New York: Harcourt, Brace & World, 1949. 195–255. Print.

Fawcett, F. Dubrez. *Dickens the Dramatist: On Stage, Screen, and Radio.* London: W. H. Allen, 1952. Print.

Glavin, John. *After Dickens: Reading, Adaptation and Performance.* Cambridge: Cambridge University Press, 1999. Print.

Grove, Allen. Afterword. *Pride and Prejudice and Zombies.* By Jane Austen and Seth Grahame-Smith. Philadelphia: Quirk, 2009. 354–357. Print.

Guida, Fred. *A Christmas Carol and Its Adaptations: A Critical Examination of Dickens's Story and Its Productions on Screen and Television.* Jefferson: McFarland, 2000. Print.

Hancher, Michael. "Grafting *A Christmas Carol*." *SEL* 48.4 (2008): 813–827. Print.

Hutcheon, Linda. *A Theory of Adaptation.* New York and London: Routledge, 2006. Print.

Kelly, Richard. Introduction. *A Christmas Carol.* Ed. Richard Kelly. Peterborough, Ontario: Broadview, 2003. 9–30. Print.

Keyser, Lester J. "A Scrooge for All Seasons." *The English Novels and the Movies.* Ed. Michael Klein and Gillian Parker. New York: Frederick Ungar, 1981. 121–131. Print.

Orr, Christopher. "The Discourse on Adaptations." *Wide Angles* 6.2 (1984): 72–76. Print.

Riley, Michael M. "Dickens and Film: Notes on Adaptation." *Dickens Studies Newsletter* 5.1 (1974): 110–112. Print.

Roberts, Adam. *I Am Scrooge: A Zombie Story for Christmas.* London: Gollancz, 2009. Print.

Seuss, Dr. [Theodor Geisel]. *How the Grinch Stole Christmas!* New York: Random House, 1957. Print.

Smith, Grahame. "Dickens and Adaptation: Imagery in Words and Pictures." *Novel Images: Literature in Performance.* Ed. Peter Reynolds. London and New York: Routledge, 1993. 49–63. Print.

———. *Dickens and the Dream of Cinema*. Manchester: Manchester University Press, 2003. Print.

Van Doren Stern, Philip. "The Greatest Gift." *Zoetrope: All-Story* 5.4 (2001): n. pag. Web. 26 Dec. 2010.

Waters, Catherine. *Dickens and the Politics of the Family*. Cambridge: Cambridge University Press, 1997. Print.

Weeks, Jerome. "What the Dickens? Turning Marley's Face into a Doorknob Is Just Problem Number One for *Carol* Adaptors." *American Theatre* 17.10 (2000): 24–28, 85–86. Print.

FILMOGRAPHY

An American Carol [*Big Fat Important Movie*]. Dir. David Zucker. Perf. Kevin Farley, Kelsey Grammer, and Leslie Nielsen. Mpower Pictures, 2008. Film.

Blackadder's Christmas Carol. Dir. Richard Boden. Perf. Rowan Atkinson, Tony Robinson, and Miranda Richardson. BBC, 1988. Television.

A Carol Christmas. Dir. Matthew Irmas. Perf. Tori Spelling, Dinah Manoff, William Shatner, and Gary Coleman. Hallmark Entertainment, 2003. Television.

A Christmas Carol. Dir. Edwin L. Marin. Perf. Reginald Owen, Gene Lockhart, and Kathleen Lockhart. MGM, 1938. Film.

A Christmas Carol. Dir. Clive Donner. Perf. George C. Scott, Frank Finlay, and Angela Pleasence. Entertainment Partners, 1984. Television.

A Christmas Carol. Dir. David Hugh Jones. Perf. Patrick Stewart, Richard E. Grant, and Joel Grey. Turner Network Television, 1999. Television.

Christmas Carol: The Movie. Dir. Jimmy T. Murakami. Perf. Simon Callow, Kate Winslet, and Nicolas Cage. Illuminated Film Company/ Film Consortium, 2001. Film.

A Christmas Carol. Dir. Robert Zemeckis. Perf. Jim Carrey, Gary Oldman, and Colin Firth. Walt Disney Pictures/ImageMovers Digital, 2009. Film.

How the Grinch Stole Christmas! Dir. Chuck Jones and Ben Washam. Perf. Boris Karloff. The Cat in the Hat Productions/MGM Television, 1966. Television.

It's a Wonderful Life. Dir. Frank Capra. Perf. James Stewart, Donna Reed, and Lionel Barrymore. Liberty Films, 1946. DVD.

Mister Magoo's Christmas Carol. Dir. Abe Levitow. Perf. Jim Backus, Morey Amsterdam, and Jack Cassidy. United Productions of America, 1962. Television.

The Muppet Christmas Carol. Dir. Brian Henson. Perf. Michael Caine, David Goelz, and Steve Whitmire. Jim Henson Company/Walt Disney Pictures, 1992. Film.

Scrooge. Dir. Henry Edwards. Perf. Seymour Hicks, Donald Calthrop, and Robert Cochran. Twickenham Film Studios, 1935. Film.

Scrooge [A Christmas Carol]. Dir. Brian Desmond Hurst. Perf. Alastair Sim, Kathleen Harrison, and Jack Warner. George Minter/Renown Pictures Corporation, 1951. DVD.

Scrooge. Dir. Ronald Neame. Perf. Albert Finney, Alec Guinness, and Edith Evans. Waterbury Films/Cinema Center Films, 1970. Film.

Scrooged. Dir. Richard Donner. Perf. Bill Murray, Karen Allen, and John Forsythe. Paramount Pictures, 1988. Film.

PART II

MODIFYING THE VICTORIANS

ADAPTATION AND SHIFTS IN CULTURAL VALUES

CHAPTER 4

THE POWER OF MONEY

BROWNING'S "THE PIED PIPER" AND EGOYAN'S *THE SWEET HEREAFTER*

Mary Sanders Pollock

Atom Egoyan's 1997 film *The Sweet Hereafter* is based on Russell Banks's 1991 novel of the same title, a tale of grave errors and terrible consequences that begins when a school bus slips off an icy embankment into a flooded quarry. Fourteen children drown, and one, the beautiful and talented teenager Nichole Burnell, will be crippled for life. The plot thickens as a group of parents file negligence suits against the bus manufacturer and the governmental bodies that are responsible for the road and quarry. Banks's novel resonates with Robert Browning's murder story *The Ring and the Book* in its ethical indeterminacy and its narrative structure of interior monologues, which stand in dialogic relation to one another as each narrator tries to make sense of what has happened. But Egoyan's film is more obviously indebted to another poem by Browning, "The Pied Piper of Hamelin; A Child's Story."[1] Egoyan faithfully represents Banks's story to movie audiences while making Browning's poem new for contemporary adult readers.

The narrative structure of Banks's novel—with its four conflicting and equally weighted points of view—would present significant challenges for any filmmaker attempting to preserve the narrators' individual subjectivities under the scrutiny of the camera's dominating gaze. Obviously, a film cannot effectively replicate such a structure, but Egoyan does represent the perspectives of the narrators evenhandedly by revealing the internal conflicts of each within the screenplay. His cinematographic style situates close-ups of the main characters' faces within a context of snowy landscapes, and montage sequences are strategically placed to show what each of the four main characters is thinking or doing at the same moment in time.[2]

These strategies are enough to preserve the perspectives of Billy Ansel, whose twins die in the accident; the tort lawyer Mitchell Stevens; and the bus driver Dolores Driscoll. However, preserving the subjectivity of the fourth narrator, Nichole Burnell, under the camera's scrutiny presents a thornier problem because children, young women, and disabled persons are typically reified by the unitary gaze of a movie camera, as they are within consumer cultures. Yet it is essential for the meaning of the story that Egoyan convey Nichole's individual perspective and ontological worth. If the dead children become commodities because their tragic deaths are worth large sums of money, Nichole Burnell's commodification is more overt and consequential because she is still living. In monetary terms, she is worth more injured than whole. She is not interested in money, yet the lawsuits pursued by her parents will require that she relive, in depositions and court battles, the traumatic moments which changed her life. Banks represents Nichole's point of view simply by giving her one of the interior monologues of which the novel is composed. But Banks's text is intransigent: in order to develop the theme of the child as a commodity while at the same time preserving the child character's subjectivity on screen, Egoyan had to go against the grain of conventional Hollywood practices and resort to extreme measures.

Because of these significant challenges, the "attitude toward adaptation" of Egoyan's film, for which he wrote the screenplay, coincides with what Dudley Andrew calls "intersecting": an intersecting film "records its confrontation with an ultimately intransigent text" (99). This confrontation between film and written word may be revealed in a variety of ways, from an exact transfer of language from the original into the screenplay to the seemingly clumsy, old-fashioned device of pages turning behind the opening credits and elsewhere. Egoyan resorts to both of these strategies: much of the screenplay quotes directly from the novel, and the film spectator looks over Nichole's shoulder as she reads aloud from Browning's poem in a book illustrated by the Victorian artist Kate Greenaway. Although the novel is primary for Egoyan, the film is nevertheless a four-way intersection of film, novel, poem, and illustrations; this complicated intertextuality is key to preserving the child's subjectivity at the center of Banks's story. The episodes of reading aloud or remembering lines from Browning's poem are central in Egoyan's development of Nichole's character as well as the themes of the film. Thus, the "record" of the confrontation between Banks's story and Egoyan's film exists, paradoxically, in yet another text.

Egoyan's interpolation of Browning's poetry in these scenes is inspired. Although in the novel Nichole remembers reading to the twins from Jean de Brunhoff's picture books about Babar and his friends—child-like bipedal elephants dressed in crowns and formal wear, stumbling into and out of minor mishaps—this is a minor detail. "The Pied Piper," in contrast, is a serious story about criminal greed, betrayal, and kidnapping. The poem was originally written for Willie Macready, the precocious invalid son of actor-manager William Macready, who produced several of Browning's verse dramas in the early 1840s. Browning first wrote "The Cardinal and the Dog" for Willie to illustrate. The project so pleased Willie that Browning followed with "The Pied Piper," a longer and richer work.[3] These two poems are Browning's only forays into children's literature. It is useful to remember that they were written for one particular child, an invalid like Nichole Burnell, and were conceived as the basis for pictorial images. The poem was first published in *Dramatic Lyrics* in 1842. When Greenaway, at the time a wildly popular illustrator and tastemaker, met Browning thirty years later, she undertook a series of paintings which emphasize the faces and attitudes of the characters, underscoring the fact that Browning's poem, like Banks's novel, is driven more by psychology than story. The plots of the novel, poem, and film are predicated on a town's reactions to the loss of its children, and the adult characters struggle to identify the agents of their loss—the society which commodifies the children and the "Piper" who carries them away. Finally, Browning, Banks, and Egoyan alike probe the allure of money.

The plots of the poem and the Egoyan/Banks story are roughly parallel, as are the demands these different works make on their audiences. If the greed of some parents motivates them to seek money in exchange for their dead children, other parents understand the tragedy as an accident and wish to grieve in silence and peace. Therein lies the conflict, as most of the townspeople understand it. But, the accident is also the ultimate tragic moment in a history of hidden pain. Beneath the superficial layer of conflicting fiduciary interests lies another layer of internal struggles within families and individuals: old emotional wounds inflicted by illness, lost love, parental failures, and parental crimes are deepened or ripped open by the accident and its aftermath, and questions of money exacerbate the pain instead of soothing it. The film and the novel urge audiences to participate in making the ethical meanings of the story from a perspective of sympathy, and the representation of conflicting views in both texts requires readers and spectators to make judgments about who is right and who is wrong.

"The Pied Piper," inserted into the film as a structuring and a thematic device, makes similar demands on both adult readers and mature child readers. When the town of Hamelin has become overrun by rats and mice, the desperate townspeople turn to the city council. In equal desperation, the council members hire an itinerant Piper, dressed in red and yellow, who offers to solve the problem—for a princely sum. After the Piper leads away all of the rodents to the sound of his pipe (except for a crippled elderly rat, who is left behind to tell the fabulous tale), the council members realize that paying according to their contract will deprive them of the luxuries of office, so they renege on their promise. Without further ado, the Piper steps back into the street and seduces the town's children with his music, just as he had earlier seduced the rats. All but one, a little lame boy who "could not dance the whole of the way" (l. 233), follow him through a magic portal in the mountainside. They are never seen again, although it is rumored that they eventually show up in Transylvania, where to the locals their clothes seem outrageous (red and yellow motley, perhaps?). The mayor searches for the children and the Piper without success; the townspeople erect a memorial column by the mountainside and place a stained glass window in the church. The burgers remember, too late, that it is easier for a camel to pass through a needle's eye than for a rich man to enter heaven.

On the surface, the moral is obvious and easy to digest. The last section, spoken in Browning's own jocular voice to Willie Macready, is even simpler:

> So, Willy, let me and you be wipers
> Of scores out with all men—especially pipers!
> And, whether they pipe us free fróm rats or fróm mice,
> If we've promised them aught, let us keep our promise!
> (ll. 300–303)

Older children and adults are likely to recognize the irony of the comically understated moral tag, which only affirms that rat-killing flautists should be paid. The Hudibrastic rhymes and forced rhythms intensify the silliness. Neither the townspeople in their grief nor the moral tag delve into the perils of monetary greed, the easy commodi-fication of a town's children, the unintended consequences of thought-less actions, or the ineffectiveness of memorials in assuaging grief. As I have argued elsewhere, the "moral" of "The Pied Piper" is manifestly inadequate: "the discrepancies between the conclusions to the poem and the weight of the previous narrative show that Browning was no more inclined to peddle platitudes for a child audience" than he was for adults (Pollock, 145).

Browning's tale ends, at best, with resignation. Egoyan omits the sentiments of the poem's ending, which is ironic in any case, in favor of examining the ethical content of "The Pied Piper" in other ways. The film, too, ends with resignation.

Browning's ironic perspective is always behind and underneath "The Pied Piper." In the novel, however, there are four storytellers. In the film that is derived from it, the perspective floats. The first perspective is bus driver Dolores Driscoll's, and Dolores also appears early in the film. In the most literal sense, she is the pied piper who has taken away the town's children, an impression that is heightened in the film by the emergence of the flute in Mychael Danna's musical score after a group of children board the bus. Dolores's memories approach no closer to certainty about that fateful morning than her stroke-disabled husband Abbott's sphinx-like pronouncements on the subject. In the film, he blurts out barely comprehensible words to the effect that participation in the suit would mean selling her soul to the devil.[4] She remains caught between a loss as deep as that of any parent—conveyed in the film by an early scene in which she drives the joyful children to the county fair—and a sense of guilt which she can neither accept nor deny, conveyed by the almost frozen close-ups of Gabrielle Rose, the actress who plays her part.

For Billy Ansel, the only eyewitness outside the bus when it slides over the embankment, the tragedy is nothing more or less than an accident. Billy sees the lawyer as a pied piper who seduces the other bereaved parents. A widower, Billy himself has already come to believe that terrible loss is a condition of life, and the lawyer's insistence to the contrary enrages him against the parents who join the suit in the hope of gaining monetary rewards. He breaks off his affair with Risa Walker, whose son also died in the bus, when he realizes that she and her husband are participating in the suit in order to save their failing motel. Drowning himself in work and drink, Billy Ansel simply waits, a state Egoyan shows through the close-ups of actor Bruce Greenwood's pained face and hollow eyes.

Late at night, visiting the bus where it has been parked behind his garage, swathed in police tape, he encounters the lawyer examining the bus. Ansel observes (in the novel) that the lawyer has "bright blue wide-open eyes that were impossible to read and sharp small features. He was clean-shaven, and his skin was pink and taut. It was...the face of a smooth talker" (83). Played in the film by Ian Holm, Stephens is the twin of Browning's Pied Piper—with "sharp blue eyes, each like a pin" and "lips where smiles went out and in; / There was no guessing his kith and kin" (60, 63–64). The impression is heightened in the film's soundtrack by the reemergence of the flute after Stephens's conversations with parents.

For Stephens, an award of damages against the perpetrators has become the only punishment that can be inflicted on them. In his view, these unknown wrongdoers are pied pipers who are responsible for the disappearance of the children. However, what really drives Stephens is not the money or even a simple sense of justice, as Billy Ansel instinctively knows. What Billy cannot know is that Stephens is driven by his daughter's desperate drug addiction, the reason for the lawyer's undirected rage. Stephens admits that he practices the arts of seduction with the townspeople, but his daughter's seduction by drugs is far closer, from his perspective, to the destructive power of the Pied Piper. As he counsels his clients to do, Stephens turns the case into a channel for his own rage against failure and loss, ironically reducing the dead and living children even more into commodities. And, because Ansel cannot be persuaded to join the suit, Stephens finds a better use for him, as an eyewitness who can swear that Dolores was driving the speed limit, thereby casting the blame entirely away from her and onto those people with deeper pockets. Like Nichole, Ansel too becomes the tool of monetary interests.

More than any other character, Nichole Burnell is an agent and a victim, a hero and a sinner. Nichole is not just a reliable teenager who takes care of her younger siblings or the neighbor's children. She is a "star," a young folk rock musician whose talent is showcased at the county fair. Egoyan casts the young Sarah Polley in this role; a talented singer, Polley projects unformed and unfinished beauty.

Nichole perceives the accident as a visible sign of inward suffering, which has been caused by Sam Burnell's intermittent pattern of slavishly worshiping his talented daughter and then sexually exploiting her. When she learns that she will be paralyzed for life, Nichole longs to join the dead children. However, by the end of the story, she reaches a different conclusion. As a "wheelchair girl," she realizes she is no longer a focus for her father's sexual fantasies but the possessor of a powerful secret which may be used for self-protection. In the film, during a family meeting with Stephens, Sam Burnell asks the lawyer when the monetary awards will be made. In a quick succession of close-ups, Burnell's eager face is replaced by Stephens's anxious one, and his by Nichole's face, her eyes narrowing slightly as she realizes that if she is no longer an erotic object for her father, she is still a valuable commodity.

Nichole is commodified, then, in two ways: sexually and monetarily. But, even though her secret separates Nichole from everyone else, her confinement to a wheelchair has given her a heightened awareness of community. She realizes, partly through eavesdropping, that blame cannot be assigned without further injuring those concerned, and she becomes the agent of not only her own emotional healing but also the potential emotional healing of the town. Nichole is the only eyewitness besides the driver who was in the bus at the time of the accident, and therefore she is a critical witness for the prosecution. When she is deposed, to the surprise of everyone, especially her father and her lawyer, Nichole changes her story, testifying that Dolores Driscoll was driving twenty miles over the speed limit when the bus went over the embankment. In one unexpected lie, she thus deprives her parents of the money they would gain by exploiting her disability and saves Billy Ansel from the ordeal of reliving his children's deaths in subpoenaed testimony.

Nichole's lie is not harmless, however; she knows that Dolores will have to absorb the blame. At the end of her second monologue in the novel, Dolores comments that she and Nichole are both "solitaries living in a sweet hereafter," along with the lost children (254). This passage provides the title for the novel and the film and resonates profoundly with the children's fate in "The Pied Piper." In the film, the passage is given to Nichole in a voice-over, in a scene with Mitchell Stephens when he catches sight of Dolores helping travelers in and out of an airport shuttle as attentively as she treated the children on her bus, but sadly different. As always, she acts the part of the Pied Piper, without being one.

Egoyan's film ends with one last flashback, with Nichole once again reading "The Pied Piper" to the Ansel twins. She kisses them goodnight, turns off the bedside lamps, and walks toward a bright light at the end of the hallway, which then quickly fades out. This scene exemplifies what Egoyan, speaking of his own work, has called lyrical style. As Steven Dillon remarks, the film "comments intentionally on its own consolations and ghostly beauties, which suggests…that Egoyan has most fully captured the inexplicable accident and lack of consolation that Banks's novel promised" (229).

For all of the storytellers whose voices are heard directly or indirectly in the film—Browning, Banks, Egoyan—human beings are flawed but deserving of sympathy. Adults are not to be trusted, and neither are children. Although the iniquities of which children are capable may have more limited consequences, children are not necessarily more innocent than the adults who control and use them. They are, in most cases, simply less powerful. Nichole is the exception to the rule: she is more sinned against than sinning, but in the end, she is neither innocent nor a helpless victim.

The weight of cinematic technology and convention makes representing such a character a treacherous undertaking. The overwhelming temptation of the filmmaker is to portray injured children, especially in films for adults, as innocent heroes or innocent victims, and in that way to objectify child characters, just as conventional film practice tends toward the objectification of women. What Laura Mulvey postulates in her classic essay "Visual Pleasure and Narrative Cinema" is also true about children in cinema for an adult audience:

> In a world ordered by sexual imbalance, pleasure in looking has been split between active/male and passive/female…. Traditionally, the woman displayed has functioned on two levels: as erotic

> object for the characters within the screen story, and as erotic
> object for the spectator within the auditorium, and with shifting
> tension between the looks on either side of the screen. (19)

As a child, a woman, a person confined to a wheelchair, and an erotic
object in an incestuous relationship with her father, the character of
Nichole Burnell is a minefield for the filmmaker who wishes to represent her subjectivity. Egoyan must display actress Sarah Polley in such a
way that instead of functioning as an erotic object for the film spectator,
she instead arouses in the film spectator a sense of outrage against Sam
Burnell, for whom she is an erotic object. However, in order to enlist the
film spectator's judgment against Burnell successfully, the actress must
simultaneously convey enough eroticism for his erotic attraction to be
plausible.

The spectator's attraction to the actress thus must be balanced on an
almost impossibly fine point. The editing and cinematographic techniques by means of which Egoyan preserves all of the narrators' subjectivities are a part of his strategy for balancing the portrayal of Nichole
on this fine point. Casting an actress with such understated beauty and
without "cuteness" is, of course, another of Egoyan's strategies. She
is beautiful in the same way Kate Greenaway's children are beautiful,
with their regular features and grave looks which border on sadness and
vacancy. Nichole's age-appropriate winter clothing also insulates her
from the audience's erotic gaze.[5] The ambiguity of the disturbing but
truncated "love scenes" between Sam Burnell and his daughter prevents
the child character from ever lapsing completely into the status of an
erotic object for the gaze of the camera or the spectator. Giving Nichole
a singing voice, even though it fuels her father's fantasy, nevertheless
adds another dimension to her power of self-expression and thus to her
potential for self-determination and agency.

A character's speaking voice can be an even more powerful strategy
for asserting her agency against the totalizing gaze of the camera and
conveying her own internal life, even if it is conflicted. For Nichole, the
"immoral" moral center whose ethics are situated in her own broken

body, the lawsuits are wrong because they harm Billy, whose children she too has loved, and allow her parents to profit from her own injury. *Not* taking control of the situation would be wrong because she herself is being commodified and has been abused with no consequences to her parents, and not challenging her father's greed would allow his terrible secret life to go on. However, the lie is wrong because, as she knows to her own cost, lies are always dangerous, and this particular lie harms Dolores Driscoll.

Nichole cannot communicate her internal conflicts to the other characters through dialogue, and voice-over narration that communicates directly with the spectator would lose its effectiveness if it were used too often. Many filmmakers are indeed chary of using voice-over at all because it has sometimes served as "an emergency cord that a filmmaker pulls when he or she is unable to think of another way to convey information" (Dick, 41). Similar, but less fraught by a history of misuse and more embodied, is the technique of voice-off; in this technique, the voice track is related to the action but not simultaneous with it. Even more than the voice-over, the voice-off splits the human image from the voice, calling attention to the fact that the image is only the surface level of the character who is presented within the frame. (Voice-off is a common feature of *film noir*, a genre which rivals *The Sweet Hereafter* in psychological darkness and complexity.) As Mary Ann Doane points out, the voice, particularly as deployed in voice-off, "appears to lend itself readily as an alternative to the image, as a potentially viable means whereby the woman" can be heard (374). Obviously the same is true for a "wheelchair girl." Egoyan most powerfully emphasizes Nichole's subjectivity and avoids reifying the character through a combination of voice-over and voice-off. What one sees is only a part of what one gets.

The other dimension of Egoyan's problem in representing this character is deciding what Nichole can say that will not propel her account into the position of the controlling discourse of the whole story, thereby denying the insights of the other characters and absolving the spectator from having to make his or her own ethical judgments. In six different scenes in the film, Nichole recites lines from "The Pied Piper" in various combinations of voice-off and voice-over, remembering lines from the poem or reading aloud within the *mise en scène* to Billy Ansel's twins. In one of the earliest scenes in the film, the audience sees her reading to the twins at bedtime:

> Rats!
> They fought the dogs and killed the cats,
> And bit the babies in their cradles,
> And ate the cheeses out of the vats,
> And licked the soup from the cooks' own ladles,
> Split open the kegs of salted sprats,
> Made nests inside men's Sunday hats,
> And even spoiled the women's chats
> By drowning their speaking
> With shrieking and squeaking
> In fifty different sharps and flats. (ll. 10–20)

In this subtly constructed montage sequence, first Nichole fills the frame with the cover of her open book. Then an over-the-shoulder shot of a picture of the Piper, followed by a crowd of brightly clad and glassy-eyed children, fills the frame. Next, the camera focuses closely on Mason Ansel as he listens to the poetry. Finally, Nichole is once more at the center of the frame. Although in this scene Nichole reads only the first two stanzas, it is clear from Mason's questions that the children have heard the poem before. Why is the Piper not able to use his magic to make the townspeople pay instead of taking the children away? Is he bad? Nichole answers with an analysis: the Piper is motivated by anger more than money, so he is not a bad man. Already, early in the film, the spectator is alerted to Nichole's ability to make fine moral distinctions that enable her, at the end of the story, to distinguish good from evil, anger from corruption.

Nichole remembers more lines from the poem, spoken in a voice-off, when her father drives her home after her evening with the Ansel children. She remembers that when Hamelin's children follow the Piper, the townspeople express an unfounded confidence that the mountain will stop his progress,

> When, lo, as they reached the mountain-side,
> A wondrous portal opened wide,
> As if a cavern was suddenly hollowed;
> And the Piper advanced and the children followed,
> And when all were in to the very last,
> The door in the mountain-side shut fast.
> Did I say all? No! One was lame,
>   And could not dance the whole of the way.
>   (ll. 226–233)

The spectator briefly looks over Nichole's shoulder at Greenaway's illustration of the little lame boy, with his crutch, sober brown coat, and lost expression.

These lines, repeated several times during the film, suggest that Nichole's engagement with the poem helps her gradually to comprehend her own physical and emotional injuries. The voice-off delivery of the passage in this scene has an indeterminate status—as both a flashback to the evening Nichole spent reading to the Ansel children and a flashback that is much closer to the diegetic present of the film (the months after the accident), after she learns to identify more profoundly with the little lame boy who is left out of the pleasures promised by the Piper. What follows the ride home in the dark is a scene in the barn behind the Burnells' home, when Nichole and her father embrace in the hay. The cliché "roll in the hay" asserts itself in the spectator's mind, even though it is not in the script, and the danger of incest is suggested by a dozen lit candles surrounding Nichole and her father in the hayloft. Like the children trapped in the mountain, Nichole is trapped in her father's erotic objectification of her. And, like the little lame boy, Nichole is crippled—by her father's toxic attentions. The remembered lines suggest that she longs for escape through a magic portal, to a place where she is unreachable and beyond exploitation. Even before the accident, Nichole is both the hearty child, lost to the Piper, and the lame child, left behind.

Nichole awakens as a member of her damaged community soon after her injury. After she arrives home from the hospital, this time in the bright light of day, "The Pied Piper" is quoted again as a voice-off. Spectators who are familiar with the poem will appreciate the irony: within the context of the film, these lines seem to refer to family members who are bereft when the children disappear into the mountain. But within the poem, the lines refer to whole families of rats who follow the Piper into oblivion. Significantly, Greenaway's illustration of the rats following the music is not a part of this scene, and Egoyan's screenplay omits the line (italicized in the following quotation) that would identify these charac-ters as rats, whom Browning describes with far more verve and color than the human inhabitants of Hamelin:

> Fathers, mother, uncles, cousins,
> *Cocking tails and pricking whiskers.*
> Families by tens and dozens,
> Brothers, sisters, husbands, wives. (ll. 114–117, emphasis added)

The omission of this line from the film script erases the difference between humans and rats, and if it is remembered by the spectator within the context of the film, the language of the omitted line—"Cocking tails and pricking whiskers"—has, for the human family, disturbing sexual connotations. In this way, Egoyan suggests the importance of family and, at the same time, the vexed and marginal nature of the support fam-ily members provide for one another when a family member follows not a fairy tale Piper, but a real seducer to a different kind of doom. The omission is part of a dense and subtle intertextual web.

Months later, in the diegetic present of the film, Sam Burnell visits his daughter as she lies in bed the night before her deposition. He is clearly uncomfortable in her presence, and Nichole intensifies his discomfort by reminding him of the promise he made before she was crippled—to build her a stage lit with candles. On the way to the deposition, a voice-off by Nichole again reminds the spectator of Browning's lines about the little lame boy, excluded from the wonders promised by the Piper and left outside the wondrous portal:

> Did I say, all? No! One was lame,
>> And could not dance the whole of the way;
> And in after years, if you would blame
>> His sadness, he was used to say,—
> "It's dull in our town since my playmates left!
> I can't forget that I'm bereft
> Of all the pleasant sights they see,
> Which the Piper also promised me.
> For he led us, he said, to a joyous land,
> Joining the town and just at hand,
> Where waters gushed and fruit-trees grew
> And flowers put forth a fairer hue,
> And everything was strange and new." (ll. 232–244)

This time, the remembered lines resonate with all of Nichole's injuries—her physical confinement as well as the emotional wounds she has suffered, first from her father's erotic fixation on her and later, perhaps, from his physical withdrawal.

Egoyan emphasizes that Nichole's behavior at the deposition is a defense against her father by inserting his own quatrain, which echoes the verse form of "The Pied Piper" not only rhythmically but thematically. As she slowly and carefully considers her false statement before saying it out loud, Nichole's eyes fill with tears, and the audience once again hears poetry, voice-off:

> And why I lied, he only knew,
> But from my lie, this did come true:
> Those lips from which he drew his tune
> Were frozen as the winter moon.

An extreme close-up shows Sam Burnell's lips as they register his astonishment. Burnell is indeed the most depraved, and the weakest, of all the Pied Pipers in the story. Thus, he cannot punish or question his daughter. He can only tell Stephens what the lawyer already knows, that his daughter has lied. It is probably not accidental that Nichole's voice-off lines also echo Browning's "Childe Roland to the Dark Tower Came" (1855), a dark, angry, and ambiguous work about a failed quest:

> My first thought was, he lied in every word,
>   That hoary cripple, with malicious eye
>   Askance to watch the working of his lie
> On mine, and mouth scarce able to afford
> Suppression of the glee, that pursed and scored
>   Its edge, at one more victim gained thereby. (ll. 1–6)

Like Nichole's morally indeterminate monologue in Banks's novel, these lines in the manner of Browning, added to the film script, convey that in its effect, her lie is more potent than the simple truth, which would have allowed lies and abuses (probably of her younger sister Jennie) to continue. Both the film and the novel suggest indirectly that such a lie may be an immoral means to a moral end. The poetry by Browning and in the manner of Browning reveals, as nothing else could, that Nichole's self-awareness is whole and her subjective existence is intact, even though she has been physically and emotionally devastated.

The last scene of the film is also dominated by Nichole's voice-off quotation from Browning's poem, one more time, as she remembers reading to the Ansel children about a place:

> Where waters gushed and fruit-trees grew
> And flowers put forth a fairer hue,
> And everything was strange and new. (ll. 242–244)

This paradise of pleasure and plentitude lies not only in the past but in the fiction of a past. Significantly, Egoyan omits Greenaway's illustration of this bucolic scene, in which vacant-eyed children dance in a circle or lean on the Piper as he plays his flute. In fact, Greenaway's mentor and correspondent John Ruskin objected to it on the basis of her pastel palette and the regularity of the composition. He could just as well have objected to her doing it at all, because the picture gives substance to what is, in Browning's poem, only an isolated little boy's fantasy.

Finally, in a moment that did not occur (or occurred differently) in the "real" time of the story, Nichole closes the book, turns off the twins' bedside lamps, and walks to the dark window at the end of the hallway. The darkness changes briefly to a brilliant light filtering through translucent curtains, before fading out one last time.

This cinematic move resonates with Browning's poetry, in which truths may be everywhere, but the essential meaning of any single tale remains elusive. The intersection of Banks's novel with Browning's poems and Greenaway's illustrations enables Egoyan to foreground ethical complexity, including the ethical complexity of cinematic representation, while it conveys psychological complexity. "The Pied Piper" may be "A Child's Story," but the protagonists, except for the little lame boy, are not children. Like the protagonists in the novel and film, the adults in "The Pied Piper" are flawed, selfish, angry, and sad.

The poem's appeal to the child audience lies partly in the madly diverting characterization of humans, animals, and the fantastic Piper figure; the bouncing tetrameter laden with odd anapests and dactyls; and the silly Hudibrastic rhymes. However, the themes that are developed outside the simplistic morals are surely also a significant part of its appeal for the child reader. In *Language and Ideology in Children's Fiction*, John Stephens argues that most children's fiction has in common the theme of transition "within the individual from infantile solipsism to maturing social awareness" (3), as well as "an impulse to intervene in the lives of children. That is, children's fiction belongs firmly within the domain of cultural practices which exist for the purpose of socializing their target audience" (8). The same could also be said of most children's poetry, from Christina Rossetti's "Goblin Market" to Shel Silverstein's *Where the Sidewalk Ends* (not to mention Silverstein's even more obviously didactic modern children's classic in prose, *The Giving Tree*). Browning's poem is different: "The Pied Piper" says nothing at all about the individual child's passage into maturity, and, like Browning's poetry for adults, this narrative poem is both profoundly moral and profoundly resistant to didactic reduction. "The Pied Piper" also says nothing about how children should behave. Because the Piper's seductive claims to

Hamelin's rodents and its children may or may not be true, the poem makes no direct or indirect statement about avoiding seduction, although, if the poem does intervene at all, that intervention can be construed as undermining childish innocence with a warning against adults. Indeed, the real "moral" of the story is aimed at the adult who is reading aloud to the child, and it can be overheard by the listening child: adults should not selfishly endanger or exploit children. In Egoyan's film, which is emphatically not for the child audience, this message is intensified as the poem is read aloud by one exploited child to her younger charges.

According to Stanley Kaufmann, writing for *The New Republic*, the themes of *The Sweet Hereafter*—"the love of children" and "the idea of community"—are uncharacteristic for a filmmaker whose attention is typically riveted on global issues, urban settings, and, self-reflexively, the camera's eye and the medium of film (qtd. in Yamada). Another way to place *The Sweet Hereafter* within the larger body of Egoyan's work, however, is to note that this particular small town is not immune from the powerful social and economic forces that are at work in the rest of society, and its secret life is no less corrupt than the secret lives of cities. And if, in this instance, Egoyan omits his usual reflections on the nature of the medium through which he expresses himself, it is only to take a long, retrospective look at the power of other, more time-honored narrative technologies—the published poem and the children's picture book. The insights and sensory seductions offered by Browning's poem and Greenaway's illustrations are no less powerful than Egoyan's usual subjects.

ENDNOTES

1. Three feature films have been made of "The Pied Piper": the first in 1957, featuring Van Johnson, and the second in 1984, as a part of Shelley Duvall's "Faerie Tale Theatre" series. Wesley Snipes is the jazz-playing Piper in "The Pied Piper—Happily Ever After," released in 1998. Not surprisingly, these films, in which Browning's grim story is sweetened and expanded, are less faithful to the spirit and letter of Browning's story than Egoyan's adaptation, in which the poem is clearly secondary to the novel. In addition to films, "The Pied Piper" has inspired dance, opera, children's theatre, pictorial art, and countless picture books besides the Kate Greenaway version that is discussed in this chapter. Jack Herring's *The Pied Piper in the Armstrong Browning Library* lists 165 items of all sorts assembled before 1969. Since then, the Pied Piper industry has continued apace: a quick check on Amazon uncovers a T-shirt, a costume, a CD for children by Donovan, a Peanuts version, framed posters and prints, modern reprints of the Greenaway volume, and numerous other picture books.

2. Banks's narrative strategy offers deeper challenges, of course, than preserving continuity or limiting the length of the film. Some changes must always be made to adapt the written word to the moving image and to keep a film within the normal length that will be tolerated by most mainstream audiences. Egoyan's Nichole is a singer but not a beauty queen. Billy Ansel's memory of a miserable family vacation in Jamaica, during which his small daughter was temporarily lost, is omitted. In the film, the story of Mitchell Stephens's drug-addicted daughter Zoe is filled out in an airplane conversation with Zoe's childhood friend Allison, a character who does not appear in the novel. A demolition derby described by Dolores Driscoll in the last section of the novel is replaced by a shorter and more evocative scene which underscores the themes of loss and resignation which are central in this story. Finally, in Egoyan's film, upstate New York becomes an unidentified location across the border in Canada, the filmmaker's adopted country. None of these changes from the original novel significantly alters the outline of the story, its thematic structures, the atmosphere, or the portrayal of the characters.

3. Willie's illustrations for both poems are in the Armstrong Browning Library and have been reprinted on several occasions.

4. My thanks to Nancy Vosburg, who could understand Abbott's statement when I could not.
5. One exception is a scene in which Nichole, alone, tries on the clothes of Lydia Ansel, Billy's dead wife. Billy insists Lydia would want Nichole to have them.

BIBLIOGRAPHY

Andrew, Dudley. *Concepts in Film Theory*. Oxford: Oxford University Press, 1984. Print.

Banks, Russell. *The Sweet Hereafter*. New York: HarperCollins, 1991. Print.

Browning, Robert. "The Pied Piper Hamelin; A Child's Story." *The Poems*. Vol. 1. Ed. John Pettigrew and Thomas J. Collins. New York: Penguin, 1981. 383–391. Print.

Dick, Bernard F. *Anatomy of Film*. 5th ed. Boston: Bedford/St. Martin's, 2005. Print.

Dillon, Steven. "Lyricism and Accident in *The Sweet Hereafter*." *Literature Film Quarterly* 31.3 (2003): 227–230. Print.

Doane, Mary Ann. "The Voice in the Cinema: The Articulation of Body and Space." *Film Theory and Criticism: Introductory Readings*. Ed. Leo Braudy and Marshall Cohen. 5th ed. New York: Oxford University Press, 1999. 363–375. Print.

Herring, Jack. *The Pied Piper in the Armstrong Browning Library*. Baylor Browning Interests 20. Waco: Baylor University Press, 1969. Print.

Holme, Bryan. *The Kate Greenaway Book*. New York: Viking, 1976. Print.

Mulvey, Laura. *Visual and Other Pleasures*. Bloomington: Indiana University Press, 1989. Print.

Pollock, Mary Sanders. "'Undue Levity': The Moral Complexity of Browning's 'Pied Piper'." *Children's Literature Association Quarterly* 24 (Fall 1999): 141–147. Print.

Stephens, John. *Language and Ideology in Children's Fiction*. New York: Longman, 1992. Print.

Yamada, Yuki. "Atom Egoyan." *Contemporary Authors Online*. Thompson Gale. http://galenet.galegroup.com. Web. May 15, 2006.

FILMOGRAPHY

The Sweet Hereafter. Dir. Atom Egoyan. Perf. Ian Holm, Sarah Polley, Bruce Greenwood, and Gabrielle Rose. Alliance Atlantis. 1997. DVD.

CHAPTER 5

MAKING PRIVATE SCENES PUBLIC

CONRAD'S "THE RETURN"
AND CHÉREAU'S *GABRIELLE*

Gene M. Moore

Joseph Conrad's story "The Return" was written in 1897, one year before *Heart of Darkness*, and published in Conrad's first story collection, *Tales of Unrest*. Critics have never liked it. Albert Guérard—who helped to define the Conrad canon for academic purposes once F. R. Leavis had welcomed Conrad into what he called the "great tradition" of English writers—deplores it as "Conrad's worst story of any length, and one of the worst ever written by a great novelist" (96). But bad stories often make good films, and good films often send viewers back to the story to discover things that remained latent or implicit in the text, aspects or even characters which the emotive power of film is able to dislodge and make visible or "scenic" on the screen. It is the business of film to make scenes.

The business of society, on the other hand, is to avoid scenes. As Conrad's friend and collaborator Ford Madox Ford puts it:

> English people of good position consider that the basis of all marital unions or disunions, is the maxim: No scenes. Obviously for the sake of the servants—who are the same thing as the public. No scenes, then, for the sake of the public. (342)

Gabrielle, Patrice Chéreau's 2005 film adaptation of "The Return," provides an occasion to explore the relationship between making social scenes and making filmic scenes as well as an opportunity to consider the sense in which, on film as in good society, the servants "are the same thing as the public."[1]

"The Return" has a simple and elegant plot: a wealthy businessman returns home from work early one day to find a letter in which his wife of five years (ten years in the film) announces that she has left him for another man. He is scandalized, outraged, and wishes she were dead. This situation transcends the conventions that govern his life: "He thought of her as a well-bred girl, as a wife, as a cultured person, as the mistress of a house, as a lady; but he never for a moment thought of her simply as a woman" (Conrad, "Return" 128). Just as he begins to come to terms with the situation (culminating in his muttering, "Damn the woman"), his wife returns. She has changed her mind, lacking the courage to change her life. The rest of the story involves their confrontation: his rage and her silence, his efforts to hold her accountable for her action, and her refusal to acknowledge his right to judge her. When he announces that he "forgives" her, she breaks out in hysterical laughter so loud that he silences her by throwing a glass of water in her face. When he professes his love for her, she replies, "If I had believed you loved me...I would never have come back" (177). She clearly has all of the best lines. In the end, her husband's frustrations become so unbearable that he himself leaves, and the story ends with the implausible proclamation that "[h]e never returned" (186).

Conrad's tale is basically the story of the uncomprehending husband, told by an omniscient narrator who both mocks and sympathizes with him; Chéreau's film adaptation is the story of the wife. In Conrad's tale, she is nameless, anonymous, yet she appeals to her husband by name more than once ("Alvan!"), and at one point he reminds her, "[Y]ou are still Mrs. Alvan Hervey" (158). Chéreau not only gives her a name— Gabrielle—but makes her the eponymous heroine of the film, which becomes her story. In Conrad's tale, the wife's curt, oracular replies cause her to appear far more complex and interesting than her husband; her transgression, and its failure, have given her a knowledge that he lacks and to which he feels entitled. But they are incapable of dialogue: he can speak only in platitudes, whereas she simply does not want to engage in discourse. Hervey's jealousy reveals a void in his own life that he cannot ignore but which he now hopes to assuage by the repossession of his wife. What she says is sharp and pointed, in ironic counterpoint to his patronizing self-delusion and his inability to comprehend the unconventional: "You might say something human," he tells her. "You misunderstand everything I say.... Your mind is unhinged" (163). Each of them is ashamed, but in diametrically different ways: Hervey is ashamed of being humiliated by a wife who breaks the rules, whereas his wife is ashamed of her lack of courage to break them thoroughly. How can one "make scenes" that express the inward drama of two characters who are unwilling and unable to communicate with each other? Conrad made a specialty of scenes in which characters misunderstand each other utterly and often fatally, but films require more explicit or at least more visual solutions to the problem of inwardness.

Both Conrad and Chéreau confront the challenge of how to present a story in which not much happens and there is very little dialogue. Conrad's ironic narrator responds with metaphorical insistence, placing Hervey's outraged and despairing reactions in a context of cosmic cataclysm. The earth moves for Hervey when he finds his wife's letter—"he experienced suddenly a staggering sense of insecurity, an absurd and bizarre flash of a notion that the house had moved a little under his feet" (125)—and thereafter, Conrad's narrator regularly "zooms out" from the paneled and cushioned interior of the Hervey mansion to invoke by hyperbolic extension a world of "horrors" (155) and massacres, of volcanoes, tidal waves, and other images of violence on a vast scale. The emotional turmoil of Hervey's private life remains utterly at odds with the conventionality of his domestic arrangements. The cosmic hyperbole of his emotional state is comic in effect: the overblown imagery of Conrad's satire appears to dwarf its subject, and the technique easily becomes wearisome. In the "Author's Note" in *Tales of Unrest*, Conrad acknowledges that rereading the story twenty years later produced in him

> the material impression of sitting under a large and expensive umbrella in the loud drumming of a furious rain-shower. It was very distracting. In the general uproar one could hear every individual drop strike on the stout and distended silk. Mentally, the reading rendered me dumb for the remainder of the day, not exactly with astonishment but with a sort of dismal wonder. (viii)

The wife's presence in the story remains muted, limited to her oracular and maddening one-liners. Chéreau and Ann-Louise Trividic, the scriptwriters of the film, realized that Gabrielle is actually a far more interesting character than her husband, whom she considers (in Conrad's words) either "unpardonably stupid, or simply ignoble" (177). She has no need for her husband's forgiveness, but she cannot forgive herself for lacking the social courage to leave him, and she blames both of the men who are involved. As Conrad says, she was "filled…with bitter resentment against both the men who could offer to the spiritual and tragic strife of her feelings nothing but the coarseness of their abominable materialism" (176). The film is the story of Gabrielle's failure to escape from materialism.

In both the story and the film, the setting and furnishings of the Hervey mansion, where all of the action takes place, make a major scenic contribution to the viewer's sense of what Conrad calls "the gospel of the beastly bourgeois" (*Collected Letters*, 393), whether in the Jamesian West End of London, as in Conrad's story, or in an elegant Parisian *quartier* near the Parc Monceau. (*Gabrielle* won César awards both for its set design and for its costumes.) But scenery is by definition static and not narrative, because nothing is allowed to change. The narrative is conveyed by a kind of choreography of pain, in which suffering spouses lash out at each other through a series of fitful scenes.

In the film, Gabrielle (played by Isabelle Huppert) is the main focus of interest; one not only hears what she says but can also see her double life as both a society hostess and a woman who is capable of secret and scandalous passion. Conrad's wide-ranging and magnifying metaphors are replaced in the film with a variety of devices for rendering states of mind, some of them familiar (such as narrating Hervey's thoughts in voice-over or the use of music versus silence) while others are more innovative (such as alternating black and white with color or using transparent placards containing written messages, or rather fragments of messages, because these superposed words are too large for the screen).

Among the most curious of the film's innovations is the use of servants as Jamesian *ficelles* (literally "bits of string") to counterpoint and draw out the character of Gabrielle. In Conrad's story, the servants are all female, according to the wife's wishes, but the couple manage to keep their guilty secret from them and avoid "making scenes" in their presence. In Chéreau's film, by contrast, the house is literally swarming with servant girls dressed in sober, impeccable black and white. When Hervey arrives home, three of them are on hand to help him remove his hat, his coat, and his cane. The filmic Herveys are literally waited on hand and foot and have no part of their mansion entirely to themselves. Moreover, Hervey is not alone even when he is alone, because the mirrors on the walls of the dressing room multiply his image into a crowd of identical clones. Conrad's narrator plays upon this mechanical reproduction to satirize Hervey as a stereotypical member of his social class without an individual identity.

Unlike their English and fictional counterparts, the filmic and French Herveys abandon decorum in the presence of their servants and break the maxim that governs home life for "English people of good position." They make scenes—the husband grossly and blindly, and the wife in a nastier, more personal way. One understands the filmmaker's need to find a way to draw Gabrielle out, to give her not only reactions but also memories and wishes, but her abuse of the servants is cruel and provides an interesting chance to test the ways in which, for spectators, the servants are indeed "the same thing as the public."

Chéreau's willingness to break the rule forbidding scenes is perhaps a sign of cultural differences between English and French servants or of temporal differences between the rules of 1895 and those of 1930 or 2005. In any case, the convention by which servants are considered absent presences except when they are invoked provides Chéreau with something like a silent chorus of young women whose very readiness to be of service stands in sharp contrast to the brutality to which the Herveys subject each other. By the rules of their profession, the servants are prohibited from reacting as "real" people would to the scenes that are made in their presence. Gabrielle exposes her inner thoughts to the servants by confiding in them, by thinking out loud in their presence and then blaming them for her own discomfort. She engages in private and intimate scenes with one young servant in particular, as if she were willfully oblivious to the unspoken contract that governs master/servant relations.

Gabrielle's husband, being less clever, forgets himself not only in front of the servant girls but even in front of his invited guests, making scenes in public that will disgrace the couple regardless of the outcome of their personal struggle. At the end of Conrad's story, the Herveys are condemned to a hell without love, from which the husband escapes when he realizes that his wife's experience has left her with no "gift" (176) to share with him. At the end of the film, Gabrielle offers herself—her own naked body—to her husband, not as a gift but as a sacrifice, and the devastating consequences are visible to viewers. As Chéreau and Trividic comment in the shooting script, "[I]t's rather painful to watch" ("C'est assez pénible à voir"; 62). Several reviewers on the Internet Movie Database (http://www.imdb.com) remarked that it was a good thing that the film was only ninety minutes long.

By almost all accounts, the final scene is flawed in both the story and the film. It is simply not credible that (as the story reports) a mindless, materialistic brute should experience an epiphany that causes him to renounce his life and wealth forever. In Chéreau's ending, Isabelle Huppert offers herself to her husband not like a wife (repentant or unrepentant) but like a corpse on a slab in a morgue, inviting him to commit necrophilia in a house of the living dead. The scene is creepy enough to frighten her husband and send him reeling down the stairs, and it provides an explanation that is more convincing than Conrad's for why he never returns. However, the continued existence of Hervey without his wealth and his house and all his material appurtenances is unimaginable. In this final scene, Gabrielle offers herself as an object, becoming physically what she has always been in essence, thus confirming the lifeless materialism of the "good position" to which she is condemned.

In summary, Conrad's story contains wonderful elements of social satire and interior discourse, but the elements are out of balance, the character of the nameless wife is underdeveloped, and the ending is artificial and implausible. Chéreau has turned Gabrielle into a personality, only to show her committing an act of social self-destruction that ultimately destroys her husband as well. Conrad's couple maintains appearances and obeys the maxim of "No scenes," whereas Chéreau uses the violation of social rules as a postmodern sign of passion or desperation. This strategy may give one insight into the personality of Gabrielle (and the relative boorishness of her husband), but it also involves a loss of credibility, precisely because the servants are "the same thing as the public," which includes the viewers and voyeurs sitting in the audience. Paradoxically, the glimpses of inner life that Gabrielle exposes to the servant girl reveal her own deficient humanity, her lack of consideration for the confusion and powerlessness of an underling whose duties do not include psychological counseling and whose replies are never to be construed as personal. The girl's embarrassed response—"*Madame se moque de moi*" ("Madame is making fun of me") —generates an instability similar to that created by the narrator's mockery of the protagonist.

"The Return" may well be an overblown tale turned into an uneasy film, but *Gabrielle* can help to illustrate the problem in film adaptation of making unspeakable thoughts and feelings visible and dramatic. How can one make scenic a world in which "making scenes" is forbidden?

In the world of the Herveys, scenes are forbidden for the sake of the servants, who are "the same thing as the public." But the film-going public demands scenes, even at the expense of servants whose discomfort the viewers are made to share. Viewers are, after all, not bothered by the sight of hundreds of filmic flunkeys and subalterns dying horrible deaths in the margins of action-adventure films, forgetting that the proletarians of evil dictatorships are also men with wives and families. By contrast, it is surprising that the psychological abuse of servants by ruthless members of a spoiled bourgeoisie should be so painful to witness, and that a strategy designed to make visible Gabrielle's sufferings should also make visible the ways in which she causes others to suffer.

ENDNOTE

1. A previous film adaptation under the title "Jej powrót" ("Her Return") was made for Polish television in 1974.

BIBLIOGRAPHY

Chéreau, Patrice, and Ann-Louise Trividic. *Gabrielle* [shooting script]. 2006. ARTE video DVD. Print.

Conrad, Joseph. *The Collected Letters of Joseph Conrad*. Ed. Laurence Davies et al. Vol. 1. Cambridge: Cambridge University Press, 1983. Print.

———. "The Return." *Tales of Unrest*. London: J. M. Dent & Sons, 1947. Print.

———. *Tales of Unrest*. London: J. M. Dent & Sons, 1947. Print.

Ford, Ford Madox. *Parade's End*. New York: Knopf, 1950. Print.

Guérard, Albert. *Conrad the Novelist*. Cambridge: Harvard University Press, 1958. Print.

Leavis, F. R. *The Great Tradition*. London: Chatto & Windus, 1948. Print.

FILMOGRAPHY

Gabrielle. Dir. Patrice Chéreau. Perf. Isabelle Huppert and Pascal Greggory. Azor Films, 2005. DVD.

CHAPTER 6

TOTALLY CLUELESS

HECKERLING AND QUEER SEXUALITY IN AUSTEN'S *EMMA*

Michael Eberle-Sinatra

Remaking, rewriting, "adaptation," reworking, "appropriation," conversion, mimicking…of earlier works into other media is an important feature of the current landscape.

—Wiltshire, 2

Seldom, very seldom, does complete truth belong to any human disclosure; seldom can it happen that something is not a little disguised, or a little mistaken.

—Austen, 122

This chapter offers a new reading of the sexual politics that are at play in Jane Austen's 1816 novel *Emma* through the exploration of film director

Amy Heckerling's retelling of Austen's original story. Heckerling's 1995 film, *Clueless*, can be understood as a free translation of *Emma* which allows an interrogation of some of the novel's received readings, especially those related to its male characters. Following Ellis Hanson and Robert Lang in their studies of films and queer theory, I use the term "queer" as it refers to "a rejection of the compulsory heterosexual code of masculine men desiring feminine women" (Hanson, 4). I intend to revisit Austen's *Emma* and its issue of homosexuality[1] by questioning the performance of Frank Churchill in Highbury through Heckerling's interpretation of that character.[2]

The title of this chapter might seem provocative, given the critical debates that have raged unabated since 2000, when Jill Heydt-Stevenson made a highly convincing case for a more sexually charged Austen. The attacks on Heydt-Stevenson seemed all the more excessive because as far back as 1975, Alice Chandler had already insisted that it was "a truth universally acknowledged" that Jane Austen's novels are "very much about sex" (88). Jan S. Fergus, too, relied on an amusing anecdote about a "tweedy Englishman" to contend that "Jane Austen and sex" were hardly "mutually exclusive" subjects (66). Film adaptations, however, have greatly helped combat the still-prevalent notion that Austen's fictions merely embody good manners and rules for proper conduct.

Released in 1995 to both critical acclaim and unusual commercial success for a small-budget film, Amy Heckerling's *Clueless* offers a stimulating reading of class and gender issues in Highbury/Beverley Hills and an unconventional take on Frank Churchill's sexual identity. Douglas McGrath's 1996 film and the A&E 1996 television adaptation of *Emma* directed by Diarmuid Lawrence both depict with great insistence Churchill's heterosexuality, whereas *Clueless* differs quite significantly from these adaptations by depicting him as gay.

Transposing the characters and action of Austen's novel into a film that takes place in the late twentieth century makes possible alternate readings, for the director as well as for the audience. As Linda Hutcheon asserts, "[w]hatever the motive, from the adapter's perspective, adaptation is an act of appropriating or salvaging, and this is always a double process of interpreting and then creating something new" (20). Projecting this novel of social mores from Austen's Highbury to 1990s Beverly Hills allows Heckerling to explore subtexts in a way that would be difficult in a period piece.[3] Heckerling is free to notice subtler social clues in *Emma* and to explore them more fully in *Clueless*. Developing a queer reading of a novel in film often consists of making explicit a homosexual or bisexual subtext that may or may not be present in the original story. Heckerling's decision to transform the apparently heterosexual character Frank Churchill into a gay character, now named Christian Stovitz, in her film adaptation of Austen's novel invites readers of Austen's *Emma* to reconsider the character of the novel's Frank Churchill, particularly in light of Eve Kosofsky Sedgwick's concept of "homosocial desire."

In Jane Austen's novel, the character of Frank Churchill constantly plays with words and manipulates the society around him while concealing his secret engagement with Jane Fairfax. The film version of this character remains the object of affection for the Emma character (renamed Cher in *Clueless*), and Christian, likewise socially problematic, embodies the figure of mystery, social class, and sensuality that Austen's Churchill represents in Emma's eyes. However, Heckerling transforms "straight" Frank Churchill into "gay" Christian, which serves to underscore Cher's "cluelessness," because she fails to recognize Christian's sexual preference and falls in love with him.[4]

Heckerling encourages the audience to smile at Cher's insensitivity to Christian's sexual orientation from the moment they first meet and he comments admiringly on her shoes. Heckerling then bombards the audience with one gay stereotype after another to exaggerate Cher's self-absorption and naiveté: Christian is reading William Burroughs's fictional memoir *Junky*, he is a great dancer, he dresses well, he knows and appreciates modern art, and, to quote Cher, "he had a thing for Tony Curtis." He is also shown dancing with another man briefly and chatting up a male bartender at a party, but Cher mistakes his obvious lack of interest in other girls as proof of his romantic attachment to her. One of the funniest scenes in *Clueless* occurs at Cher's house when she tries to charm Christian. After he has admired Cher's father's art collection (showing again his knowledge of, and his sensitivity to, modern art) and declined her invitation for a late-night swim, Christian suggests that they watch one of the films he brought with him—*Some Like it Hot* and *Spartacus*. The next scene shows Cher and Christian lying on Cher's bed in front on a television set. While Tony Curtis as a slave in *Spartacus* speaks about "the children of my master to whom I taught the classics," Cher attempts unsuccessfully to seduce Christian. The irony of this scene is obviously lost on Cher, but most likely not on the audience, who recognizes the iconic status of *Spartacus* as a gay film, as well as Heckerling's own tongue-in-cheek nod to Austen's *Emma* in this reference to "the classics."

The following scene takes place the next day when Cher tells her friend about the evening with Christian and tries to find reasons to explain why nothing happened between them. Overhearing the conversation between Cher and Dionne, Tyron rather bluntly tells Cher that Christian is "a Cake Boy, a disco dancer, Oscar Wilde reader, Streisand ticket holder, friend of Dorothy, you know what I'm saying?" In case there was any room left for doubt (and Cher certainly wants to remain doubtful at first), Dionne clinches the argument by commenting that "[Christian] does like to shop, and the boy can dress." Although Heckerling includes an apparent alternative to the heterosexual norm with the character of Christian, he remains on some level the token gay man, who has artistic taste and a sense of fashion and who is allowed to shop happily with Cher but not to have a sexual relationship himself, although all of the other characters do. Ultimately, Christian's homosexuality is only one element of Heckerling's modernization of *Emma*, yet many viewers see it as the most radical departure from Austen's novel. Is it, in fact, really such a departure?

Heckerling's film invites readers of *Emma* to think more carefully about Frank Churchill's sexuality, the mystery and secrecy surrounding this character, and the relationship that exists between Knightley and Churchill in Austen's original novel. True to her source, Heckerling retains the spark of jealousy that triggers Josh, her Knightley character, to reconsider his feelings for Cher, just as Knightley recognizes his sentimental attachment to Emma through his jealousy of Churchill. Tom Hoberg suggests, however, that "Christian is neutralized as Josh's romantic rival for Cher's affection because he is gay" (123). I would argue that through the character of Christian and his open homosexuality, Heckerling provides an alternative interpretation of Churchill's secrecy and his apparently trivial and even effeminate traits, such as insisting on going to London in order to get his hair cut[5] and his musical abilities as a singer and dancer in a society where artistic inclinations are considered effeminate.[6]

Several critics have discussed Emma's attachment, and even attraction, to other female characters in the novel, including Mrs. Weston, then Harriet Smith, and finally Jane Fairfax. Some good articles have in fact been written about Emma's potential lesbianism and her unusual position of power as a wealthy, independent, single person who does not need to worry about money, unlike all of the other female characters in the novel.[7] It is thus fair to state that Emma's position of power was commonly associated with men in her society at that time, and this is the first clue for a reconsideration of the gender politics in Austen's novel.

If one were to borrow René Girard's model of the erotic triangle, as described in *Deceit, Desire, and the Novel*, Emma would be positioned at the apex as the apparent object of desire for both Knightley and Churchill. Girard's insistence that the bond that links two rivals is as potent as the one linking the rivals to the beloved opens many directions for discussions of male relationships. Sedgwick has amply demonstrated this in her influential study *Between Men: English Literature and Male Homosocial Desire*, where she expands on this triangular relationship to consider homosocial bonding that may verge on homosexual attraction but is rendered safe because of the presence of a woman in this configuration. The Girardian triangle is, however, slightly more complex than two heterosexual men lusting after a woman. Indeed, Knightley and Emma behave more like the men in this triangle in terms of their positions of authority and independence within their world and their interest in other women. Emma's slightly unusual social status is underscored when, for example, Knightley's brother, John, remarks, "You and I, Emma, will venture to take the part of the poor husband. I, being a husband, and you not being a wife" (Austen, 62). As for Churchill, he chooses to conform to his aunt's wishes and thus, according to Knightley, does not behave like a man, because he shirks his other social duties in so sacrificing his independence of movement. It is thus tempting to reconfigure this Girardian triangle with Churchill as the feminine apex, or more precisely, to read the triangle no longer in terms of Knightley and Churchill gravitating toward Emma, but rather with Knightley gravitating toward Emma, Emma toward Churchill, and Churchill toward Knightley.

Perhaps because Austen's novels primarily focus on female characters rather than on male ones, the majority of criticism written about male characters reads them in relation to the females or in comparison with other males. But what about the relationships between male characters? Frank Churchill is important for Knightley because it is the latter's growing jealousy that motivates him to examine his feelings for Emma. Until the arrival of Churchill, Knightley's relationship to Emma was either paternalistic, given his seniority of sixteen years, or fraternal, given his connections through his brother's marriage to Emma's sister Isabella. Emma and Knightley are also aunt and uncle to five nieces and nephews. Overall, these familial relations, introduced early in the novel, heavily color the characters' and the readers' perceptions of their relationship. Yet, many critics have argued that the ultimate romantic relationship between Emma and Knightley appears to be inevitable because of the fact that their social class would not really allow them to marry anyone else in Highbury.

There has been a rather large amount of scholarship devoted to Austen's novels, including *Emma*, over the last fifty years. But no one, to my knowledge, has explored the underworld of Austen's novels, the diurnal and nocturnal activities that were quite current in England at that time for young men such as Frank Churchill. John Cleland's novel *Memoirs of a Woman of Pleasure; or Fanny Hill*—"that most licentious and inflaming book" as Boswell puts it (qtd. in Wimsatt, 81)—famously contains an exploration of the world of prostitution, but it also condemns what Fanny considers "unnatural practices," including sodomy and male homosexuality.[8] Scholars have debated the fluid gender identity of Austen's female characters, but what about her male characters? Do the overtly masculine, heterosexual male characters in her novels really think about nothing apart from their businesses, their social standing, and upholding the values of the heterosexual society they inhabit by marrying by the end of the story? How can one qualify their relationships to other male characters? As Robert K. Martin's work on Melville and nineteenth-century American male friendship shows, one must not always assume that male or female friendship "means" homosexuality, although one must not assume either that "friendship and sexuality are opposite ends of a pole" (126). I would argue that more work needs to be done on male friendships, or the apparent absence of such friendships, and male homosocial relationships in Jane Austen's novels.

Returning to Frank Churchill, I would suggest that the fact that he ends up marrying Jane Fairfax is not in itself a conclusive argument for his heterosexuality because pressures to conform to heterosexual norms were extremely high at the time. Austen's society frowned upon single men as well as marriages between people of different classes, as is illustrated in *Emma* by Churchill's reluctance to tell his wealthy aunt about his engagement to Jane Fairfax, who is poor and thus otherwise destined to become a governess. Though it was difficult to marry outside of one's given class, one's sexual preference remained in any case a nonissue. In late eighteenth- and early nineteenth-century England, pressures from one's family and society meant that many young men who frequented "molly houses," the taverns and socializing places for men who were interested in other men throughout the seventeenth and eighteenth century, at one point or another in their lives had no choice but to marry.[9] Thus, Churchill's marriage to Jane Fairfax could very well be an instance of a marriage of convenience that would rescue Fairfax from her life as governess and provide her with a wealth that is implied by Churchill's purchase of one of the most expensive pianofortes available at that time. That marriage would also allow Churchill to pursue his chosen homosexual lifestyle. In any case, the topic would never be discussed, and the absence of public recognition or even the vocabulary to describe such behavior contributed to a silence that lasted famously until Oscar Wilde's trial, where the "love that dare not speak its name" became a topic of public knowledge and discussion. In fact, as Jeffrey Weeks's work on male prostitution demonstrates, there was a noticeable absence of judicial vocabulary and a misperception of the number of male prostitutes in England until the later half of the nineteenth century.

Discussing what remains unspoken in Austen's novel brings to mind Michel Foucault's comment that

> there is no binary division to be made between what one says and what one does not say; we must try to determine the different ways of not saying such things.... There is not one but many silences, and they are an integral part of the strategies that underlie and permeate discourses. (27)

Austen may have been a conservative, heterosexual woman, but she never married. Thus, she did not share the lifestyle she apparently promoted in her novels, but rather lived out her years dependant on her relatives. She was also well versed in Gothic literature, as her parody *Northanger Abbey* demonstrates, and the Gothic, as Sedgwick has convincingly argued,

> was the first novelistic form in England to have close, relatively visible links to male homosexuality, at a time when styles of homosexuality, and even its visibility and distinctness, were markers of division and tension between classes as much as between genders. (91)

An interpretative exploration of the kind I offer in this chapter is inconclusive by nature. Rather than draw a firm conclusion on the presence or absence of homosexuality in Austen's work, I want to suggest that the assumptions with which readers approach the sexuality of Austen's characters in her novels should be examined more carefully. Austen's *Emma* contains a number of social clues about its characters that could be read in quite a different light than the majority of criticism published so far would suggest, even including the queer-oriented readings that are currently available. For instance, is Austen perhaps hinting at more than one possible reason for Churchill's use of Emma as a blind for his secret life? What about his insincerity and his callous public behavior toward Jane Fairfax? Is there any truth to his apparent disdainful and manipulative attitude toward women or in the fact that Knightley finds Churchill's behavior offensive because it is "unmanly"? Toward the end of volume 2, Mr. Woodhouse refers negatively to Churchill by saying "he is not quite the thing" (205), and later on he asks, "[C]ould he be queer?" (207). Mr. Woodhouse's description is more accurate than he realizes, both for a nineteenth-century reader who understands "queer" as meaning "fake"—thus reinforcing my discussion of Churchill's performance as a heterosexual man—and for a modern reader who interprets "queer" for its sexual connotations.

If Hollywood and its set of cultural values imposes a restrictive viewpoint of the sexuality of Austen's characters, Amy Heckerling's film, *Clueless*, suggests a number of possible avenues of inquiry encouraging more challenging approaches to *Emma*. Austen's novel is replete with sexual innuendos, as scholars have discussed with regard to the well-known "Kitty" charade and the lesbian undertones that are present in Emma's relationship to other women. Various critics have convincingly argued for Austen's awareness of the exchange of sexual favors for promotion in the army and the issue of sodomy in the navy. I hope that this chapter will contribute further to a discussion of the sexuality of Austen's male characters, particularly when they do not adhere exclusively to the heterosexual norm.

I also hope that this chapter has proven that, contrary to Virginia Woolf's distrust of the adaptation process, the alliance between cinema and literature is not always "unnatural" or "disastrous" to both forms (42). In fact, the symbiotic relationship that exists at present between film and literature, especially in the hearts and minds of twenty-first-century viewers and readers, deserves further exploration for new readings of canonical texts.

ENDNOTES

I want to thank Cara Lane for her useful comment on an earlier version of this chapter, as well as Jason Camlot and Alan Bewell for inviting me to Concordia University and the University of Toronto, respectively, to discuss my views of Austen and *Clueless* with their students and colleagues.

1. Throughout this chapter, I use the words "heterosexual," "gay," and "homosexual" for the sake of clarity, but I am of course aware of the apparent historical fallacy of using terms that were not in existence until the end of the nineteenth century, when, as Michel Foucault famously declared, the homosexual emerged as a "species" (43).

2. As Penny Gay suggests, Churchill "is never, in Emma's imagination or experience, divorced from his theatricality" (135). Gay discusses the theatricality of Emma's world at length in her study. She also notes that "[i]n so far as they are actors, Frank Churchill and Mr. Elton are effeminate, rather than admirable men" (129), thus reinforcing my reading of the possible undertone of Churchill's sexual politics in light of his anti-male behavior that remains a performance throughout the novel.

3. The Beverly Hills 90210 setting anticipates other teen-oriented shows and films such as *Sabrina* and *Buffy the Vampire Slayer*. Though Heckerling plays fast and loose with Christian's sexuality, she has a rather conservative take on 1990s girls' sexuality. Furthermore, even though Heckerling includes several black and Hispanic characters, the culture she depicts is dominantly white and upper class.

4. Roz Kaveney suggests as well that "Christian's sexuality is Heckerling's way of demonstrating that Cher is not seriously pursuing love so much as the social status of having a boyfriend, partly because, as we realize before she does, her heart is already taken by Josh" (118).

5. Readers find out eventually that Churchill actually went to London to purchase a pianoforte, but the true reason is not known for a while and thus allows for a reading of that character along the lines I suggest.

6. See, for instance, the scene in which Churchill sings a duet, first with Emma and then with Jane Fairfax, thus performing, in the words of Penny Gay, "an unmanly display of elegant accomplishment rather than action" (138).

7. See, among others, Heydt-Stevenson, Hudson, and Tuite.

8. The two-paragraph description of a homosexual encounter witnessed by Fanny was in fact removed from most eighteenth-century editions of Cleland's novel.
9. For a detailed discussion of "molly houses," see Bray, 102–103.

BIBLIOGRAPHY

Austen, Jane. *Emma*. Ed. Stephen M. Parrish. 3rd Ed. New York: W. W. Norton, 2000. Print.

Axelrod, Mark. "Once Upon a Time in Hollywood; or, the Commodification of Form in the Adaptation of Fictional Texts to the Hollywood Cinema." *Literature/Film Quarterly* 24.2 (1996): 201–208. Print.

Bray, Alan. *Homosexuality in Renaissance England*. London: Gay Men's Press, 1982. Print.

Chandler, Alice. "'A pair of fine eyes': Jane Austen's Treatment of Sex." *Studies in the Novel* 7.1 (Spring 1975): 88–103. Print.

Fergus, Jan S. "Sex and Social Life in Jane Austen's Novels." *Jane Austen in Context*. Ed. David Monaghan. Totowa, NJ: Barnes & Nobles Books, 1981. 66–85. Print.

Foucault, Michel. *The History of Sexuality. Volume I: An Introduction*. Trans. Robert Hurley. New York: Pantheon, 1978. Print.

Gay, Penny. *Jane Austen and the Theatre*. Cambridge: Cambridge University Press, 2002. Print.

Hanson, Ellis. Introduction. *Out Takes: Essays on Queer Theory and Film*. Durham: Duke University Press, 1999. 1–22. Print.

Heydt-Stevenson, Jill. "'Slipping into the Ha-Ha': Bawdy Humor and Body Politics in Jane Austen's Novels." *Nineteenth-Century Literature* 55 (2000): 309–339. Print.

Hoberg, Tom. "The Multiplex Heroine: Screen Adaptations of *Emma*." *Nineteenth-Century Women at the Movies: Adapting Classic Women's Fiction to Film*. Ed. Barbara Tepa Lupack. Bowling Green: Bowling Green State University Popular Press, 1999. 106–128. Print.

Hudson, Glenda A. *Sibling Love and Incest in Jane Austen's Fiction*. Basingstoke: Macmillan, 1999. Print.

Hutcheon, Linda. *A Theory of Adaptation*. New York: Routledge, 2006. Print.

Kaveney, Roz. *Teen Dreams: Reading Teen Film and Television from Heathers to Veronica Mars*. London: I. B. Tauris, 2006. Print.

Lang, Robert. *Masculine Interests: Homoerotics in Hollywood Film*. New York: Columbia University Press, 2002.

Martin, Robert K. Introduction. *English Studies in Canada* 20.2 (1994): 125–128. Print.

Sedgwick, Eve Kosofsky. *Between Men: English Literature and Male Homosocial Desire*. New York: Columbia University Press, 1985. Print.

Tuite, Clara. "Period Rush: Queer Austen, Anachronism and Critical Practice." *Re-Drawing Austen*. Ed. Beatrice Battaglia and Diego Saglia. Rome: Liguori, 2004. 294–311. Print.

Weeks, Jeffrey. *Against Nature: Essays on History, Sexuality, and Identity*. London: Rivers Oram Press, 1991.

Wiltshire, John. *Recreating Jane Austen*. Cambridge: Cambridge University Press, 2001. Print.

Wimsatt, William K. Print. Jr., and Frederick A. Pottle, eds. *Boswell for the Defence*. New York: Longman, 1959. Print.

Woolf, Virginia. "The Movies and Reality." *New Republic* (August 4, 1926): 39–47. Print.

FILMOGRAPHY

Clueless. Dir. Amy Heckerling. Perf. Alicia Silverstone, Stacey Dash, and Paul Rudd. Paramount, 1995. DVD.

Emma. Dir. Diarmuid Lawrence. Perf. Kate Beckinsale, Mark Strong, Samantha Bond, and Bernard Hepton. A&E, 1996. DVD.

Emma. Dir. Douglas McGrath. Perf. Gwyneth Paltrow, Jeremy Northam, Juliet Stevenson, and Ewan McGregor. Miramax, 1996. DVD.

CHAPTER 7

FROM VICTORIAN TO POSTMODERN NEGATION

ENLIGHTENMENT CULTURE IN THACKERAY'S AND KUBRICK'S BARRY LYNDON

Louise McDonald

Whereas much has been written about the artistic achievement of Stanley Kubrick's *Barry Lyndon*, the central ideology of William Makepeace Thackeray's source novel has received little attention by adaptation studies critics. Wrongly dismissing it as a crude example of the picaresque and a simplistic study of villainy, they have ignored the importance of the fully developed anti-Enlightenment philosophy which shapes Thackeray's text to Kubrick's postmodern lament for the human condition. I am mindful of James Naremore's criticism of the tendency of traditional adaptation studies to be too "inherently respectful of the precursor text" (2). However, by reconsidering the novel in the light of the film, this study intends to redeem Thackeray's *The Memoirs of Barry Lyndon, ESQ*, by showing that its attack on Enlightenment culture is every bit as sophisticated as the film's, but that its specifically Victorian sociopolitical concerns substantially differ from Kubrick's postmodernist stance. Reading the Enlightenment from a different historical vantage point, Kubrick extended Thackeray's pessimistic deconstruction of eighteenth- and nineteenth-century ideology while disregarding his sociopolitical details. The film adaptation is informed by twentieth-century masculinist postmodern philosophical and aesthetic considerations, and thus it foregrounds some of Thackeray's deepest concerns, those that are most relevant to the postmodern viewer, and understates others that are less culturally relevant for a twenty-first-century audience.

In *Knowledge and Postmodernism in Historical Perspective*, Joyce Appleby identifies the tenets of eighteenth-century Enlightenment thought which have since been rejected by postmodern theorists and philosophers—among them "[t]he free development of liberated persons (the autonomous individual)" (18). That the human subject is the constructed product of myriad cultural references is particularly pertinent to any discussion of Thackeray's perennial skepticism. In the *Roundabout Papers*, for instance, Thackeray declares the "impossibility of knowing one's self accurately" (Shillingsburg, 123) and demonstrates a "philosophical conviction that uncertainty dogs every aspect of human knowledge" (103). This "Derridean" outlook extends to his rejection of another Enlightenment principle: the "truth" of a text or "the capacity of language to describe the external world" (Appleby et al., 18). For Thackeray, knowledge, particularly self-knowledge, is unattainable, and narratives are consequently dogged by falsity. Of "On a Hundred Years Hence," Thackeray comments,

> every story retold, whether by a new hearer or by the same person at some subsequent occasion, suffers the distortions of memory and misunderstanding, and [is] embellished by the teller's desire to entertain or to shine by contrast. Truth, whatever it may be, has precious little to do with it. (Colby, 32)

Thackeray's outlook was shaped by his reading of Victor Cousins's "Cours de l'histoire de la Philosophie," which proposed that because "men are scarcely ever more than halves and quarters of men," truth was visible only in "the diversity of humanity" and not in the work of any one privileged and rational individual (Colby, 32, qtd. in Shillingsburg, 130; Colby, 30, qtd. in Shillingsburg, 129).

Cousins provided a frame of reference for Thackeray's "fragments of humanity," each with what Cousins called an "incomplete or partial view of things" (Colby, 34). The novelist's butts are the destructive and self-destructive overreachers who are sanctioned in a culture of innovation, individualism, and "progress," who employ "rationality" to manage their freedom only for their own self-aggrandizement.

Kubrick's adaptation foregrounds Barry Lyndon as one such fractured subject. An eighteenth-century cultural construction, he is a self-deluded and consequently spurious storyteller, the antihero of a political novel which deconstructs the period's hegemonic confidence in "the mastery of the cause-and-effect relations that run the world" (Appleby et al., 18). Kubrick has said of his 1971 film, *A Clockwork Orange*, that there is "something in the human personality which resents things that are clear, and conversely, something which is attracted to puzzles, enigmas and allegories" (Miller, 1360). Thackeray provided Kubrick with one such enigma.

Rather than interpreting Kubrick's Barry Lyndon as a fractured subject, most adaptation critics have read the film as an indictment of cultural institutions that limit the protagonist's opportunities. They assume that Kubrick has transformed an archetypal villain into a sympathetic victim. For Peter Cosgrove, the film "completely reverses the theme of Thackeray's book": "instead of being a satire on upward mobility, Kubrick's adaptation becomes an elegy for the destruction of the low-born hero by an unyielding class system" (21–22). Neil Sinyard describes Barry as "an active, violent rogue in the novel; a resourceful but vulnerable character in the film" (133), and Donata Meneghelli considers that "the Barry Lyndon in the film, as opposed to his counterpart in the novel, is a character destined to gradually lose his innocence and the illusions which mark him out in the early sequences" (6). Willem Hesling and R. P. Kolker go further in their sympathetic interpretation of Barry. Hesling writes that the film's omniscient narrator depicts Barry as a lonely man who reaches out to Lady Lyndon in a spirit of dissatisfaction with the emptiness of his life, and whose "misbehaviour...serves a respectable project: climbing the social scale and founding a family" (6). Both Kolker and Mark Crispin Miller also defend Kubrick's Barry against the film's narrator, whom they read as deliberately unreliable, damning Barry through references to events and behavior for which there is no visual evidence. For Miller, Barry's "warmth denies the meaning of propriety, and so he seeks immediate closeness everywhere" (1375); his emotional neediness defines his superiority to his passionless peers.

Clearly, both novel and film similarly dramatize the impact of an inflexible class system upon an individual, and Thackeray's central didactic purpose is not to condemn the overreacher, who is conceived as neither wholly good nor wholly evil, as much as the political and philosophical system which corrupts and then destroys innocence. The juxtaposition in the film of Bryan Lyndon's birth and his father, Barry's, whoring, which Miller interprets as evidence of Barry's intense and mostly admirable passions, could well be interpreted as demonstrating a gross betrayal of his suffering wife (indeed, this detail should perhaps be read in both ways at once). Barry's affectionate dealings with his son have been interpreted as signifying essential goodness, but Kubrick has no need to depart from his source to dramatize both Barry's fatherly feelings and the temporary reconciliation of the Lyndons after Bryan's death.

It is also misleading to suggest that "Kubrick eliminates the sordid aspects of Thackeray's story and restores emotional undercurrent to moments of death and departure" (Miller, 1367); individualized suffering is in fact a significant theme in the novel. Thackeray's Barry is more than a rogue and a bounder: sensitive to early degradations and prone to depression, he "had serious thoughts of committing suicide, so great was [his] mortification" (77). In the novel, Barry is also plagued by homesickness, nostalgia, and an enduring romantic attachment to Nora.

Kubrick translates this assemblage of woes into melancholia, indicated by the slow pace of the film and its evocative soundtrack.

Such elements no doubt contribute to Meneghelli's argument that Kubrick converts Thackeray's picaresque text into a *bildungsroman* (6). To read the novel as picaresque, however, is to ignore its overtly political purpose. In a picaresque novel, the reader witnesses the triumph of the adventuring hero without paying much attention to the socializing effect of his culture. Thackeray's text, in contrast, calls the picaresque into question by incorporating its principal conventions into an anti-*bildungsroman* in which he shows the "innocent" boy hero unable to retain his integrity in the face of faulty socialization and education. Sinyard observes the operation of neglect and cruelty in Kubrick's film:

> Barry is seen to be as much victim as villain. Deprived of his father in the first shot of the film, seduced and then abandoned by his cousin, tricked in a duel, robbed, caught up in a war, it is small wonder he looks for a more comfortable position. His tactical marriage is understandable, given that a fortunate position in that society seems the only way of surviving its hellish cruelty. (133)

This is indeed so, but if one examines the details of Thackeray's plot, one can see that his young hero struggles to survive the same intolerable conditions, and Kubrick effectively retains the anti-*bildungsroman* genre of his source.

Cultural construction is at the heart of Thackeray's didactic purpose; it is crucial that in his youth Barry should contain a mixture of good and evil and become wicked through circumstance. Thackeray's depiction of Barry's mother as cold and grasping is consistent with Kubrick's representation of a universal "frozen" quality in all of Barry's acquaintances. In Thackeray's text, however, the mother tyrannizes her young son and subjects him to "fits of anger…and…reconciliations, which used to be still more violent and painful" (*Memoirs* 224). Not only is he abused, bullied, and neglected by immoral and ignorant parents, but his father, a drinker and gambler, appropriately dies of a heart attack at a race course. This is the man who is held up to Barry as a model of gentlemanly conduct by his mother, who teaches her son, too, how to live a dissipated, fashionable life.

Here and elsewhere, Thackeray treats the concept of a gentleman with devastating irony. Bad fathering is self-perpetuating. Bryan is raised as an arrogant and aggressive chip off the old block, who absorbs his father's misguided notion of what constitutes honorable and gentlemanly behavior. Kubrick encapsulates Barry's bad influence on his son in a macabre bedtime "reading" ritual, in which Bryan listens with relish to his father's account of the atrocities which he committed when he was in the army. In Kubrick's film, the novel's focus on early abuse is retained only in embryonic form (the omission is perhaps surprising in the light of Kubrick's interest in family violence in *The Shining* [Kolker, 151]).

But parental encouragement of hypocrisy is only one aspect of Thackeray's anti-Enlightenment views. As Appleby explains, the values of the Age of Reason were fully embedded in Thackeray's world:

> [T]here was a clear consensus during the nineteenth century that its knowledge came from the liberation of reason, indeed, that truth and falsehood were stamped upon the universe waiting for the discerning discriminator to make the distinctions public. Like a heat-seeking missile, human curiosity was presented honing in on reality and detonating its protective cover. Completely absent from this account of how the West built its formidable fortress of information was the play of human passion, of prejudice, of power, of reason in the service of the collective ego. (17)

Against the grain of his culture, the novelist was ambivalent not only about the power of individual reason but also about the inevitability of human progress. In *Barry Lyndon*, "education," "progress," and "rational" thought appear to have produced a culture of powerful, patriarchal bullies. Thackeray persistently questions the social conduct that is encouraged by a so-called enlightened civilization. As a young soldier, Barry struggles to make sense of the Seven Years' War. Despite his limited intellect, he understands that textbook military history misrepresents war's brutal reality, poignantly realized in the fate of the "poor little ensign, so young, slender and small, that a blow from my pig-tail would have dispatched him, I think, in place of the butt of my musket, with which I clubbed him down" (Thackeray, *Memoirs* 79). Barry's army reflections read less like his usual confused, contradictory, and ill-informed rants and rather reveal Thackeray's perspective on the discrepancy between the reputation of King Frederick of Prussia as a model of Enlightenment principles and the war crimes that were committed in the name of these principles by a brutalized and press-ganged militia:

> It is well for gentlemen to talk of the age of chivalry; but remember the starving brutes whom they lead—men nursed in poverty, entirely ignorant, made to take a pride in deeds of blood—men who can have no amusement but in drunkenness, debauch, and plunder. It is with these shocking instruments that your great warriors and kings have been doing their murderous work in the world; and while, for instance, we are at the present moment admiring the "Great Frederick", as we call him, and his philosophy, and his liberality, and his military genius, I, who have served him, and been, as it were, behind the scenes of which that great spectacle is composed, can only look at it with horror. (79–80)

Kubrick certainly dramatizes the war's hardening of Barry's resolve to prosper at whatever cost, but the film also understates army atrocities both in the *mise en scène* and in the narrative voice-over. Perhaps, as Kolker suggests, the director was too sensitive to accusations of gratuitous overemployment of violence in *A Clockwork Orange* to make another film in the same vein (147). Whatever the reason, the mood of the film is elegiac rather than satirical, and Kubrick's treatment of war is milder. Kubrick's Barry is chronically melancholic, but his melancholy is not directly related to soldiering as it is in Thackeray's text, in which, gradually dehumanized by what he experiences, Barry is made suicidal.

Barry's moral deterioration, brought about by his role models and his participation in the organized violence of war, is indicated in his adoption of the corrupt perspective of the aristocracy. In the novel, Barry continues to be aware of his indebtedness to his poor childhood friends and behaves generously to servants. In contrast, Kubrick's representation of the self-aggrandizement of individual aristocrats is not countered by any establishment of warm humanity in the hearts of the peasantry; he "loses" Thackeray's class consciousness and political critique.

Kubrick also departs from the source novel in his treatment of Barry Lyndon's misogyny. In both the novel and the film, Barry's social ascendancy is achieved through matrimony. Just as the marriage nearly destroys the woman, in a number of earlier subplots, women are kidnapped, falsely imprisoned, forced into marriage, and even murdered. There are no equal unions in which women have freely given consent. The more powerful the abuser, the more extreme is the abuse, and Thackeray anticipates Foucault in his representation of the relationships among institutional power, the creation of knowledge, and the mistreatment of the powerless. The conspiracy which masks the murder of Princess X as the suicide of a madwoman indicts state power, here epitomized by her husband and the medical and scientific institutions which are subject to his authority. The princess suffers the extreme penalty for challenging the patriarchal code, and her execution is a lurid dramatization of institutionalized violence meted out in the "knowledge" that a wife's infidelity merits death. In such episodes, "Thackeray's fiction manages to put the women's view forward, even when the male characters fail to see it. The author and the reader, together, assess the unhappy results of ordinary men behaving ordinarily" (Shillingsburg, 45). Thackeray shows that the maltreatment of women is wrongly regarded more as roguish and foolish than as a mark of complete villainy. That Barry behaves according to cultural norms is also confirmed by *Barry Lyndon's* reliable fictional editor:

> From these curious confessions, it would appear that Mr. Lyndon maltreated his lady in every possible way; that he denied her society, bullied her into signing away her property, spent it in gambling and taverns, was openly unfaithful to her; and when she complained, threatened to remove her children from her. Nor indeed, is he the only husband who has done the like, and has passed for "nobody's enemy but his own": a jovial, good-natured fellow. (Thackeray, *Memoirs* 260)

In contrast, endemic misogyny is absent from Kubrick's film, whose Sir Charles is not represented as having married his wife for financial gain. In the novel, Lady Lyndon is a heroine in the Gothic tradition, subjected to a sustained bullying campaign; once Barry has compromised her reputation, she has no choice but to concede to his marriage proposal. By softening Barry's treatment of Lady Lyndon; eliminating Barry's previous, carefully planned seduction of Countess Ida; and excluding the violent subplots, Kubrick eliminates much of the horror and melodrama which darken Thackeray's text. Kubrick's protagonist makes only one attempt to marry into wealth, and his Lady Lyndon is a fusion of the two women in the novel. In the novel, after the marriage, Barry blackmails, threatens, imprisons, and regularly beats his wife, to whom he is chronically unfaithful. In the film, it is suggested that Barry's "whoring" is a temporary aberration; Barry and his wife are united in their disapproval of Lord Bullingdon's behavior, and there is not the slightest hint of domestic violence. Estrangement, rather than brutality, defines the relationship.

In the novel, the reader is encouraged to sympathize with Lady Lyndon's dignified demeanor and behavior. If one examines Lady Lyndon's actions, it is quite possible to read her as a serious intellectual with modest and pious habits. Her version of the courtship and marriage is voiced in her correspondence with her friends and "lover," George Poynings, and to give weight to her perspective, Thackeray adds to the epistolary narrative a letter from young Quinn to substantiate what she has said about her husband's villainy. This strategy confirms Barry's mendacity, conveys Thackeray's concern with the complexity and relativity of truth, and coincides, to a degree, with Thackeray's feminist agenda.[1]

Unlike Thackeray, Kubrick represents Lady Lyndon with a complete disregard for feminism and is open to accusations that he indulges his aesthetic sensibilities at the expense of political comment. Thackeray's indictment of the oppressive patriarchal foundations of eighteenth-century reason is largely replaced in the film by homage to the beauty of Marisa Berenson. As a result, in the film, Barry is the sole rounded center of narrative interest; his wife remains a peripheral and stereotyped conception—a beautiful, inanimate, and ageless possession who delights both her husband and the voyeuristic viewer. Although the screen Lady Lyndon is for the most part voiceless, possibly because of the fact that the inexperienced actress's performing abilities were largely untested (Combs), her silence does serve to maintain the enigmatic qualities that are suggested in the novel: although she is persecuted by her husband, she supports him financially until her death, retains her preference towards him over her surviving son, and was, apparently, "never out of love with" him (323). The screen character's silence also precludes the possibility of an impassioned or intellectual performance, but it serves to reinforce her intense vulnerability and deathly stasis, most visible in the very funereal "bathroom" scene, in which Barry's attendance on his wife resembles a candlelit vigil for a dead woman. In her death-in-lifeness, Kubrick powerfully dramatizes the life-draining impact of a culture of oppression. The quietness of Kubrick's Lady Lyndon prevents any reading that suggests her superior education and intellect, and thus, although Thackeray's feminist agenda is not violated in the film, it is muted.

Similarly, Thackeray's concerns about the landscape and rural nature are minimized by Kubrick's aesthetic. As Enlightenment ideology developed into nineteenth-century theories of progress, environmental "invasion" became widely sanctioned. It was generally accepted that "the world as a given to be understood, accepted—even cherished—yielded to the spirit of inventiveness, to the drive to plan, improve, and replace" (Appleby et al., 9). The preservation of the countryside and rural culture was important to Thackeray in the same way that it would become for Hardy, and, like the mistreatment of his wife, Barry's mistreatment of the land, local traditions, and ancient buildings signifies his collapsing integrity. In accordance with popular eighteenth-century perceptions, Barry believes that in order to become a gentleman, he must subject his land and property to alteration, and so he ransacks Hackton's house and has "the place new-faced, under a fashionable architect, and the façade laid out in the latest French-Greek and most classical style. There had been moats, and drawbridges and outer walls; these I had shored away into elegant terraces" (Thackeray, Memoirs 252). He extends his fashionable but philistine project to the surrounding landscape, and Thackeray's parodic representation of Barry as a retainer is placed in sharp contrast to the attitude of earlier preservers of the land. Thackeray provides a wry comment on the modern enthusiasm for innovation as "progress," which his nineteenth-century readership, witnessing a revival of the medieval style which Barry rejects, would certainly appreciate.

Despite Thackeray's references to landscape to demonstrate Barry's inimical relationship with nature, there is little description in the novel of the countryside as a force of beauty. Much of the power of Kubrick's film, in contrast, derives from the visual representation of rural Europe. It could be said that Kubrick sacrifices a sense of authenticity in order to create a beautiful spectacle; his visual aesthetic is disturbingly pleasurable. The film certainly reads as a kind of choreographed drama, but it is also a death dance, a pageant of decadence which fleshes out and transcends Thackeray's political indictment of nineteenth-century culture. Kubrick's beautiful pastoral settings contrast with the ugliness of man: they are a gorgeous backdrop to the decadent activities of the people who are dwarfed by them, little in their hopeless greed and frozen hearts. The film features no physical act of despoilment, but the further the protagonist falls, the further he is physically and psychologically removed from his rural roots and from the outdoor world where growth and adventure are possible. In the second half of the film, he increasingly inhabits worldly internal spaces.

In forcing Barry deeper and deeper into a claustrophobic interior world, Kubrick recreates the novel's traditional biblical pattern of fall, punishment, and (a degree of) repentance, as justice is meted out to Barry according to his crimes. Thackeray's protagonist is a plotter who is brought down by a clever plot. He locks up his wife, so he is duly punished through a gradual journey which takes him to prison. He abuses his land, and it is taken from him. Because his villainy is not unequivocal, the reader's responses are complicated. Barry comes to regret some of his actions and victims, expressing relief that he failed to kill Quinn, wishing he had not wounded Poynings, and in the end, remarking that he would have liked to apologize to Fakenham.

The film reconstructs the novel's violent spirit through the synthesis of many skirmishes and altercations into a few violent episodes, culminating in a final duel with Lord Bullingdon which generates what can be interpreted as a final act of repentance. One important difference between the purpose of the duels in the novel and those in the film is that in the former, many are figments of Barry's imagination, and

> it will be observed, in one or two other parts of his Memoirs, that whenever he is in an awkward pass, or does what the world does not usually consider respectable, a duel, in which he is victorious, is sure to ensue. (*Memoirs* 122)

These duels indicate Barry's unreliability as a narrator of an exceedingly self-deluded memoir. In Kubrick's adaptation, however, these scenes are fully realized and function as a series of beacons to signify Barry's development in terms of his rise and fall in honor and gentlemanly conduct. Thus, Kubrick omits Thackeray's contrast between true gentlemanly conduct and Barry's faulty notion of it, but he charts Barry's fall from a received cultural code which the audience will recognize.

Although all of the fight episodes are allotted significant screen space to indicate their importance, the final engagement, when Barry throws the fight, is even more prolonged. There are many ways to interpret Barry's decision to allow Bullingdon to defeat him. His customary melancholy may be so exacerbated following the death of his son that he no longer wishes to live, or he may finally behave like the gentleman he has aspired to become, sacrificing himself to his stepson to atone for his former wrongdoings. Fought in a church ruin with narrow windows through which streams a "godly" light, with cooing doves in the background (Barry has not heard birds since his first duel in Ireland), this final duel may offer a partial return to innocence. Barry's ultimate fate, hobbling with one leg through Europe in a state of poverty, indicates Kubrick's ultimately pessimistic disavowal of redemptive possibilities.

But what of the other characters? Do they receive what they deserve? The film differs from the novel in relation to Lady Lyndon's fate. In Thackeray's text, her wealth and freedom are restored, but she is prevented from retaining her romantic attachment to George Poynings by the return of the truant Lord Bullingdon. Kubrick adapts her partial triumph in ridding her of Barry and restoring her as the mistress of Hackton Hall, but it is uncertain whether she will be able to recover the fortune which her husband has lost. The key difference between the novel and the film is in the level of social critique. Though Kubrick's Bullingdon may be slightly foolish, he is an obedient and respectful son, whereas in Thackeray's narrative, he inherits the controlling role which Barry is forced to relinquish, becomes the next in a line of patriarchs, and continues the culture of oppression which Thackeray sought to expose.

Kubrick's eighteenth century is distasteful, dishonest, decadent, and languid, but it is not filled with people whose cruel and oppressive behavior reflects a misunderstanding of progress. Being closer to the century which Kubrick can observe through rosier glasses, Thackeray critiques a political system which oppresses women, the poorest classes, and nature. He could count on his readers to see the relevance. In contrast, the filmmaker disregards the prevailing cultural consciousness of his own late twentieth-century liberal audience; given the importance of gender and environmental issues for this audience, it is particularly significant that he disregards Thackeray's treatment of the reification of both human beings and nature in the interests of postmodern critical distance. Kubrick's adaptation also rejects any affiliation with the popular postmodern heritage tradition in cinema, which locates a fictionalized progressive present in a safe historical haven and "takes us back on a tourist trail to an England that never was" (Hutchings, qtd. in Tambling, 9). Paradoxically, resisting the popular postmodern practice of nostalgia exploitation signifies a "nihilism of satiety" (Howe, 24) and an uncompromising postmodern political critique of the strategies of reassurance that are adopted in mainstream cinema. Kubrick's *Barry Lyndon* is designed not for the audience as much as for the cinema, and this quality may explain the esteem in which it is now held in the academic world of film criticism (as well as the lack of commercial success which it experienced on its cinematic release).

Kubrick situates postmodern man in a film which is as much about now as about the eighteenth century. Hesling writes that "foolishness, weakness and wickedness, injustice of society and fickleness of fate were Kubrick's favorite themes too" (3). While transforming the overtly political content of his source, he still maintains the contradictory nature of the central protagonist, with something like Thackeray's pessimistic vision, to produce a nihilistic postmodern outcome. Twenty-first-century audiences of Kubrick's film can thus view their own destabilized and dehumanized selves reflected in the absence of self-knowledge, the political inertia, and the dissipated mental energy of the fictional protagonists.

None of the characters in Thackeray's narrative achieve a happy ending, and judgment is deferred "because, unlike the omniscient narrator of most Victorian fictions, he does not know the end and does not trust what he knows" (Shillingsburg, 12). No ideology is entirely pure, however. In spite of his personal skepticism, Thackeray partially assimilated the belief in progress which prevailed in the nineteenth century. As Robert Colby points out, "there is gain as well as loss," and he shows that "mankind in its stumbling way somehow manages to advance over ruins" (47). Thus, the "editor," the narrator of the novel, ends his work on a positive note: Barry's memoir is a historical document, and by the narrative present, his villainy has become the stuff of folk tale, new trees are established in Hackton Park, and Barry's Irish property has been divided into small peasant tenancies. Lyndon's land becomes a source of hope. Stability, community, conservation, continuity, and equitable distribution are apparently possible once an "angel" like Barry, corrupted by a false interpretation of Enlightenment principles, is expelled from the garden. Yet, although future regeneration is implied, it is imagined only in a landscape where the key characters and their descendents are entirely absent. Though Thackeray offers a sliver of hope, Kubrick provides no final panoramic scene of peasants in fields within a stable and happy community. As a postmodern subject, he attests to the contemporary view that redemptive possibilities and human progress are myths of an earlier system of thought, and his audience bears final witness only to the end of progress and of hope. Kubrick seems to say that such is the essentially limited nature of humanity.

ENDNOTE

1. Thackeray's intention was to champion Lady Lyndon. He modeled her on his good friend, Caroline Norton, who countered her own abusive ex-husband's claim to all of her income, her property, and her children with an outpouring of letters and pamphlets advocating rights for married women and pleading for new legislation related to separation, divorce, and child custody. Such was Thackeray's commitment to her cause that his later novel, *The Newcomes*, was a deliberate, "central and effective instrument in the passage of the Marital Causes Act of 1857" (Shillingsburg, 100). By supporting the cause of women through his narrative treatment of the Lyndons' marriage, he was challenging eighteenth-century patriarchal culture and the continuation of its abuses into the nineteenth century. Indeed, Thackeray's perspective is shared by early postmodern feminists, who critiqued the tendency of Enlightenment thinkers to support the rights of the individual man but ignore oppressions that were perpetrated against women.

Bibliography

Appleby, Joyce, Elizabeth Covington, David Hoyt, Michael Latham, and Allison Sneider, eds. *Knowledge and Postmodernism in Historical Perspective: A Reader from 1700 to the Present*. London: Routledge, 1996. Print.

Colby, Robert. *Thackeray's Canvass of Humanity*. Columbus: Ohio State University Press, 1979. Print.

Combs, Richard. "Barry Lyndon." *Monthly Film Bulletin* 43.504 (Jan. 1976): n. pag. Web. 3 March 2007.

Cosgrove, Peter. "The Cinema of Attractions and the Novel in *Barry Lyndon* and *Tom Jones*." *Eighteenth-Century Fiction on Screen*. Ed. Robert Mayer. Cambridge: Cambridge University Press, 2002. 16–34. Print.

Hesling, Willem. "Kubrick, Thackeray and the Memoirs of Barry Lyndon, ESQ." *Literature Film Quarterly* 29.4 (2001): 264–278. Print.

Howe, Irving. "Mass Society and Postmodern Fiction." *Postmodernism: A Reader*. Ed. Patricia Waugh. London: E. Arnold, 1992. 24–31. Print.

Hutchings, Peter J. "A Disconnected View, Modernity and Film." *E. M. Forster New Casebooks*. Ed. Jeremy Tambling. Hampshire: MacMillan, 1995. 213–228. Print.

Klein, Michael, and Gillian Parker, eds. *The English Novel and the Movies*. New York: Frederick Ungar Publishing, 1981. Print.

Kolker, R. P. *Cinema of Loneliness*. New York: Oxford University Press, 1988. Print.

Meneghelli, Donata. "What Can a Film Make of a Book? Seeing Literature through *Apocalypse Now* and *Barry Lyndon*." *Image and Narrative* 8 (2004): n. pag. Web. 11 Jan. 2011.

Miller, Mark Crispin. "Kubrick's Anti-Reading of *The Luck of Barry Lyndon*." *MLN Comparative Literature* 91.6 (1976): 1360–1379. Print.

Naremore, James. *Film Adaptation*. New Brunswick: Rutgers University Press, 2000. Print.

Shillingsburg, Peter. *William Makepeace Thackeray: A Literary Life*. London: Palgrave, 2001. Print.

Sinyard, Neil. *Filming Literature: The Art of Screen Adaptation*. New York: St. Martin's, 1986. Print.

Tambling, Jeremy. "Introduction." *E. M. Forster*. Ed. Jeremy Tambling. Hampshire: MacMillan, 1995. 1–10. Print..

Thackeray, William Makepeace. *The History of Pendennis*. London: Smith, Elder, 1849. Print.

———. *The Memoirs of Barry Lyndon, ESQ*. 1856. Harmondsworth: Penguin, 1975. Print.

Tillotson, G. *A View of Victorian Literature*. Oxford: Clarendon Press, 1978. Print.

FILMOGRAPHY

Barry Lyndon. Dir. Stanley Kubrick. Perf. Ryan O'Neal, Marisa Berenson, and Patrick Magee. Warner Bros., 1975. Film.

CHAPTER 8

INTERTEXTUALITY IN SIMON RAVEN'S *THE PALLISERS* AND OTHER TROLLOPE FILMS

Ellen Moody

As my companions in this volume make abundantly clear, screen adaptations mirror their makers as much as—or more than—they reveal the authors of their source texts. At the same time, comparing the adaptation to the original work sheds new light on the source text itself. Nowhere is this principle more apparent than in juxtaposing the screenplays written by Simon Raven for several twentieth-century Trollope adaptations to the Trollope adaptations written by Alan Plater, Andrew Davies, and Henry Herbert. The latter three writers react to, engage with, or attempt to replace Raven's cynical Tory Trollope with a humane, liberal Trollope for modern times and thus influence not only viewers, but readers of Trollope's novels as well.

As in other British quality television, the screenplay writer dominated the adaptation process (Cardwell, *Andrew Davies* 14–17), but Simon Raven was no film buff. He never owned a television and did not frequent films, but he was active at a distance in day-to-day filming and script editing. Although Raven wrote of himself that he "would probably have consented, as Spike Milligan observed, to dramatize the telephone directory had the price been right" (Barber, 210), he took the form seriously and produced still-respected film adaptations. His vocation was that of a writer, and he read omnivorously (Barber, 187–188).

It is my argument that nonimpressionistic intertextual studies of *The Pallisers* (1974) and *The Barchester Chronicles* (1982) must form the basis of an understanding of Anthony Trollope films by various makers. The original airing, many replays of these two miniseries, and the successful sales of videocassettes and DVDs are among the most important and underestimated late twentieth-century "sociological events" to have happened to Trollope consumers—equivalent in influence to the much-discussed 1981 Granada adaptation of *Brideshead Revisited* and the 1995 *Pride and Prejudice*. Artistically and thematically, *The Pallisers* anticipates *Brideshead Revisited*, which has been wrongly credited with the invention of motifs that are intrinsic to film adaptations of high-status books. The Barchester novels are as much political fables as Trollope's Palliser novels; however, because *The Barchester Chronicles* is but seven episodes (a common length), is closely and literally associated with Church of England politics, and belongs to the genre of adaptations that are set in a pastoral English environment, I will focus on intertextuality in *The Pallisers* and then only briefly turn to *The Barchester Chronicles*.[1] I begin with Raven's use of literary allusion, then describe his characters, and finally analyze the structure of and two scenes from two parts of *The Pallisers*.

VICTORIAN IDYLL AND THE TEXTURE OF ALLUSION

The Pallisers announces itself as a visual Arcadian Victorian experience, richly Trollopian from its opening scene of well-known Trollope characters walking, playing croquet, and waltzing to a band in a vast green park. It is done in the 1970s miniseries style: actors are filmed as if they are on a stage in long, psychologically-nuanced scenes whose thematic content builds and is complicated over a course of cyclically conceived episodes in historically accurate and archetypal settings. Twenty-six nearly hour-long *Palliser* parts encompass more than the traditional six *Palliser* books: *Can You Forgive Her?*, *Phineas Finn*, *The Eustace Diamonds*, *Phineas Redux*, *The Prime Minister*, and *The Duke's Children*. A seventh novel, *The Small House at Allington* (much of 1:1 is taken from this book and provides the thematic framing for the series as a whole), is also central. Matter also comes from *Dr. Thorne*, *The Noble Jilt* (a play by Trollope that is vaguely alluded to in *The Eustace Diamonds*), and *The American Senator*. The *Pallisers*' central ironic choral figure, Dolly Longstaffe, derives more from *The Way We Live Now* than *The Duke's Children* (and in cynicism borrows from *All About Eve*). George Pickering as Dolly imitates George Saunders as Addison.[2] Arcadian gatherings (with which the series not only opens but transitions from book to book; 1:1, 3:6, 5:10, 9:19), weddings (2:1), trial scenes (9:18–9:19), funerals (8:15, 12:26), and even police interrogations (7:13) and (seemingly) Venetian seascapes (11:22) define, punctuate, and provide choral moments for the series. Televisual blocking makes the characters into allegorical figures across the small screen— all in imitation of other popular Victorian melodramas and elegiac ceremonial events that were on television.

Original illustrations for many of Trollope's novels, all chosen from the idyllic style that was favored by the author (Moody, *Trollope* 127–154), generate lavish costume and production design. For example, Plantagenet Palliser's voice-over meditation as he walks past a flower woman near a church is configured to imitate G. H. Thomas's drawings of Josiah Crawley in *The Last Chronicle of Barset* in his anguished meditation walks. A dialogue between George Vavasour and Palliser is a replay of Josiah's conversation with the Barsetshire working man (3:5, episode 23). When Major Tifto mounts a table and proposes a toast, John Ringham's body stance and gestures imitate those of a salesman in *Orley Farm* during an evening's cavorting in a tavern (12:25, episode 38). Across the series, one repeatedly returns to the elegantly barred bow windows of Matching to see meditative women reading or making gestures of imprisonment in elegiac light, a paradigm of reverie or intense frustration.

But elegy is mixed with other elements in Raven's adaptations. Asked about how he would like to see the world change, Raven wrote as someone who is dependent on patronage, instancing Balzac: "Less compassion and more independence: more *Balzacian* world, in which everyone pursues his own business" (Barber, 187). Indeed, Balzac's *Splendeurs et Misères des Courtisanes* (*The Pallisers* 1:2 and 2:3, parts that correspond to *Can You Forgive Her?*) are read obsessively by Lady Glencora in the face of her husband's disapproval. The book is also an amusement to the sycophantic labor politician Mr. Bott, and it is found under sofa pillows at Matching Priory (having been left there after other networking characters have dipped in). Functioning as a prop, the novel signals that viewers are in a Balzacian countryside, and thus it is suggested that many of Trollope's characters will sell themselves utterly. The suggested emotional pain and danger lie in people's dependence on one another.

In another instance of intertextuality, references to Meredith's *Beauchamp's Career* (*The Pallisers* 9:18, episode 1)—a book that is studied by a depressed Phineas Finn when he is in prison and commented on by Phineas's political mentor Monk—signal that Phineas's ordeals parallel those of Meredith's hero. Both defend their own integrity; both are trapped in illiberal, repressive, patronage-ridden communities; and both are stifled or defeated when they fail to conquer. Beauchamp ends up dead; Phineas nearly ends up so (he is saved by a fairy tale key and a wealthy wife).[3]

The emotionally pessimistic outlook here is made explicit in Raven's *Edward and Mrs. Simpson* (1978); like his *The Pallisers*, it is dependent on Frances Donaldson's biography of Edward VIII and *Blackheath Poisonings* (1992), a transposition adaptation of Julian Symons's Victorian pastiche crime novel. These two films and Raven's *The Pallisers* form a dialogic debate: *Edward and Mrs. Simpson* takes seriously and finds value in a Talleyrand-like sweet, luxurious life controlled by hierarchical dynasties; *Blackheath Poisonings* exposes the miseries of people whose lives are perverted by dynasties; and *The Pallisers* veers between the two.[4]

Stanzas of poetry, often heavily erotic, are also scattered throughout the series, making an ironic case for an authentic solitary life. Tennyson's *Maud*, which can be enjoyed only when one is alone, makes Lady Glencora go off into gales of laughter (*The Pallisers* 2:3, episode 13). Byron's *Childe Harolde* ("There is a rapture on the lonely shore/There is society where none intrudes") is repeated by Lizzie Eustace as Frank Greystock watches over her (6:12, episodes 16, 18). There are also passages from Shakespeare and Swinburne which have gay subtexts—from *Henry VI, Part 2* where Hal rejects Falstaff, and Swinburne's "Atlanta in Calydon" (*The Pallisers* 8:15, episode 31, and 10:20, episode 13)—and proverbial events from the Bible. Other allusions are to classical works and possibly from contemporary women's writing—as when Lady Glencora wishes she could travel (2:3, episode 11). The texture of allusions in Raven's scripts shapes Trollope's novels into a filmic, disillusioned political vision, which justifies patriarchy in an ameliorated inegalitarian society and which is dependent on the self-erasure of women whose emotional and social support is needed to sustain it.

CHARACTER-DRIVEN POLITICS

Raven's scripts for *The Pallisers* took him almost five years to write (1969–1973). He described his revamping frankly but abstractly and acknowledged only that he rewrote the five books so as to make all of the stories he took over "parts, large or small, of Glencora" (played by Susan Hampshire, whose looks resemble those of the female in the original illustrations).[5] Raven's pouring of his life experience into his characters—female and male—is reflected in his strong empathy for Lady Glencora as a tormented rebel and salonnière, even as she also sustains the role of a conventionally loyal and loving wife; Raven's characterization is somewhat at odds with Trollope's portrait of a still-resistant woman. Similarly, Raven's sympathy shows for Madame Max Goesler (later Mrs. Finn) as a version of the European archetypal ideal super-female, although she is eventually tamed into a chaste, wary nurse-companion to an old man, as found in Trollope's novels.[6] Raven's Madame Max unites the Phineas and Palliser stories, sustains her role across the series, and displaces Lady Laura Standish Kennedy—whom Trollope declared "the best character" (*Autobiography*, 320) in the Phineas books—as the series' second remarkable female. The "tragic misery of Lady Laura," which Trollope attributes "to the sale she made of herself in her wretched marriage" (Trollope, *Autobiography* 320), was transferred to the type of woman careerist that is still frequently seen in films—someone who mistakes her "better" female nature. Trollope's Laura is incapable of remorseless ambition and cannot overcome her love.

The film story is made riveting by Anna Massey and Derek Godfrey's performances of two people beginning well and gradually hardening. Raven's derivation from Trollope's candid scenes of the wife's refusal to have sexual relations with her husband shows much greater pity for Kennedy; Raven's Kennedy longs for companionship (*The Pallisers* 8:15, episode 31) and experiences an agonized frustration which (in the film) edges into violence towards his wife (cf. *The Pallisers* 5:9, episodes 2–3, and *PF* 332–336). Both film characters are lonely people (4:7, episode 33; 5:10, episode 10) whose natures lead to ostracized lives. The conflict between them resembles that which Raven presents in *Blackheath Poisonings*, in which Isabel Collard, the framed adulteress, finds herself in conflict with her seething, transvestite, secretly crazed murderer-husband George and with her lover Roger Vandervent, who is in most respects a sympathetic character.

Raven's adaptations of *The Decline of the Gentleman, Boys will be Boys*, and Donaldson's *Edward VIII* make visible and explicit the attitudes underlying his presentation of Trollope's males. For Raven, the central hero in the Trollope series is Plantagenet, dramatized as ethical and honorable, yet ontologically different from the man his upbringing shaped him to be, and thus disabled when he must interact with those around him. (In this respect, he resembles Edward VIII as played by Edward Fox). Similarly, Raven's Phineas Finn is a man who knows how to live conventionally while hiding the fact that he contains within himself "the other" (not just that he is Irish, but that he is motivated by thoughts that have been formed independently).[7] The series ends with Philip Latham as Palliser and then the Duke of Omnium reluctantly but resiliently adapting to a bourgeois, liberal ideal of an individually authentic existence. The duke marries for love and returns to Parliament with a lesser post than he had before. Both decisions are acts of the free spirit—a spirit that Glencora was never permitted.

The exemplary male of the series is Donal McCann as an appealing, gradually maturing Phineas. His rhetorical speech, excoriating the bullying macho norms which seek openly to deride the duke, is the political climax of several public lives—Phineas's own, the duke's, and Glencora's. Raven's Phineas treats Lord Chiltern's demand for a duel as that of a predatory bully: the camera shows Phineas shooting up into the air (*The Pallisers* 5:9, episode 5, 5:10, episode 6). By focusing on a heckler as one who is anxious to wound "in order that he may be gratified by seeing the pain which he inflicts," Raven arranges Trollope's theatrical parliamentary scene so as to focus on Phineas's attempt to shame his opponents (cf. *The Pallisers* 11:23, episode 29; *PM*, 493–495).

In *Boys will be Boys*, Raven makes an argument about men that is analogous to that made by feminists about women: men are not born, but as boys, they are coerced into learning the role of macho heterosexuals, driven to practice war (bullying), and corrupted by a "sinister" militarist culture in schools (27–38). Several of Raven's males are explainable if they are seen as hiding homosexual tendencies: Derek Jacobi as an easily humiliated Lord Fawn uninterested in women, for example, and Ferdinand Lopez as a man with a hidden background.[8] Different from Trollope's Lord Chiltern and Gerard, Raven's versions of these characters do not so much reject a work ethic and political ideals as they respectively loathe and disdain modern networking and careerism. Terence Alexander effectively plays Lord George de Bruce Caruthers as ironically amused by Protestant hypocrisies. Raven's Caruthers is a (quietly) kept man to Helen Lindsay's Mrs. Jane Carbuncle, a character whom (in *The Eustace Diamonds*) Trollope expects his readers to dislike intensely: she is an obdurate, mercenary bully who shatters the sanity of her (probably) illegitimate daughter, Lucinda Roanoke.

Indeed, Raven's revisions of Trollope's female characters are as striking as his revisions of the male characters of his source stories. Raven's Jane Carbuncle is reconfigured as a quick-witted, genial demimondaine who mothers Lizzie Eustace in a companionable bedroom scene when she gives Lizzie the good advice—at least from her own and Lizzie's perspective—to break up the fabulously valuable necklace Lizzie is tenaciously holding onto and sell it (cf. *The Pallisers* 7:12, episode 20; 7:13, episode 21; and *ED*, 428–429). This Mrs. Carbuncle appreciates a good meal with wine (she stays "jolly" that way), and she knows that her safety lies in obscurity. She aims only to escape with a small percentage of the take. In their last scene after George secures for them Lizzie's rent, they evade creditors and police. George remarks, "We'll change the check into cash without telling anyone and then just slip away quietly in two or three days time." Her answer is a strong, amused, answering face. He again: "You'll have to look sharp and travel light, but it won't be the first time, what?" Darker memories register on her face, but she laughs as she turns "to get away without that lot watching" (7:14, episode 29). Raven's Mrs. Carbuncle corresponds to the mostly unnamed women in Trollope's *oeuvre* who run boarding houses where sex is quietly for sale by other desperate women.[9]

Raven erases most of Trollope's carefully nuanced, virtuous victim-heroines in the novels: gone from his adaptation of *The Eustace Diamonds* are the victim-governess-paid-companion Lucy Morris, her employer Lady Fawn, the nightmare figure Lady Linlithgow, and Lucinda Roanoke. And, Raven sometimes works to create distaste or even outright antagonism towards a heroine Trollope engaged and identified with, such as the depressed Alice Vavasour in *Can You Forgive Her?* Sometimes, powerful women in Trollope become salacious prudes (such as Lady Midlothian in *CYFH?*, inane (such as Griselda, Lady Dumbello, in

The Small House at Allington), or spoilt childlike fools who make trouble for others as well as themselves (such as Raven's hollow Lizzie Eustace in *ED*). Female characters Trollope saw in genuine, if limited, feminist terms become women who have foolishly rejected the sexually alluring men they really wanted (such as Violet Effingham in *PF/PR*). Anna Carteret as Lady Mabel Grex (in *The Duke's Children*) retains some of the desperation and capability of genuine love that Henry James gave his treacherous women in need, but in contrast, a rare forthright, intelligent female character, Adelaide Palliser, becomes a comic "hors-y" woman, allured by Gerard Maule's male cruelty. Raven's Adelaide even participates (with Jacobi as Fawn) in a slapstick comic repeat of the proposal scene between Elizabeth Bennet and Mr. Collins in *Pride and Prejudice* (*The Pallisers* 8:17, episode 43). Left unexamined by Raven are the innocently enthralled (the seduced and well-meaning Mary Flood Jones, *PF*, and the wistful and ethical Lady Mary Palliser and Isabel Boncassen, *The Duke's Children*), the women who kindly mother men, and those women who live happily without men (Lady Baldock in *The Pallisers* 5:9, episode 7, and Aspasia Fitzgibbon, played superbly by Rosalind Marshall, who saves Phineas from the nagging debt collector Clarke in *The Pallisers* 5:9, episode 2).

Raven's condescending and discouraging revisions are partly explained by his attitudes towards women in general and towards Trollope's women in particular. These attitudes are seen in his introduction to Trollope's *An Eye for An Eye*. Trollope's contemporary and best Victorian periodical critic, Richard Holt Hutton, reads this novella as a powerful poetic tragic romance, in which Trollope explores the ways in which human nature can be violated when, answering to "social obligations" (Smalley, 447), the weak protagonist, a young Protestant English lord, is pressured and persuaded into deserting the Catholic Irish girl he has impregnated outside of marriage. In a withering scathing commentary to the contrary, Raven argues that Trollope is "writing between the lines" about a "ferocious" priest, a "scheming and vindictive...mother," and a "witless" girl (Introduction, x–xii). Raven is not writing tongue-in-cheek here: for him, Trollope's women are minor characters, presented as manipulative sex objects (when they are young) and as domineering (when they are older) (Barber, 104–106; McSweeney).

Raven's interest typically lies with the male characters. *The Pallisers*—and Alan Pater's *The Barchester Chronicles*, which appeared partly in its wake—dramatizes the problems men in their public roles have in getting through life under the burden of 1970s and 1980s masculine norms, which demanded aggression, competitiveness, sexual and financial success, protective behavior over women, and successful coping with the domineering, mistaken, and entrapping women in their lives. In Raven's versions, what liberties women should be allowed are severely limited (Stewart, 163–164, 166–171). A greater range of liberty is allowed the male characters. Some of the male characters in these series succeed according to these norms, some fail, and some fall in between. Some succeed ethically, some unethically. But their success is always the point of interest.

The two story lines of *The Barchester Chronicles* derive from the contradictions resulting from a rigid, privileged, exclusive caste order and the qualities with which chance endows particular individuals. Raven typically shows male characters as living in a world of intense vacillation and confusion—for example, they are surreally driven (such as Alan Rickman as the seething Slope, George Watson as George Vavasour, and Stuart Wilson as the resentful Lopez), well-meaning but inept and/or comically ineffective (such as Nigel Hawthorne as Archbishop Grantly and Derek Jacobi as Lord Fawn), without sufficient stamina to bully others (such as Jonathan Adams as Mr. Quiverful), or with no trajectory for advancement and dependent on women because they lack money, connections, ambition, or will-power (such as Martin Jarvis as Frank Greystock and Terence Alexander as Lord de Bruce Carruthers).

It is worth noting that Alan Plater, the writer of *The Barchester Chronicles*, seems as little amused as Raven by genially corrupt insiders (such as Peter Blythe as Bertie Stanhope and Neil Stacey as Lawrence Fitzgibbon). In both miniseries, women's sexual desires (which are much more on display in *The Pallisers*) and moral conflicts are presented as problems that are posed for men until the women submit to the socially safe marriage.

NARRATION INTO DIALOGUE, DESCRIPTION INTO SPEECH

The Pallisers is nevertheless a masterpiece of fascinating televisual art. The substance of Raven's characterizations, which have affected how Trollope's novels are read and how Trollope novels are adapted ever since the first airing, is seen in the series' justifying dramatizations of coercive institutions and family life, the men's as well as the women's experience of courtship and marriage, relationships between children (adolescent and grown) and their parents or their aunts and uncles, and relationships between siblings.[10] Political campaigns are presented as an opportunity for one set of men to fleece another, and parliamentary politics are shown as a game for coercing men into obedient groups in order for them to stay in power. Much of the action in these adaptations occurs in the men's clubs, Lady Glencora's political gatherings, and (less frequently) behind the scenes with incidents of pressure and bribery (for instance, when Slide, the newspaper proprietor, hounds Phineas). Now and again, one treads the dangerous streets and returns to landscapes (estates and public parks). Once, the camera moves into a police station, where, contrary to Trollope's original, Phineas successfully bribes a police officer (*The Pallisers* 4:8, episode 39; *PF*, 237–238). In spite of the numerous small alterations in setting, the sheer variety of places and the vigor and sheer energy of the characters, moods, and incidents does reflect Trollope's approach to human beings in their natural habitat. There seems never to be a lull—in Raven's screenplays, as in Trollope's fiction.

In this miniseries, Raven's most successful Trollopian scenes are the longer, intimate ones where one watches two characters who know one another very well communicating or gouging one another competitively, or those in which people in a larger group interact to reveal competitive, corrupt, and messy parliamentary politics. In such scenes, Raven translates the original language more or less faithfully into the screenplay while at the same time creating a political emphasis of his own. A comparative study of the context and content of two such scenes from parts 8:15 to 8:16 (a medial pair), both out of *Phineas Redux*, will show how Trollope's text was typically successfully adapted in *The Pallisers*. As with all twenty-six parts of the miniseries, these two parts are self-contained unified segments with interwoven themes, moods, palettes, and carefully composed scenes. *The Pallisers* 8:15 is mournful: many scenes are set at night, and the characters age and face irretrievable loss, for example, when Lord Brentford realizes he would have nothing to return to were he to find himself in London. In the second dominant scene, which takes place in Dresden, Lady Laura opens her heart to a Phineas who is no longer in love with her. Here, Laura is a very Trollopian character—someone who has made a terrible decision from which she cannot retrieve herself (episode 31).

This scene contrasts with the death scene of the disreputable, unrepentant, self-satisfied, and supine Duke of Omnium, who is watched over by the loving noble, Madame Max. (This latter scene, in episode 34, is indeed the high point of the part and is thematically important for the whole miniseries). By continual small alterations of a few paragraphs of free indirect discourse, punctuated by fragments of dramatic naturalistic speech (*PR* 1:226), Raven alters Trollope's emphasis: Trollope's duke's "continual trust in the greatness and goodness of God" (*PR*, 226) vanishes, as does his trust in the efficacy of his rank, even in the afterlife. Roland Culver as Raven's Omnium tells Barbara Murray as Madame Max that he has received the sacraments for Lady Glencora's sake, although they meant nothing to him, indeed, less than the broth Madame Max is feeding him because the broth was touched by her hand. His words, which come early in Trollope's paragraphs, become the definitive last statement of the scene: She: "It is nearly finished." He: "The thing is done. No. I hope for nothing. Fear nothing." There is a moment of silence, and he dies. Madame Max goes round the bed and takes a stance that parallels Philip Latham Plantagenet's in a previous scene, when Omnium refuses to see Lady Hartletop (who decades before was one of the duke's lovers) because she is now old and ugly. To explain his feelings about seeing Lady Hartletop, the duke has asked Plantagenet to complete some lines he finds apt and amusing from *Henry IV, Part 2*. Palliser finds them apt too, though from a very different perspective, and he quotes Shakespeare's Hal's opening lines in which Hal rejects Falstaff: "I know thee not old man.... How ill white hairs become a fool and jester" (8:15, episode 31). The duke, oblivious, has continued to laugh. In the scene that is under consideration now, Madame Max utters the phrase (which with Trollope's narrator ends the chapter) as a valediction: "You hoped for nothing, feared nothing. But no man should live as idly" (*The Pallisers* 8:15, episode 34). Using a nearly transposed text, Raven (along with the director, actors, script editor, and assistant editors in the cutting room) has transformed Trollope's ethical perspective into an atheist death scene.

THE INVENTED SCENE

By contrast, the second exemplary scene under consideration is a wholly invented dinner party, a multiperson drama developed out of a single narrated paragraph in which no such party is mentioned (*PR* 1:357–358). Still, in this scene, Trollope's complicated meanings are conveyed more or less faithfully. As in the scene discussed earlier, the duchess's (Lady Glencora's) dinner is the climax of a thematically coherent, nearly one-hour program. It is also crucial for the plot design of the next four parts: treacherously, insidiously, she encourages the career politician Mr. Bonteen—a malleable, sycophantic, and envious enemy of Phineas Finn, as well as an expert in matters of trade—to become drunk and, in Trollope's words, sufficiently make "an ass" (*PR*, 161) of himself, so that he is refused the position of chancellor of exchequer which has been promised to him. Bonteen becomes enraged and in turn enrages Phineas, who is then accused of murdering him "for advancement" (8:17, episode 45). Episode 8:16 is dominated by scenes of active insider politics, alternating with scenes in which the insiders (such as Barrington Erle) justify themselves and the excluded complain. The episode opens with a drawing-room gathering to which Phineas has not been invited (episode 36). The characters manipulate and plan tactics (Lady Glencora) or are crotchety (Lord Brentford). Two scenes focus on women as wistful: Madame Max gazes at the duchess, who gazes at herself with a crown as she meditates the price she continues to pay for this bauble (episode 38). Back in London and out of mourning (in autumnal yellow and browns, which match her now rich-looking auburn hair), Laura is eager to know what to do to help Phineas, even though her very presence hurts him (episode 39). The dominating shades of brown in this part are somber, but the rooms and parks (where Adelaide Palliser vies with Gerard Maule) are lit with morning sun and soft blue afternoon light. The scene darkens only in one confidential talk between a despairing Phineas and (dressed in rich purples) Madame Max (episode 38). Donal McCann as Phineas is the center of this part in the sense that, like Hamlet, his status is on everyone's mind; however, the actor who is given the most to do and who is seemingly omnipresent is Peter Sallis as Mr. Bonteen, a venomous obstacle to Phineas's need for office. Bonteen's antagonistic encounters with Phineas, from 7:14 to 7:30, are memorable.[11]

The dinner party is, then, a bravura theatrical epitome of the personal losses and outward political maneuvering that fuel the scenes of the entire part. The camera focuses on Sallis as Bonteen, an overweening man who has had too much to drink. Maurice Quick as Collingwood is also continually present as he unobtrusively does her ladyship's bidding (here, he keeps filling Bonteen's glass). Deluded by Lady Glencora, the growingly unsteady Bonteen loudly spouts his hard-earned knowledge of trade in such a way as publicly to expose his ambition to replace Plantagenet (who is sitting at the other end of the table), control powerful banks, and make the Irish do his bidding. Susan Hampshire delivers her honeyed phoniness here with a steel-like smile, and Dolly Longstaffe delivers his shafts at this "liberal" bunch and their duchess with stringent bitterness. In some ways, Raven's Bonteen elicits sympathy, just as Trollope's narrator evidently intended, in a nearby briefly narrated scene in *Phineas Redux* (which is not dramatized). When the prime minister (no one else will do it) informs Mr. Bonteen that he is not to be in the cabinet after all, "The proposition very nearly broke the man's heart" (*PR* 1: 361). In the novel, there follows a deliciously ironic paragraph from the narrator on how "the secrets of the world are very marvelous" and how what makes things happen is often not what the readers had supposed (362).

Here, Raven and the team have brought to life Trollope's grave and scintillating political novel, this time by semioriginal invention. The scene that seems closely transposed turns out to undergo significant changes in order to dramatize current "anxiety-provoking issues" (Rose, 2): old age, death, and looking back on a life with comic or anguished uneasiness. In dramatizing a public experience which many viewers may identify with or may have seen—a humiliating career defeat for the scene's chief figure—Raven's wholly invented scene conveys what Trollope's nineteenth-century work briefly hinted at and described not at all.

RAVEN IN CONTEXT

Understanding films, particularly those that are adapted from source texts, requires, as I have said, a close comparative reading. A look at these two ways of adapting Trollope—through the transposed text and the invented scene which compresses and alters the original materials—reveals the Victorian author's transformed presence. If it is carried farther, such an examination would reveal, as well, the fact that all other adaptations of Trollope engage as much with Raven as with Trollope himself.[12]

For example, a review of the transposed (yet transformed) scene allows one to distinguish Plater's perception of Trollope from Raven's. Quite a number of Plater's closely transposed dramatic scenes and narrator's monologues develop Trollope's meaning into a mild feminism or strong academic satire (Showalter, 5). A scene from *The Barchester Chronicles*, written by Plater, reveals a perhaps unexpected connection with Trollope's *He Knew He Was Right*. Susan Hampshire, playing the crippled Signora Madeline Neroni, has been listening to her sister, Charlotte Stanhope, urge their penniless brother Bertie to court the widowed Eleanor Bold in order to marry Eleanor for her money.

Obstacles include the heavy mourning Eleanor wears. Madeline's reply shows the same kind of significant small changes that are seen in Raven's death of the Duke of Omnium. Directly from Trollope comes Madeline's response: "I hate such shallow pretenses. I'd let the world say what it pleased and show no grief [for a dead husband] if I felt none—perhaps not show it if I did." When her brother and sister say nothing, she continues,

> [Y]ou both know in what way husbands and wives generally live together. You know what freedom a man claims for himself and what slavery he would exact from a wife and you know how wives generally obey. Marriage means tyranny on one side, and deceit on the other, and a man is a fool to sacrifice his interests to such a bargain. The tragedy is a woman generally has no other way of living.

But, Plater reinforces Madeline's vulnerability and reminds one of her crippled state when Bertie and Charlotte laughingly anticipate their father's death as a way of "getting something." Madeline replies sharply: "I think we'll inherit his debts as well." When Peter Blythe as Bertie then chuckles, Hampshire again counters or makes melancholy the bright hardness of the original scene with a tone of sudden anguish and the words, "Besides I like him, and I should be sorry to lose him." Unlike Trollope, Plater has his Madeline voice her dependence on her father for safety (cf. 1:4, episode 5; *BT*, 125–126).

For his semi-invented dramatic scenes from Trollope, the kind of texts Raven drew on are narrated indirect discourse and the ironic monologues of Trollope's narrator. Partly as a result of this miniseries' heavy reliance on studios, and on one location, Sudeley Castle (which served as Matching Priory and Gatherum), Raven rarely develops Trollope's descriptive powers, especially when it comes to mountainous terrain, bleak landscapes, and heaths. Trollope's landscape pictorialism and frequent resort to epistolary narration is kept to a minimum (voice-over is rare in *The Pallisers*) in Raven's scripts. In *Malachi's Cove*, Mally remembers her mother and father's death by drowning three times, and this is dramatized three times; she visits their gravestones near a Romanesque church, and shots liken her to a bird that is seen across a cliff. In Trollope's story, her orphan state is mentioned briefly. Phrases and images of stones that include a sense of centuries of human history felt in the Cornish landscape are suggested by mention of the cliffs and waters of Tintagel.

In contrast, in Davies's adaptation of *The Way We Live Now*, twenty-first-century computerized camera and sound bring to more fully realized sensual life what Trollope's narrator tells or briefly suggests. One such scene is Paul Montague's hard work on the railway in the United States. Others include Felix Carbury's several trysts with Ruby Ruggles in the woods (*TWWLN* 1:1, episode 12, 1:2, episode 4; *TWWLN*, 149) and scenes in a tavern and a music hall (*TWWLN*, 1:2, episode 8; *TWWLN*, 569, 574). Because their original equivalent is usually an epistolary narrative, the semi-invented scenes in Davies's scripts are most frequently presented as dialogues between two and three characters. One notable example: Davies turns a correspondence between Anne-Marie Duff, as the coldly selfish Georgiana Longstaffe, and Jim Carter, as her generous-spirited Jewish banker-suitor Breghert, into an intimate confrontation. Breghert earnestly and decently tells Georgiana that for a while he will not be able to provide her with a house and pay for a season in London; her response is immediately to lash out against having anything to do with his "Jew children." Breghert is thus forced to see, and then admit aloud, that she has no feeling for him or his relatives, and he resolutely turns away. To her indignation and painful astonishment, Georgiana finds herself standing alone (*TWWLN* 2:4, episode 7; *TWWLN*, 634–643). Davies's script has done justice to an unusual moment in Trollope: an exposure of anti-Semitism. The paradigmatic televisual performance moment also visualizes a core idea of Trollope's *The Way We Live Now*: that living according to a code of commercial transactions impedes human bonds and the fulfillment people yearn for.[13]

The 1974 *Pallisers* and the 1982 *Barchester Chronicles* continue to be considered the standards for Trollope adaptations. More attention also should be paid to the other adaptations, whatever is known of the screenplays of the others, and to Trollope's texts, too, as the product of his distinct art and genius. For when one studies the ways Trollope's texts have been adapted, one uncovers their value, discovers how each group of filmmakers recreates them, and may surmise why readers turn to and away from them.

ENDNOTES

1. This is not to deny the miniseries' importance or its brilliance. Barsetshire is a mythic Trollopian place. Giles's use of a spiritual quietism and communal characters, strictly Victorian costumes, and storybook and pastoral *mise en scène* for *The Barchester Chronicles* is repeated in the Exeter Close scenes of the 2004 BBC/WGBH *He Knew He Was Right* and the 2007–2009 *Cranford Chronicles*. Its predecessors include Giles's 1970 BBC *Little Women* and the 1971 BBC *Sense and Sensibility*.
2. See Barber, 187–191; Moody, *The Pallisers*.
3. Monk comments on *Beauchamp's Career* and Trollope's *American Senator* in *The Pallisers* 9:18, episode 1. Wilding's essay reveals the close alignment between *Phineas Redux* (a darker book) and *Beauchamp's Career*.
4. I adhere to the tripartite division of film adaptations that is used in many film studies (see Brian McFarlane, *Novel to Film*). In a transposition, or apparently faithful film, the filmmakers have attempted to match the original story and to reproduce most of the characters, with some allowance for modernizing interpretations. In a commentary, or the critical and departure type of adaptation, the filmmakers intend to maintain considerable fidelity, but attempt this through departures from the original which often include altering central pivotal events and the way in which the events are presented dramatically in order to comment on or alter the original author's theme. In analogies, or free adaptations, filmmakers have abandoned historical costume drama in the central story but make the film manifestly intelligible as an adaptation.
5. "A is a boring and apparently superfluous woman: I shall delete her [major characters deleted include, from *CYFH?*, the Widow Greenow and her suitors; from *PF*, Mr. and Mrs. Low; from *ED*, Lucy Morris, Lady Fawn, Lady Linlithgow, Lucinda Roanoke, and Mr. Camperdown; from *PR*, Mr. Maule; from *PM*, Arthur Fletcher and Mrs. Roby; and from *The Duke's Children*, Lady Cantrip and Lord Popplecourt]. But if I delete her I also delete most of the motive power behind her husband, B, who is a social climber and a minor but essential piece of mechanism. All right: let us have B motivated, not by his wife A, but by his old crony, C. A very neat suggestion [e.g., Barrington Erle and Mr. Monk's roles are expanded to motivate and link actions]—were it not that B and C have quarreled in the second chapter and refuse to talk to each other for the next seven-eighths of the novel. Very well: delete their quarrel. I can't because the quarrel is the delayed fuse

which detonates the grand dénouement 700 pages later; whichever way I look at it, I cannot substitute C for A as the driving force behind B. All right: bring back A after all. But somebody has to go, indeed half of them have to go, and it is the same trouble with everyone I try to get rid of: they all keep pushing themselves back in again for seemingly ungainsayable reasons" (Barber, 243).

6. "I have lived almost constantly with them ['Trollope's *people*']: eaten and drunk, scoffed and prayed, gambled, cheated and intrigued with them, won and lost with them" (Barber, 190). Raven's Lady Glencora corresponds to the sexually chaste, relatively less wise (than her husband), loyal, respectful, good wife type in popular movies. The European super-female is a woman who is not interested in marriage, a career, or public power—someone who is sexually alluring, good in bed, a quiet and civilized manipulator, intellectual, and lightly flirtatious (see Haskell, 153–188)—for example, Stephane Audan as Carla, Lord Marchmain's companion in *Brideshead Revisited*. Raven adheres to the terms of hostility to career woman in movies (see Basinger, 19–66).

7. On Raven's handling of Phineas's dual lives as a homosexual perspective, see Toibin.

8. Dellamora argues that Trollope's text invites one to read Lopez as a homosexual male (104–108).

9. See Moody, "Trollope's Comfort Romances."

10. Only recently has Trollope's presentation of older and fatherly-like men agreeing to or pursuing coerced marriage with young women been openly characterized as (what even he—in, for example, "The Editor's Tales"— recognizes it as) male sexual predation.

11. In Trollope, Bonteen is mentioned twice in *Phineas Finn* and once in *The Eustace Diamonds*, and in *Phineas Redux*, chapter 33, he is a suddenly emerged complex living presence. Raven builds Bonteen up from 7:14 on: as a part of Lizzie Eustace's story, with two early scenes of insult, and needling Finn (8:15, episodes 6 and episode 30).

12. Three—*Malachi's Cove*, *He Knew He Was Right*, and *The Way We Live Now*—turn Trollope's texts into filmic critical exposures of the suffering, self-destructive, and cruel behavior that was elicited by Victorian systems of social, economic, and gender privilege and power as well as lingeringly memorable depictions of ordinary people's lives at the time without departing from the norms of transposition-type adaptation.

13. Trollope empathizes with another ostracized and wounded Jewish hero, Anton Trendellsohn (who has his initials), in *Nina Balatka*; see Moody,

Trollope 92–93 ("our Christian heroine, Nina, and her Jewish lover, Anton Trendellsohn, live in a segregated world which imprisons their minds in its hatreds, avarice, shame and distrust"). Davies's last brief scene of Georgiana Longstaffe seated alone at the piano (for life, as it were) is, however, harder on Georgiana than Trollope's busier ending of Georgiana's desperate elopement with a clergyman who has no income (*TWWLN* 2:4, episode 12; *TWWLN* 769–771). Some of the pairs or trios have textual authority: Felix, Marie, and Didon (whom Davies places in an ironically Arcadian garden; 1:2, episode 11) meet variously in the book. Other pairs are wholly invented: Davies adds scenes between Hetta Carbury and Marie Melmotte (e.g., 2:3, episode 1; 2:4, episode 12) to provide a naturalistic opportunity for Marie to confide her bitterness and maturation (she speaks with scorn of her stepmother's dependence, stating that she does not want to be "like her").

BIBLIOGRAPHY

Barber, Michael. *The Captain: The Life and Times of Simon Raven.* London: Duckbacks, 1996. Print.

Basinger, Jeanine. *A Woman's View: How Hollywood Spoke to Women, 1930–1960.* Hanover: Wesleyan University Press, 1993. Print.

Cardwell, Sarah. *Adaptation Revisited: Television and the Classic Novel.* Manchester: Manchester University Press, 2005. Print.

————. *Andrew Davies.* Manchester: Manchester University Press, 2005. Print.

Cleere, Eileen. Rev. of *The Politics of Gender in Anthony Trollope's Novels: New Readings for the Twenty-First Century,* ed. Deborah Denenholz Morse, Margaret Markwick, and Regenia Gagnier. *Victorian Studies* 52.3 (2010): 506–509. Print.

Dellamora, Richard. *Friendship's Bonds: Democracy in the Novel in Victorian England.* Philadelphia: University of Pennsylvania Press, 2004. Print.

Gibbs, John. *Mise-en-Scene: Film Style and Interpretation.* London: Wallflower Press, 2002. Print.

Hagen, John. "*The Duke's Children*: Trollope's Psychological Masterpiece." *Nineteenth-Century Fiction* 13 (1958): 1–21. Print.

Haskell, Molly. *From Reverence to Rape: The Treatment of Women in the Movies.* New York: Holt, Rinehart and Winston, 1973. Print.

McSweeney, Kerry. "The Novels of Simon Raven." *Queen's Quarterly* 78 (1971): 106–116. Print.

Moody, Ellen. "Can You Forgive Her," "Orley Farm" and "The Last Chronicle of Barset." *On the Original Illustrations of Trollope's Fiction.* Ellen Moody's website: Mostly on English and Continental and Women's Literature. Web. 11 Jan. 2011.

————. "*The Pallisers*." *Film Adaptations*. Ellen Moody's website: Mostly on English and Continental and Women's Literature. Web. 11 Jan. 2011.

————. "Partly Told in Letters: Trollope's Art of Story-telling." *Trollopiana: The Journal of the Trollope Society* 48 (2000): 4–31.

————. *Trollope on the 'Net*. London: Hambledon and the Trollope Society, 1999. Print.

————. "Trollope's Comfort Romances for Men: Heterosexual Male Heroism in His Work." Paper presented 18 July 2006 at the Trollope Conference, Exeter. *The Victorian Web*. Web. 7 Jan. 2011.

Morse, Deborah Denenholz, Margaret Markwick, and Reginia Gagnier, eds. *The Politics of Gender in Anthony Trollope's Novels: New Readings for the Twenty-First Century*. Farnham Surrey: Ashgate, 2009. Print.

Raven, Simon. *Boys Will be Boys*. London and Liverpool: Anthony Blond, 1963. Print.

————. *The Decline of the Gentleman*. New York: Simon and Schuster, 1962. Print.

————. Introduction. *An Eye for an Eye*. By Anthony Trollope. New York: Stein and Day, 1966. Print.

Showalter, Elaine. *Faculty Towers: The Academic Novel and Its Discontents*. Philadelphia: University of Pennsylvania Press, 2005. Print.

Smalley, Donald, ed., *The Critical Heritage*. New York: Barnes & Nobles Inc., 1969. Print.

Stewart, Garrett, "Film's Victorian Retrofit." *Victorian Studies* 38.2 (1995): 153–198. Print.

Toibin, Colm. "The Art of Being Found Out." *London Review of Books* 30.3 (2008): 24–27. Print.

Trollope, Anthony. *An Autobiography*. Ed. M. Sadleir and F. Page. Introd. P. D. Edwards. New York: Oxford University Press, 1980. Print.

————. *Barchester Towers* [*BT*]. Ed., introd. Robin Gilmour. London: Penguin, 1994. Print.

———. *Can You Forgive Her?* [*CYFH?*]. Ed., introd. David Skilton. London: The Trollope Society, 1989. Print.

———. *The Eustace Diamonds* [*ED*]. Ed., introd. Stephen Gill and John Sutherland. London: Penguin, 1969. Print.

———. *He Knew He Was Right*. Ed., introd. John Sutherland. New York: Oxford University Press, 1985. Print.

———. *Phineas Finn, or, The Irish Member* [*PF*]. Ed., introd. John Sutherland. London: Penguin, 1972. Print.

———. *Phineas Redux* [*PR*]. Ed. John C. Whale. Introd. F. S. L. Lyons. London: Oxford, 1983. Print.

———. *The Prime Minister* [*PM*]. Ed., introd. David Skilton. New York: Oxford University Press, 1994. Print.

———. *The Warden* [*TW*]. Ed., introd. David Skilton. New York: Oxford University Press, 1980. Print.

———. *The Way We Live Now* [*TWWLN*]. Ed., introd. Robert Tracy. New York: Bobbs-Merrill, 1974. Print.

Turner, Mark W. *Trollope and the Magazines: Gendered Issues in Mid-Victorian Britain*. London: Macmillan, 2000. Print.

Wilding, Michael. "George Meredith's *Beauchamp's Career*: Politics, Romance and Realism." *Sydney Studies* (1982): 46–69. Print.

FILMOGRAPHY

The Barchester Chronicles. Dir. David Giles. Screenplay by Alan Plater. Perf. Donald Pleasance, Nigel Hawthorne, Alan Rickman, Janet Maw, Geraldine McEwan, Janet Maw, and Barbara Flynn. BBC, 1982. DVD.

Blackheath Poisonings. Dir. Stuart Orme. Screenplay by Simon Raven. Perf. Christine Kavanagh, Judy Parfitt, Ian MacNeice, Zoe Wanamaker, Christien Anholt, and Patrick Malahide. Central Television/WGBH, 1992. DVD.

Edward and Mrs Simpson. Dir. Waris Hussein. Screenplay by Simon Raven. Perf. Edward Fox, Cynthia Harris, Nigel Hawthorne, David Walker, Peggy Ashcroft, and Charles Keating. Thames/BBC, 1978. DVD.

He Knew He Was Right. Dir. Tom Vaughn. Screenplay by Andrew Davies. Perf. Oliver Dimsdale, Laura Fraser, Bill Nighy, Anna Massey, Geoffrey Palmer, Geraldine James, Claudie Blakeley, David Tennant, Fenella Woolgar, Ron Cook, John Alderton, and Betsy Palmer. BBC/WGBH, 2004. DVD.

Malachi's Cove, Dir. Screenplay by Henry Herbert. Perf. Donald Pleasaunce, Veronica Quilligan, John Barrett, Peter Vaughn, Meg Wynn Owen, Arthur English, Alan Hockley, and Lillias Walker. Penrith, 1974. Film.

The Pallisers. Dir. Hugh David, Ronald Wilson. Screenplay by Simon Raven. Perf. Susan Hampshire, Philip Latham, Donal McCann, Barbara Murray, Anna Massey, and Donald Pickering. BBC, 1974. DVD.

The Way We Live Now. Dir. David Yates. Screenplay by Andrew Davies. Perf. David Suchet, Paloma Baeza, Cheryl Campbell, Shirley Henderson, Douglas Hodge, Matthew Macfayden, Cillian Murphy, Miranda Otto, David Bradley, and Anne-Marie Duff. BBC/WGBH, 2001. DVD.

PART III

TRANSLATING THE VICTORIANS

TEACHING BOOKS BY READING MOVIES

CHAPTER 9

TEACHING STOKER'S DRACULA WITH MULTIPLE FILM VERSIONS

NOSFERATU, DRACULA, AND PAGES FROM A VIRGIN'S DIARY

Sarah J. Heidt

To detail the pedagogical horizons that teaching multiple film versions of a single novel can open, I will focus on the final unit of one of my junior- and senior-level English courses at Kenyon College, "Page, Stage, Screen: Nineteenth-Century Novels Transformed."[1] In this class, students read Bram Stoker's *Dracula* (1897) against a backdrop of six films: the German Expressionist classics *The Cabinet of Dr. Caligari* (1919) and *Nosferatu* (1922), the Universal Studios *Dracula* directed by Tod Browning (1931), the blaxploitation picture *Blacula* (1972), Guy Maddin's neo-silent ballet film *Dracula: Pages from a Virgin's Diary* (2002), and Francis Ford Coppola's ambitious and tellingly flawed *Bram Stoker's Dracula* (1992).

In just over three weeks, my students gained exposure to distinct cinematic traditions from Germany, the United States, and Canada, as well as to film history controversies and developments in both the Hollywood studio system and independent cinema. Reading *Dracula* while studying this historical range of films allowed them to consider what it means for Stoker's novel and characters to represent themselves as living on the razor's edge of modernity—at the very moment, in fact, of the cinema's invention. Ronald R. Thomas has noted that "the cinema and *Dracula* are twin children of the same cultural forces" (303). My students and I, in turn, used this unit to explore the ways in which these twin children of the late-Victorian period have aged together. As we did throughout "Page, Stage, Screen," we also confronted a range of formal and cultural/ historical issues that might have remained more or less hypothetical in a course reading *Dracula* against only one of its seemingly innumerable adaptations. I have particularly sought to destabilize the hierarchy of high- and low-cultural forms, as well as the ideas that one can usefully study a film adaptation only after completing a reading of its source text and that the chief goal of watching film adaptations should be to assess their fidelity to source texts.[2]

We began studying *Dracula* with a double-feature, screening Kino International's restored versions of *The Cabinet of Dr. Caligari* and *Nosferatu*.[3] As we had concluded our unit on *Strange Case of Dr. Jekyll and Mr. Hyde* in the previous week, I suggested to my students that they should wait to read their first *Dracula* assignment—chapters one through four, covering Jonathan Harker's stay in Transylvania—until after they had seen these two German Expressionist films. To facilitate this possibility, I encouraged the students simply to sit together in pitch-darkness and open themselves to the creeping dread that characterizes German Expressionist cinema's uncanny brand of horror. I suspected that most of my students would find the silent cinema's convention of tinted film—wherein (for instance) a blue tint signals night, a reddish or lavender tint signals dawn or dusk, and a standard grey signals daylight or a night interior—initially bizarre but increasingly significant, just as the Victorian novel's mechanics can seem a bit unwieldy before their narrative and thematic opportunities reveal themselves.

Thus, I framed our viewing of these two films both as an opportunity to experience a kind of cinema (and its visual and emotional lexica) with which most of my students were completely unfamiliar and also as a way to prepare themselves for the techniques through which Stoker builds his novel's terrors. With its emphasis on duplicitous lives and psychologies, as well as on the shadowed area between sanity and madness, *The Cabinet of Dr. Caligari* functioned as a segue out of our Jekyll and Hyde unit. As the earliest surviving adaptation of Stoker's novel, *Nosferatu* served as a touchstone for our discussions of *Dracula*'s first nine chapters.

For much of our first day of discussing Stoker's novel, I projected a single image from Murnau's film on the screen in my classroom: the iconic profile-view shadow of Nosferatu as his clawed right hand reaches for the Mina-figure Ellen's bedroom door, only five minutes before the film's end (1.27:30).[4] This image organized our thinking about *Dracula* in multiple ways. It works as a figure for many twenty-first-century readers' experience of Stoker's novel: many readers come to *Dracula* shadowed by expectations that have been generated through its main character's diffusion into Anglo-American culture, only to find themselves crept up on by stranger terrors than any glimpsed cinematic or televised vampire has led them to imagine.[5] In a sense, my students' experience of *Dracula* is not entirely dissimilar from the experiences that Jonathan Harker (in the novel) and Hutter (in *Nosferatu*) face within their respective works: they confess to plunging in briskly, cheerily, thinking that they know in advance what they are about to encounter. But, within these first reading and viewing assignments, they find themselves, like Harker, "all in a sea of wonders," feeling Stoker's novel to be, like Transylvania itself, "the centre of some imaginative whirlpool" (49, 32).[6] Harker's experiences in Transylvania radically destabilize his senses of himself and of his world—as can the viewer's witnessing, at this late moment in *Nosferatu*, yet another instance of the vampire's predatory powers, which invest even his shadow with penetrative agency.

With this image of Nosferatu's shadow fixed on the screen at the front of my classroom, I encouraged my students to identify specific moments in which Stoker shows how Harker's life is upended in Dracula's castle. They pointed immediately to his initial idealism, to his self-characterization as an up-and-coming young professional who has done his research and believes himself to have prepared well for his first important business trip. "I had visited the British Museum, and made search among the books and maps in the library regarding Transylvania," Harker reports in his first journal entry, going on to express delight that his hotel is "thoroughly old-fashioned, for of course I wanted to see all I could of the ways of the country" (31–32, 34). When the hotel owner's wife tries to persuade him not to venture to Castle Dracula on St. George's Eve, Harker rebuffs her: "[T]here was business to be done, and I could allow nothing to interfere with it.... [M]y duty was imperative" (35). Harker's particularly English skepticism about superstitions and religious symbols alike appears when he bemusedly accepts a crucifix: "I did not know what to do, for, as an English Churchman, I have been taught to regard such things as in some measure idolatrous, and yet it seemed so ungracious to refuse an old lady" (35). As the students drew quote after quote out of Stoker's first four chapters, they also gestured to corresponding earlier moments in *Nosferatu*: Hutter's cheery preparations at his mirror (2:25), his laughing off the innkeepers' proffered book about vampires (17:57), and his disregarding the coach driver's refusal to proceed to Orlok's castle (20:20). Even after Hutter awakes after his first vamping, he seems manifestly unconcerned, first smiling and then writing a cheery letter home to his wife, detailing the "mosquito bites" on his neck (27:56).

As my students pointed out, soon after he has entered Dracula's castle, Harker begins using his journal both to document the "wild feeling[s]" that threaten his faith in reason and to maintain his sanity through creating something like a verifiable, factual record (59). Knowing that he will need "all [his] brains to get through" (58), Harker invests his journal with a saving power: "I turn to my diary for repose. The habit of entering accurately must help to soothe me" (68). As the stakes rise, the diary becomes more and more crucial because it keeps him on the lookout for facts and for "proof" of what he is experiencing (72)—both for himself and, in the case of his death, for his survivors. Harker's diary itself occasions his famous proclamation, "It is nineteenth century up-to-date with a vengeance" (67). Indeed, the characters' reliance on written records as vehicles for factuality, as preservers of sanity, and as outright weapons against an invasion by "the old centuries" (67) continues throughout *Dracula*. "I sometimes think we must all be mad and that we shall wake to sanity in strait-waistcoats," Jack Seward muses midway through the novel (313), only to begin his diary's next entry with an imperative to himself: "Let me put down with exactness all that happened, as well as I can remember, since I last made an entry. Not a detail that I can recall must be forgotten; in all calmness I must proceed" (315). Even more crucially, Van Helsing's validation of Harker's journal becomes the agent of Harker's return to health and courage:

> [A]ll I wrote down was true. It seems to have made a new man of me. It was the doubt as to the reality of the whole thing that knocked me over. I felt impotent, and in the dark, and distrustful. But, now that I *know*, I am not afraid, even of the Count. (225)

Stoker's novel focuses intensely on the textual nature of his characters' experiences—a phenomenon my students had already encountered during their earlier studies of *Frankenstein* and *Strange Case of Dr. Jekyll and Mr. Hyde* and those novels' multiple film versions. Indeed, the course's multifilm approach itself urged the students to become increasingly attuned to differences in cinematic and novelistic techniques, particularly pertaining to narrative time and form, which in turn sharpened their focus on Stoker's initial presentation of Harker's character and experience through a first-person journal. This focus on textuality finds some analogues in *Nosferatu*'s intertitles. At various moments, one reads along with Hutter and Ellen as they study a book about vampires; one also reads texts such as Hutter's letter from the castle and the ship *Demeter*'s log. A never-identified figure narrates the film as a reconstruction of Wisborg's experience with the "Great Death" in 1838. But instead of reading *Nosferatu* as having somehow done Stoker's novel a disservice by being too speedy to be textual enough, or focusing on the ways in which the film does adapt the novel's textuality, I encouraged my students to use the film's most evocative moments—such as the shadow of Nosferatu climbing Hutter's and Ellen's stairs—as vehicles for learning to read the horrors that render Stoker's characters' lengthily developed textual records vitally or even viscerally necessary. Discussing Stoker's novel under the shadow of a vampire helped us collectively to appreciate how "nocturnal existence" afflicts Harker and how "horrible imaginings" make him "start at [his] own shadow" (65).[7] In other words, this single image from late in Murnau's film allowed us to consider more deeply the emotional and thematic dynamics of the early chapters of Stoker's novel and to lay the groundwork for subsequent reading and viewing assignments.

Before that first discussion ended, we also dissected Murnau's final presentation of Nosferatu's shadow as its hand slides up Ellen's bed and over her nightdress, eventually gripping her heart and causing her to throw her head back with something that looks uncomfortably like desire inscribed on her face. This short sequence helped us to focus on how, within Stoker's novel, Harker's record of his imprisonment represents the violation of gender conventions and the displacement or rearrangement of sexual behavior as being among vampirism's key threats. With Ellen's ambiguously transported body on the screen behind me, we discussed the ways Stoker realigns gendered expectations for sexual performance during Harker's seduction by the three vampiresses at the end of chapter 3. We particularly focused on his horrified response to his own "languorous ecstasy" (70) and how that response illuminates Harker's connection between proper sexual identities and proper boundaries between humanity and monstrosity at the end of chapter 4. Harker frames his last-ditch efforts to defeat the vampiresses and maintain his manhood both with an insistence that the vampiresses cannot be women because "Mina is a woman" and also with a declaration that he would prefer even a fatal fall from Dracula's castle to being killed by vampiresses because "[a]t its foot a man may sleep—as a man" (85). Stoker's novel will ask its readers, I told my students, to consider the horror of having their world infiltrated by vampires—and the even greater horror that they might find themselves turned on by that infiltration, unable or even unwilling to fight it off by preserving "properly" performed gender identities. Such questions, of course, help bring into focus *Dracula*'s status as a novel of the *fin de siècle*, with its concerns about the New Woman, the feminization of English men and culture, and the future of marriage.

My students were thus ready for their next reading assignment's introductions to Mina Murray and Lucy Westenra, to Lucy's trio of suitors, and to the range of crucial questions about gender and sexuality that these characters bear with them not only into Stoker's novel but also in subsequent adaptations of *Dracula*. From *Nosferatu*'s presentation of the "sinless maiden" Ellen's self-sacrifice for her town's sake to *Bram Stoker's Dracula*'s swelling of Dracula and Mina's relationship into transhistorical romance and beyond, *Dracula* films' transformations of their female leads' motivations and fates have been perhaps their most crucial ways of bringing Stoker's novel "up-to-date"—often with quite a vengeance indeed. Furthermore, reading the representations of gender and sexuality in Stoker's novel against a sequence of film adaptations reveals the aptness of Nina Auerbach's claim that "the rapidity with which our Draculas date tells us only that every age embraces the vampire it needs" (145).

Through a motley mix of letters, phonographic diary entries, private journals, newspaper clippings, a ship's log, and telegrams, chapters 5 through 9 of Stoker's novel present a range of gender performances that almost threatens to become schematic. One meets Mina Murray, the professional woman who is forward-thinking enough to practice shorthand and typewriting—but traditional enough to be learning these skills for the benefit of her future husband's professional career (86). One meets Lucy Westenra, who is proposed to by three men very much of their moment—a son of a lord, a clever director of a lunatic asylum, and a rough and ready Texan adventurer—and who is sweetly (though also radically) bewildered as to why her society "can't...let a girl marry three men, or as many as want her, and save all this trouble" (91). We meet Renfield, the "zoophagous (life-eating) maniac" of whose "hallucination" Jack Seward seeks to make himself "master" in order to "advance [his] own branch of science" (103, 93–94). One watches Mina watching Lucy, "sweetly pretty in her white lawn frock" (97), noting that she "is so sweet and sensitive that she feels influences more acutely than other people do" and might be "too super-sensitive a nature to go through the world without trouble" (121–122). After Mina, like her fiancé Jonathan, has claimed that her journal "soothes" her by being "like whispering to one's self and listening at the same time" (105) and that she has thus "made [her] diary a duty" (123), one watches Lucy taking after her friend's discipline: "I must imitate Mina, and keep writing things down" (144). Perhaps most crucially, one learns the degree to which Mina conceptualizes herself as belonging to her particular cultural moment. This is apparent when she quips that she and Lucy, on an outing, "should have shocked the 'New Woman' with our appetites" (123). It is also clear when she worries over how Lucy's reputation will suffer if stories circulate about her wandering barefoot and nightgown-clad in the Whitby cemetery—and she goes so far as to cover her own feet in mud so as to hide their bareness after she rescues Lucy (126–127).

After a day's discussion of this range of identities and performances—as well as, once again, the ways in which Stoker uses textual production as one more tool for establishing his main characters' stances toward knowledge, doubt, and agency—we screened our second *Dracula* film, the 1931 Universal Studios release directed by Tod Browning and starring Bela Lugosi. By this point in the semester, my students had watched enough films for class that they were no longer expecting every one to be a masterpiece and had, in fact, learned to search out the revealing or provocative elements even of films that they found largely problematic. Thus, although all of the students raised major objections to significant portions of Browning's film—especially to its abrupt termination in a promised marriage between Jonathan and Mina—they found themselves collectively intrigued by the specific ways in which it alters Stoker's novel. In their response papers for that week, some students focused on the film's domestication of Dracula: its way (following the Hamilton Deane and John Balderston play on which it is based) of transforming the count into a suave continental gentleman and then inviting him right into the theater and the drawing room to interact openly with other characters. But more of them zeroed in on the film's other key character changes: sending Renfield, not Harker, to Transylvania (and thereby offering an explanation for his psychic connection to Dracula); eliminating Lucy almost as soon as this jazz baby version of her has been introduced; stripping Mina of the active, intellectual role she plays in Stoker's novel; and compressing the novel's men so that Dr. Seward becomes Mina's father and the Texan Quincy Morris disappears altogether.

Indeed, Browning's film offered us a way to develop further the concept of compression as a crucial technique in adapting the complexities of nineteenth-century novels to the narrative limitations (in particular, the shorter time frames) of cinematic representation. We had begun building a theory of compression earlier in the semester as we screened *Pride and Prejudice* and *Frankenstein* adaptations, looking for the characterizations and shot sequences through which a film presents a condensed or even isolated version of a source novel's more pervasive thematic energy. This idea of compression was then of particular value to us as we studied *Oliver Twist* films, offering an invaluable way to discuss how and why Dickens's female foils, Nancy and Rose, get folded into one another or preserved as distinct entities in particular adaptations, thereby affecting those adaptations' overall stances toward femininity and redemption.

The compression that most drew my students' attention in Browning's *Dracula* was the isolation of the novel's widespread concerns with madness and sanity within the film's version of Renfield. As we discussed this film, the students had read through chapter 15—nearly the midpoint of the novel—which concludes with Van Helsing's request of Arthur, now Lord Godalming, "May I cut off the head of dead Miss Lucy?" and the bereaved fiancé's response: "Are you mad, that you speak of such things, or am I mad to listen to them?" (244). The nearest Arthur approaches to an answer either way is his admission, "I cannot understand" (245). And chapters 10 through 15, taken as a whole, further develop the concerns about insanity and doubt that Harker's experiences in Transylvania introduce to the novel. In particular, Seward wonders "if [his] long habit of life among the insane is beginning to tell upon [his] own brain" (171), and upon reading Lucy's deathbed note, he asks Van Helsing, "In God's name, what does it all mean? Was she, or is she, mad?" (186). Just as Harker has done in Transylvania, and just as Lucy tries to do in imitation of Mina, Seward comes to rely on his diary for solace: "Only resolution and habit can let me make an entry tonight.... Let me get on with my work" (195). As Van Helsing explains the vampire's existence, Seward's skeptical retort captures once again Stoker's characters' faith in their age's utter modernity: "Do you mean to tell me...that such a thing is here in London in the nineteenth century?" (229). Ultimately, Van Helsing's response is simple: "I want you to believe" (230). Throughout this section of the novel, Van Helsing's discussions with Seward are interspersed with Seward's further observations of Renfield and with Mina's finally reading her husband's journal and meeting Van Helsing (who points up Mina's function as the "so clever woman" of the novel, proclaiming, "I am daze, I am dazzle, with so much light" [221]).

In Browning's film, nearly all of this focus on questions of madness versus knowledge and on the need for the rational nineteenth century to grapple with what has seemed outdated superstition becomes concentrated in Dwight Frye's Renfield, who travels to Transylvania in Harker's role as an enterprising (and dandyish) young man, then returns to England on the ship *Vesta* in the company of Dracula, who has maddened him and become his master. Indeed, my class largely agreed that one of the most frightening moments in Browning's film comes when Renfield's crazed laugh leads to his being discovered in the wrecked ship's hold (20:40): one gazes down into the hold along with the investigating authorities for a full twelve seconds while a wide-eyed and laughing Renfield stares back from the bottom of a square of bright light. "Why, he's mad!" a voice-over proclaims. "Look at his eyes! Why, the man's gone crazy!" (20:46–52). As the film continues, Renfield's plotline arguably occasions the film's greatest suspense and best acting—so that Dracula's eleventh-hour murder of him at Carfax Abbey affected my class just as much as, if not more than, Van Helsing's defeat of the count and Jonathan and Mina's final ascent toward wedded resolution. And, our class discussions of the compressing work Renfield's recharacterization does within Browning's film contributed directly to the final major writing some students produced for my course.

As we pushed toward the novel's end, my students had to complete a one- to two-page proposal for their final papers. Because their first round of eight- to ten-page critical essays had largely been solidly executed, I offered them the option of producing their own creative adaptations of one or more of the course texts, with the provisos that their proposals had to provide strategies and rationales for their imagined adaptations and that they would ultimately craft not only an adaptation but also a critical commentary on their creative work and how it illuminated its source text. Unsurprisingly, because we were in the thick of the novel, many students decided to focus their final projects on *Dracula*. And, in part because of the divergent ways in which the *Dracula* films we viewed streamlined and/or foregrounded particular characters—and in so doing, recreated the figure (and the significance) of Dracula himself—several of my writers decided to produce alternate character studies, imagining voices and perspectives, such as Renfield's, that Stoker's novel marginalizes. That is, not least because the 1931 film fleshes Renfield out in a particular way and alters Mina's character and her relationship with both Dracula and with Jonathan, these students were reading Stoker's narrative choices with ever-greater precision, viewing them as choices and analyzing them, in part, by imagining and even crafting their alternatives. One student created an overview of a new, futuristic *Dracula* film that would focus on gender inversions and perversions, not least by transforming Dracula into a female figure; her final project involved a portfolio of film stills and a lengthy description and analysis of how this version's script would use Stoker's novel. Another student produced a dynamic short story, fully inspired by but also departing richly from Stoker's novel, imagining a latter-day vampire victim's embrace of his diabolical immortality.

In one of the richest projects I received, a student who was also enrolled in Kenyon's advanced poetry seminar that semester decided to write a creative work centered on Renfield. "I was intrigued and saddened by the elusive character of Renfield, who speaks volumes both in his silence and in enigmatic revelations," she wrote in her critical commentary. "I wanted to script a part of the novel that I felt was only present subtextually and in the reader's own imagining, while trying not to pervert any information given by Stoker." Following Seward's mention of Renfield's "little notebook in which he is always jotting down something" (102), my student called her collection of prose and poetic fragments "Renfield's Black Book." In both content and form, the project functioned as an explication and expansion of Renfield's function in *Dracula*, so that (for instance) Seward's clinical notation that Renfield has consumed "his pretty family of tame sparrows" and "disgorged a whole lot of feathers" (102–103) developed into evocative stanzas:

> I will gum a sparrow to the rinds;
> A man collects sounds of dying, I collect toothpicks
> made of bone.
> A feathered enclave of hardened pellets;
> Wombed and uneasy it rests birched, resisting.

By the project's end, my student had Renfield realizing his fate, both within the text and as text: "More heroic men than I will wipe away the curse of my remembering; only in the footnotes will I find myself in definition lain."

Of course, many students who wrote about *Dracula* decided to produce critical essays on topics as diverse as the perversion of motherhood, the function of xenophobia, and anxieties over the New Woman and gender roles in Stoker's novel. What my writers had in common as they crafted their critical and creative projects, though, was an increased investment in scrutinizing the enunciation techniques and interpretive stances of the course's final mandatory films, Maddin's *Dracula: Pages from a Virgin's Diary* and Coppola's *Bram Stoker's Dracula*. The students wrote their final response papers after watching Maddin's film (and the optional *Blacula*, whose harnessing of Stoker's main character and subtextual worries in order to explicate issues of race and sexuality in 1970s Los Angeles makes it a terrific companion for Maddin's reading of the novel, despite its flagrant departures from Stoker's text). Not since *Young Frankenstein* had we watched a film that is so engaged with its source text—and its source text's previous cinematic adaptations—on so many levels simultaneously and with such thoughtful revisionary force. Maddin's film serves both as an admirably specific critical reading of the novel and also as a musing on the history of film itself, echoing as it does the cinematic techniques we had witnessed in *Caligari* and *Nosferatu* at the beginning of our *Dracula* unit. Maddin shoots the film in black and white, using tinting and selective hand coloring to convey changes in time of day and to create other emphases; even its seventy-three-minute length pays homage to early horror films' brevity. *Dracula: Pages from a Virgin's Diary* was, in all, perhaps the most revelatory and provocative of the semester's films, both for the students and for me as their teacher. In order to foster their active synthesizing of what they had learned from the semester, I allowed the students' interests and concerns to shape our discussions even more than usual in our last two class meetings, as we discussed both Maddin's film and the end of Stoker's novel.

In their response papers as well as in our class discussions, the students focused on Maddin's decision to foreground the novel's concerns with xenophobia and alterity, both by casting Chinese dancer Zhang Wei-Qiang as Dracula and through deploying outlandish intertitles and provocative cross-cutting at the film's beginning. Within the film's first three minutes, intertitles proclaim "IMMIGRANTS!!" "OTHERS!" "FROM OTHER LANDS," "From the East!" and "From the Sea!" as fake blood oozes over maps, reaching from Asia until it engulfs England (2:23–59). Maddin punctuates this schematic, hysterical warning of bloody infiltration with close-ups of Dracula's coffin and then of his face, glimpsed through cracks in the coffin's lid (in a shot that is reminiscent of Hutter's first glimpse of Orlok in his coffin in *Nosferatu*). He also uses alternating long shots and close-ups of Lucy Westenra's body—first writhing in her bed; then advancing desirously toward her bedroom door (located on the right side of the frame, so that she is reaching toward the mapped blood's flow); then, once more in bed, trying to escape the stream of blood that is now approaching her image. Maddin also reverses the trend of romanticizing Dracula and his relationships with female characters—a trend that has been developed in the last half-century by Christopher Lee, William Marshall, and Frank Langella.[8] Maddin's version of Dracula remains foreign not only because of his race but also through his cold, determined, and frighteningly erotic predations upon first Lucy and then, late in the film, Mina.

My students also noted the various ways that Maddin's film often uses very specific passages from Stoker's novel in order to produce interpretations of those passages that go more or less radically against the novel's grain. Our collective favorite such moment appears during the final confrontation in Dracula's castle, when Maddin's Harker slashes Dracula's shirt and chest—and gold coins pour out instead of blood. This moment is a direct re-presentation of the men's encounter with Stoker's Dracula in his London townhouse: Harker "had ready his great Kukri knife.... [T]he point just cut the cloth of [Dracula's] coat, making a wide gap whence a bundle of bank-notes and a stream of gold fell out" (345). Such correspondences afforded my students—whether they were writing creatively or critically in their final projects—a chance to discuss their own close reading practices once more, considering especially the uses to which particular passages can (or should) be put in reading a novel's thematic development. And, because Maddin has claimed that, in making his *Dracula*, he "decided his adaptation would be the most faithful to Stoker's 1897 novel, dance steps notwithstanding" (Rubin), we were able to reopen critical questions about what cinematic fidelity might actually mean.

Maddin's sustained reinterpretations of the novel most frequently (and provocatively) connect to portrayals of sexuality, in keeping with his contention that the novel "is really just about jealousy and male rivalry and the double standard we insist on forcing on our women" (qtd. in Rubin). Still within the film's early scenes, Maddin shows Lucy, fresh from her near-encounter with foreign blood, writing in her diary; in a frame that also contains her diary and her writing hand, an intertitle reads, "Why can't they let a woman marry *three* men?" (3:09). Maddin cuts to a point-of-view shot of Lucy's three suitors as the viewer swings toward them, then offers a full-screen intertitle— "Or as many as want her?" (3:14)—before giving the viewer the suitors' point of view, a vision of Lucy swinging away from them. Maddin thus dramatizes swiftly the novel's focus on textuality and Lucy's early decision among three men. Lucy continues to swing to and from her beseeching suitors, teasing them by repeating, "I choose..." in the intertitles. But, when she finally mouths, "I choose you," the intertitle "YOU!" appears over an image of the raging sea that heralds Dracula's arrival (3:49). While Holmwood congratulates himself for having won her, Lucy carries his proffered bouquet onto a terrace, pricks her finger with it, and marks her bedroom's lintel with her own blood (which Maddin tints red), looking seductively over her shoulder toward the sea—and Dracula (4:26–46). Even more notably, once Lucy has been vamped, has approached all three of her suitors seductively, and has encountered the film's invasively authoritative version of Van Helsing (who conducts a discomfitingly thorough medical examination of her body and also steals her diary), Maddin rereads the novel's scenes of Lucy's blood transfusions as a kind of gang rape from which her fiancé is initially excluded. Using low-angle point-of-view shots in which the viewer looks up at the clenched fists and lusting faces of Van Helsing, Morris, and Seward as they thrust their blood into her simultaneously, Maddin forces the viewer to imagine how this three-man transfusion victimizes the unconscious Lucy, even as it pinkens her cheeks (17:38– 18:31). The forced, perverse nature of these transfusions serves only to highlight, first, the unstoppable directness of Dracula's second attack on Lucy and then, more disturbingly, her apparent welcoming of and pleasure in his fatal third attack. Maddin represents this pleasure with climactic close-ups of her arching, empty hands (26:36–41), shots my students and I close read at some length, comparing them with the shots of Nosferatu's shadow and Ellen's arched neck that we had studied during our first day of discussing *Dracula*.

When Mina and Jonathan's narrative finally begins, midway through the film, Maddin further develops his idea that part of *Dracula*'s narrative mission is to represent the wrongheadedness of disciplining female bodies and sexuality. Maddin crafts Harker's sexual encounters in Transylvania as a swift flashback imagined by Mina when she reads his diary after their reunion in a convent (once again alluding to the novel's reliance on texts and documents) (45:18–43). Here, though, Mina's reading of her husband's diary does not serve to further a search for Dracula, as it does in Stoker's novel; instead, it prompts her to try to seduce Jonathan herself, in apparent imitation of the vampiresses about whom she has just read. Once Jonathan has rebuffed her three times and fled the convent, Dracula arrives to claim her and, in so doing, to reassert his potency in direct contrast to Jonathan's (and the other male characters') ineffectualness and in direct defiance of the massive image of Christ that is hanging over the convent's door (50:50–51:06). As the film culminates in confrontation after confrontation within Dracula's castle, Maddin unsettles the conclusion of Stoker's novel, problematizing its ending in happy domesticity—not least through continuing to offer a troubling version of Van Helsing's character, who, in the film's last frames, leaves the castle while tucking the petticoat he has stolen from Mina into his jacket (1.12:22–36).

Significantly, though, Maddin troubles Stoker's novel without romanticizing Dracula in the process of eroticizing him and without creating overly blatant or bizarre caricatures of the novel's other characters—in contrast with Francis Ford Coppola's *Bram Stoker's Dracula*, the last film my students watched with me. I offered them Coppola's *Dracula* both as an entertainment with which to end our semester and as a warning (to my creative writers, especially) about the dangers of proclaiming fidelity to a source text (by invoking its author) but then departing from it so radically as to render large swaths of it unrecognizable. Our

Monday-night screening of Coppola's film was our last formal course activity. However, I took it as a sign of the course's success that many students either turned up in my office during our final examination period or sent me e-mail messages, offering capsule versions of what they would have written in response papers about this last film. In a differently targeted version of this unit on Stoker's *Dracula* and its cinematic afterlife, instructors could certainly make more thorough use of Coppola's film than my students and I did. The film could also allow a class to interrogate the ways in which twentieth-century *Dracula* films increasingly developed Dracula as a romantic hero—or, as Glennis Byron puts it, the way in which "Stoker's chilling 'This man belongs to me' has fizzled away into the sentimental banality of 'Love never dies'" (25), the tagline for Coppola's film.

Indeed, in teaching *Dracula* and my course's other novels with such a range of film versions, I took enormous pleasure in the sheer inexhaustibility of each of our units—in imagining the number of other directions we might have pursued. Screening every film version of any one of these novels would be impossible, of course, but screening many film versions of each made my students increasingly hungry to explore these novels' transformations at greater length on their own. In future versions of the course, I imagine that I will supplement these films' readings of Stoker's novel both with excerpts from other films (for instance, pairing scenes from John Badham's 1979 *Dracula* with their analogues in the 1931 version) and with assigned critical readings. Thus, a discussion of Stoker's novel in light of *Dracula: Pages from a Virgin's Diary* might also be informed by Steven Arata's analysis of reverse colonization in *Dracula*; likewise, a reading of Coppola's film and other romantic Draculas might be shaped by Nina Auerbach, Phyllis Roth, or Christopher Craft. But, in making any such changes, I would strive to enhance the chief benefit of this multifilm approach to nineteenth-century novels and their adaptations: it helps students become savvier readers of novelistic and cinematic texts, both in their own particularities and in their places within historic and ongoing cultural conversations.

ENDNOTES

1. The plan of the course is fairly simple: the students read six nineteenth-century novels that have developed significant dramatic and cinematic afterlives: Jane Austen's *Pride and Prejudice* (1813), Mary Shelley's *Frankenstein* (1818), Charles Dickens's *Oliver Twist* (1837–1839), Lewis Carroll's *Alice's Adventures in Wonderland* (1865), Robert Louis Stevenson's *Strange Case of Dr. Jekyll and Mr. Hyde* (1886), and Bram Stoker's *Dracula* (1897). My students and I sample the nineteenth-century stage versions of many of these novels, including Richard Brinsley Peake's *Presumption; or The Fate of Frankenstein* (1823) and *Sikes and Nancy*, Dickens's public reading version of *Oliver Twist*. And, during a mandatory film session that adds three hours to a Kenyon course's standard 160 minutes per week, we watch as many film adaptations of those novels as we can fit into our semester. In most semesters, we screen about twenty-two films in our fourteen Monday-night screenings. Some weeks are full double-features—for instance, James Whale's *Frankenstein* (1931) and *Bride of Frankenstein* (1935) fit neatly into a three-hour viewing, as do Frank Lloyd's and David Lean's versions of *Oliver Twist* (1922 and 1948, respectively). Other weeks, we combine a full-length film with a significantly shorter artifact from the early years of cinema. Before viewing Mel Brooks's *Young Frankenstein* (1974), for example, we watch the Edison *Frankenstein* (1910), which is now widely available on the Internet. Similarly, the night we screen Gavin Millar's *Dreamchild* (1985), a fascinatingly uneven pseudobiographical riff on Charles Dodgson, Alice Liddell, and the *Alice* books' genesis, we preface it with Cecil Hepworth's *Alice in Wonderland* (1903)—at 800 feet (or about ten to twelve minutes long), the longest British film ever made at the time of its release (Brown). (One could now, of course, include Tim Burton's 2010 *Alice in Wonderland*—though I suspect I will continue using Jan Švankmajer's *Neco z Alenky* [1988] instead.)

2. Brian McFarlane explores the various limitations of focusing on an adaptations' "fidelity" (8–11); I find particularly useful his insight that an "insistence on fidelity…tends to ignore the idea of adaptation as an example of convergence among the arts, perhaps a desirable—even inevitable—process in a rich culture" (10). Similarly, in a 2007 *Bookforum* feature devoted to film adaptations of fiction, Phillip Lopate wondered, "Why even speak of [an adaptation's] betrayal when we can view these deviations as alternate paths that the novel might have taken, alternate lives it might have

lived?" (33). Throughout the semester, my students experienced what Linda Hutcheon calls "a constant oscillation" between source novels and their adaptations (xv); by the semester's end, all of the students were highly attuned to the intertextual (or, as Hutcheon puts it, "palimpsestic" [9]) nature of both novelistic and cinematic narratives.

3. I prefer the Kino versions of both of these films because of the quality of their remastering (particularly of details such as film tints), but the 2000 Image Entertainment release of *Nosferatu* (though it is twelve minutes shorter than the Kino) includes a useful audio commentary by Lokke Heiss.

4. In this chapter, I may seem to take for granted that anyone teaching a film and literature course will have appropriate projection technology in his or her classroom. However, I know that not every institution (and not every room at every institution) is so equipped. Some of the classroom strategies I will discuss could be modified for a classroom with no DVD player if an instructor could capture a screen image such as the one I am about to discuss and photocopy handouts. Similarly, a movie's dialogue track could be transcribed and presented independently of the movie itself. In my course, I found my classroom's reliable DVD player and projector to be invaluable for presenting both the components of a scene—such as isolated images or sounds—and also longer clips that allowed discussions of how such components function together to make a movie's meaning.

5. Linda Hutcheon has observed that adaptations are "haunted at all times by their adapted texts"; she claims that knowledge of source texts creates a sort of double-seeing for anyone watching an adaptation: "If we know that prior text, we always feel its presence shadowing the one we are experiencing directly" (6). In screening *Nosferatu* just as my students were beginning to read *Dracula*, I sought to reverse the expected order of such hauntings and shadowings, letting Murnau's film (and each film we subsequently viewed) shadow Stoker's novel.

6. In this iteration of my course, I used mostly Broadview editions of the novels we studied, including *Dracula*, so as better to introduce my students to the contexts and intertexts of these novels' composition and initial publication. Instructors wishing instead to emphasize twentieth-century literary and cultural criticism of *Dracula* would do well to consider the 1997 Norton Critical Edition, edited by Nina Auerbach and David J. Skal.

7. Here, of course, I am punning on the title of *Shadow of the Vampire* (2001), Elias Merhige's fantasia on the making of *Nosferatu*. Merhige pays homage to Murnau's film (incorporating some of its frames into his own work) and

to the history of cinema itself while also developing the wild premise that Max Schreck (who played Orlok/Nosferatu in Murnau's film) was actually a melancholy, Tennyson-quoting, Stoker-critiquing vampire with a thirst for the film's lead actress. Instructors with sufficient time could make excellent use of Merhige's film in conjunction with Murnau's *Nosferatu* and/or Werner Herzog's 1979 remake, *Nosferatu the Vampyre*.

8. See Auerbach's discussion of Lee's and Langella's charismatic vampires (119–147).

BIBLIOGRAPHY

Auerbach, Nina. *Our Vampires, Ourselves*. Chicago: University of Chicago Press, 1995. Print.

Brown, Simon. Audio commentary on *Alice in Wonderland* (1903). *Alice in Wonderland*. 1966. Home Vision Entertainment, 2003. DVD.

Byron, Glennis. Introduction. *Dracula*. By Bram Stoker. Peterborough: Broadview, 1998. 9–25. Print.

Hutcheon, Linda. *A Theory of Adaptation*. London: Routledge, 2006. Print.

Lopate, Phillip. "Adapt This: Fiction into Film." *Bookforum* 14.2 (June/July/August 2007): 29–34. Print.

McFarlane, Brian. *Novel to Film: An Introduction to the Theory of Adaptation*. New York: Oxford University Press, 1996. Print.

Rubin, Mike. "FILM: 'Dracula' Takes Dancing Lessons." *New York Times*, 18 May 2003. Web. 5 December 2006.

Stoker, Bram. *Dracula*. 1897. Peterborough: Broadview, 1998. Print.

Thomas, Ronald R. "Specters of the Novel: *Dracula* and the Cinematic Afterlife of the Victorian Novel." *Victorian Afterlife: Postmodern Culture Rewrites the Nineteenth Century*. Ed. John Kucich and Dianne F. Sadoff. Minneapolis: University of Minnesota Press, 2000. 288–310. Print.

FILMOGRAPHY

Blacula. Dir. William Crain. Perf. William Marshall, Denise Nicholas, Vonetta McGee, and Gordon Pinsent. MGM, 1972. DVD.

Bram Stoker's Dracula. Dir. Francis Ford Coppola. Perf. Gary Oldman, Winona Ryder, Keanu Reaves, and Anthony Hopkins. American Zoetrope, 1992. DVD.

Dracula. Dir. Tod Browning. Perf. Bela Lugosi, Helen Chandler, Dwight Frye, Edward Van Sloane, and David Manners. Universal, 1931. DVD.

Dracula: Pages from a Virgin's Diary. Dir. Guy Maddin. Perf. Zhang Wei-Qiang, Tara Birtwhistle, David Moroni, Cindymarie Small, and Johnny Wright. CBC, 2002. DVD.

Neco z Alenky. Dir. Jan Švankmajer. Perf. Kristýna Kohoutová. Channel Four, 1988. DVD.

Nosferatu. Dir. F. W. Murnau. Perf. Max Schreck, Gustav von Wangenheim, Greta Schroeder, and Alexander Granach. Jofa-Atlier Berlin-Johannisthal, 1922. DVD.

CHAPTER 10

TRANSPOSING SHERLOCK HOLMES ACROSS TIME, SPACE, AND GENRE

Tamara S. Wagner

The character of Sherlock Holmes, created by Sir Arthur Conan Doyle, is ageless, invincible, and unchanging. In solving significant problems of the present day, he remains, as ever, the supreme master of deductive reasoning.

—*Sherlock Holmes: The Voice of Terror*

In a unit that features three unlikely transpositions of Sherlock Holmes, the students in an upper-level undergraduate course on film and literature learned that loose adaptations of Arthur Conan Doyle's literary ur-text may not only expand genre boundaries but also illuminate shifting cultural formations. These adaptations involve what I call a transposition by lifting a character or set of characters from their original source text into new sets of narrative. The reconfigurations of an iconic protagonist such as Sherlock Holmes can facilitate a reinspection of such a figure's multiple cultural roles. Transpositions thereby frequently function as updates, although not all updated versions of a classic narrative necessarily involve a transposition. Indeed, a single character may be wrested from a well-known narrative in order to be confronted with a pointedly incongruous environment. The resulting defamiliarization offers a fresh interpretive framework that can prompt a re-viewing of the source text itself.

The Sherlock Holmes texts that were chosen for the course (and for a closer analysis here) provided a valuable case study of adaptive models that have not yet been captured by existing adaptation theories. At first glance, transpositions seem to affirm the validity of the so-called spoke, or sunburst, model of adaptation, discussed by Thomas Leitch in his contribution to this collection. But, the retold story of familiar fictional characters becomes more complicated when individual characters, such as Holmes, Watson, or their arch-nemesis Moriarty, are transposed into a different genre and medium. Conan Doyle's detective may share his transportability with other memorable nineteenth-century icons (Frankenstein and his Creature, Count Dracula, Jekyll and Hyde). Yet, the transpositions of Holmes are inevitably filtered through another text, a kind of second primary source text. Until such overtly revisionist films as Guy Ritchie's 2009 *Sherlock Holmes*, all Holmes films drew heavily on the Basil Rathbone versions of the 1930s and 1940s. Even those versions that endeavor to supply an alternative still do so by self-consciously referring to the Rathbone films.

Both Rathbone's Holmes and Nigel Bruce as his Dr. Watson shaped the most frequently and persistently transposed characterization of the detective and his sidekick, thus displacing Conan Doyle's actual representation of this pairing.[1] The Rathbone films thus became a conduit or lens that altered the perception of both characters in the popular imagination. Yet, the reappearance of Holmes and Watson in other times and places cannot be wholly accounted for by what Leitch describes as the "daisy chain, or genealogical," model of adaptation. The multiplicity and variety of their continual reuse demands a new model to explain the functions and effects of their reappearances. A transposition of a figure that has, like Holmes, become an icon frequently involves an "updating," although as I have stressed, it need not. The most straightforward updating simply has the classic literary character appear in the present day or brings the character (and often the entire plot) up to date. In either case, such a detaching and reinserting of familiar characters shows how they can develop lives of their own outside of their source texts. The longevity and shifting meaning of Holmes's status as a cultural icon is particularly insightful in that it has involved divergent agendas. Early on in his circulation as an adaptable figure, he began to exhibit a striking facility to be moved across time and space as well as genre confines.

The *Sherlock Holmes* series starring Rathbone and Bruce was fascinatingly aware of this ready transportability, openly suggesting that it had rendered him "ageless, invincible, and unchanging," as it is put on the title card following the opening credits of the third film in the series, *Sherlock Holmes: The Voice of Terror* (1942). This is also the first film in the series to be set in the 1940s instead of the late nineteenth century. In imbuing Holmes with this timelessness, the film suggests that this is precisely what makes him such a comforting solution to the problems of all times: "The character of Sherlock Holmes, created by Sir Arthur Conan Doyle, is ageless, invincible, and unchanging. In solving problems of the present day, he remains, as ever, the supreme master of deductive reasoning." This suggests a twofold adaptability. On the one hand, it renders Holmes's unchanging aspects a reliable, consistent factor that inspires confidence and comfort, whereas on the other hand, the appropriation this iconography invites can fit any kind of agenda and hence undergo radical changes in the process. The wartime propaganda of the 1930s and 1940s is a glaring example of an ideologically driven appropriation that ironically makes the most of Holmes's identification with changelessness.

In conceptualizing a model of transposition, I wish to stress what happens, or can happen, or can be ideologically used and potentially abused, when iconographic figures are moved across time, space, and genres. Simultaneously, I wish to bring out the creative and experimental potential of transpositions, and I wish to suggest that they offer a particularly revealing point of entry for studying and teaching adaptations. In discussing the nineteenth century's representation on film or the filming of classic literary texts in general, a focus on the most self-reflexive transpositions can be an effective way to derail any expectations of "mere" costume drama.

Sherlock Holmes: The Voice of Terror is one of three transpositions of the figure of Holmes in film and television that served as the core texts of a three-part exploration of "Holmes for the Times I–III." The first segment of the class, "Transposition & the War Effort," starts out with *Sherlock Holmes: The Voice of Terror* and is followed by "Refashioning the Biographical," exploring what I term the biographical back projections that structure *Dr. Bell and Mr. Doyle: The Dark Beginnings of Sherlock Holmes* (1999). This in turn is followed by "Transposition & Intertextuality," which takes "Elementary, Dear Data," an episode of the U.S. television serial *Star Trek: The Next Generation*, first screened in December 1988, as an example of the redeployment of an iconographic figure across genres. Stretching over three weeks, these focus points facilitate a comparative study of Holmes in popular culture as well as of the changing Holmes of Arthur Conan Doyle's writing. The three sessions on Sherlock Holmes are representative of the course's overall methodology and form the core of its central emphasis on the variety and creativity of literature adaptations. Though it is the course's main target to bring out the sheer spectrum of transpositions, updates, pastiches, and remakes, it thereby also highlights changing approaches to adaptation as a creative process. Most importantly, these three weeks also involve the most widespread inclusion of material, exemplifying first and foremost the creativity that is involved in processes of adaptation.

The first session in this threefold exploration of *Sherlock Holmes* transpositions, "Holmes for the Times I: Transposition & the War Effort," showcases how *Sherlock Holmes: The Voice of Terror* offers itself as an easily accessible example of an ideologically driven adaptation that is very conscious of the underlying processes. Produced in the middle of World

War II by Universal, this sixty-five-minute black-and-white feature film appropriates Conan Doyle's Bohemian amateur detective as an icon of Old England, reviving him to solve the problems of the present. Because students are simultaneously asked to read a number of *Sherlock Holmes* texts, including *The Sign of Four* (serialized in 1889 and published in book form in 1890), as well as "The Adventure of the Speckled Band" (1892) and "His Last Bow" (1917), they realize the irony of this iconography very quickly. The early novella depicts a violin-playing, cocaine-taking Holmes combating ennui through an aesthetic connoisseurship of crime; this figure surely is a far cry from the embodiment of English heritage under siege in World War II propaganda. Although the changing characteristics of Conan Doyle's Sherlock Holmes are notorious, a look at these well-known and often-cited texts reminds us of the vast differences between all of the "original" (i.e., Conan Doyle's) Holmeses and the iconographical version that was created by the Basil Rathbone character.

The Sign of Four opens and concludes with recourse to the cocaine bottle, Holmes's surrogate for the excitement of detection: their effects are equally "so transcendently stimulating and clarifying" (6). An artist of crime, Holmes would moreover have made a skillful criminal, as Dr. Watson pointedly phrases it: "I could not but think what a terrible criminal he would have made had he turned his energy and sagacity against the law instead of exerting them in its defense" (44). Projected into a wartime scenario, he presents something entirely different. *Sherlock Holmes: The Voice of Terror*, it is important to note, partly draws on the narrative structure of the late Holmes story "His Last Bow," which suggests a different character formation, while similarly introducing a spy story. The story has notably been seen as a response to Conan Doyle's rejection of an offer to head up a propaganda office (Klinger, xxxviii). Yet, in making Holmes fight the Nazis, the film identifies not only warfare and criminal investigation but also a revived literary figure of the past with Englishness under threat. Explicit war rhetoric is articulated both by Holmes and by a young working-class woman who sacrifices herself to ensnare a German spy. The dramatic close-ups that underscore her rallying speech to working-class men to assist in Holmes's investigations (and hence the war effort) spell out the film's agenda. Although students generally react to the overt jingoism with laughter, this feature of the adaptation also alerts them to the datedness of ideological underpinnings generally and, more specifically, showcases to what extent much of the cultural iconography of the Victorian Holmes of Old England was generated by the Basil Rathbone version.

Early on in *Sherlock Holmes: The Voice of Terror*, Holmes's transposition is externalized in a light-hearted scene: as Holmes and Watson are leaving 221B Baker Street, Holmes takes up the deerstalker hat that has become so famously associated with this literary detective from his earliest appearances on screen. Notably not a feature in any of Conan Doyle's stories, it was first introduced in the original illustrations of some of the narratives and has continued to function as one of the recognizable paraphernalia of the Victorian detective in popular culture. In *Sherlock Holmes: The Voice of Terror*, it is retired as the epitome of a reverenced, yet outmoded past. Watson reminds Holmes of a promise to update himself, and Holmes instead dons a currently conventional hat. The myth-making effects of 1940s transpositions (later films included the 1943 *Sherlock Holmes in Washington*, for example) similarly extended to a revision of Watson's character that has influenced countless adaptations since. This bumbling ignoramus as a comical sidekick who is teased and even publicly humiliated by Holmes contrasts sharply with the Dr. Watson of the original tales. A comparison with *The Sign of Four* illustrates this shift particularly well. The novella not only credits Watson's expert medical knowledge as an important contribution to the case at hand, it also highlights his significance as Holmes's chronicler and links this function to his frequently forgotten romantic side. His courtship plot is embedded within the criminal case, and the end sees him married. At the narrative's opening, moreover, Holmes ineffectually attempts to police Watson's representation of his "adventures":

> "Honestly, I cannot congratulate you upon it. Detection is, or ought to be, an exact science and should be treated in the same

cold and unemotional manner. You have attempted to tinge it with romanticism, which produces much the same effect as if you worked a love-story or an elopement into the fifth proposition of Euclid." "But the romance was there," I remonstrated. "I could not tamper with the facts." (7)

"The Adventure of the Speckled Band" opens with Watson going through Sherlock Holmes's previous "adventures":

> In glancing over my notes of the seventy odd cases in which I have during the last eight years studied the methods of my friend Sherlock Holmes, I find many tragic, some comic, a large number merely strange, but none commonplace. (227)

Both works contain explicit references to the methodology of detection and insist on its narrative potential, including its fusion with the romantic. Outlining Holmes's self-definition as the "only unofficial consulting detective" (6), the first chapter of *The Sign of Four* is tellingly titled "The Sign of Detection." The three qualities of the ideal detective consist of observation, deduction, and knowledge, and throughout the case, Holmes is repeatedly presented as proceeding with "something of the air of a clinical professor" (41). This explicit evocation of the clinical is one of the reasons I have chosen these two Holmes narratives for close analysis in class. The parallel development of the genre of detective fiction in the nineteenth century and the rise of forensic science (Thomas, *passim*) finds its most overt realization in the filming of Holmes's cultural contexts in *Dr. Bell and Mr. Doyle: The Dark Beginnings of Sherlock Holmes*. Originally conceived as a two-part miniseries, it was screened on BBC2 in January 1999 and subsequently shown as the more sensationally titled *Murder Rooms: The Dark Origins of Sherlock Holmes* on American television as a single two-hour movie in May 2000. Based on Arthur Conan Doyle's own experience as a medical student in Edinburgh, the film operates through a series of back projections. Young Mr. Doyle becomes a clerk to Dr. Joseph Bell, a leading surgeon at Edinburgh's

Royal Infirmary and a lecturer at the university. The inversion of the Holmes/Watson dynamic in that of Bell/Doyle posits the latter as the possible inspiration of the fictional relationship. Though this is only the most easily identifiable projection, it also establishes diametrically contrasting interpretations of Watson as an additional linkage between the first two lectures on Holmes.

These two transpositions pursue opposite trajectories as well as agendas. Instead of either making Holmes "ageless" and "unchanging" or evoking him as the solution to present-day concerns, *Dr. Bell and Mr. Doyle* capitalizes on a foregrounding of historical background material. Accentuating the social, cultural, and scientific discourses of the time, it suggests a curiously neopurist approach to notoriously distorted—because already variously transposed—literary legacies. The same attempt to recuperate long-obscured historical specificities characterizes a number of similar turns throughout the 1990s. Both *Bram Stoker's Dracula* (1992) and *Mary Shelley's Frankenstein* (1994), for example, exhibit a preoccupation with precise contextualization. In evoking the name of the source texts' authors, their full titles externalize their marketing as true, original versions of familiar and yet regularly defamiliarized narratives. In this, they seek to break through the cultural myths that are engendered by such earlier filmic representations as the Basil Rathbone interpretation of Holmes's character, or in a similar vein, James Whale's 1931 version of *Frankenstein*. That this marketing strategy can be misleading comes out very visibly in the prologue that was added to the 1992 version of *Dracula*, which equips the count with a formative love affair in the past. *Sir Arthur Conan Doyle's Sherlock Holmes* (2010), a British direct-to-DVD production directed by Rachel Lee Goldenberg, joins this growing list of seemingly "accurate" film versions of what the authors presumably intended. It was produced in the wake of (and clearly to capitalize on) the latest Hollywood blockbuster based on *Sherlock Holmes*, released in 2009, directed by Guy Ritchie and starring Robert Downey Jr. and Jude Law. Intriguingly, *Sir Arthur Conan Doyle's Sherlock Holmes* opens up with a frame story set during the Blitz in 1940, in which Dr. Watson begins to reminiscence on the past—generating in the process a nostalgic recall or intertextual bowing to the Rathbone versions. What I want to highlight here is how *Dr. Bell and Mr. Doyle* shares this seemingly recuperative driving force as well as the same interest in scientific or technological advancement in the nineteenth century.

In its concentration on the origins of Conan Doyle's work, *Dr. Bell and Mr. Doyle* simultaneously shows significant affinities with another, related development in recent transpositions: biographical back projections that play with a blurring of fact and fiction, art and life, and a resultant fictionalization of seeming historical reconstruction. Examples of this phenomenon include *Miss Potter* (2006), which uses cartoon animation to introduce the fictional characters Beatrix Potter envisions, and *Becoming Jane* (2007), which transposes a love affair from Austen's novels onto her life. Throughout the course, I continually endeavor to underline such developments to encourage a tracing of changing trends in adaptation and in the presentation of cultural figures.

Dr. Bell and Mr. Doyle is less representative of an experimental transposition than of a trend to heighten the effects of a dark Victorian underbelly in popular fictions of the last decades of the twentieth century. This "spicing up" of historical material can fruitfully help start off discussion. Set in Edinburgh in 1878, the film is "inspired," as the production notes included in the DVD pointedly put it, by "the real-life relationship between Arthur Conan Doyle (Robin Laing) and his tutor at Edinburgh University, pioneer forensic pathologist, Dr. Joseph Bell (Ian Richardson)." Further, according to the production notes, it is not only that the "historical evidence about the relationship between Doyle and Bell" is used "to construct a mystery in the best traditions of Sherlock Homes"; their pursuit of a serial killer "reveals the underbelly of Victorian society and inspires Doyle to create the most memorable detective of all time: Sherlock Holmes." To term Holmes "the most memorable detective of all time" unexpectedly echoes the timelessness that is posited for this "ageless, invincible, and unchanging" character in *Sherlock Holmes: The Voice of Terror*, yet this Holmes is, like the depiction of his creator, emphatically grounded in his time. He is not at all invincible, although desire for stability and a sense of invincibility might underpin his creation. In fact, the main detective plot not only involves an ultimately unsolved serial murder, based on the Jack the Ripper case of late-Victorian London (transposed into Edinburgh), it is also additionally spiced up by a fictitious love story. Mr. Doyle first meets Elspeth Scott when she assumes the disguise of a man in order to avoid the harassment that is often extended to women at the university. Women's education as a prominent topical issue of the day is then paired with the social hypocrisy that leaves the real cause of the illness of Elspeth's sister unpunished: she has contracted syphilis from her husband, who has picked it up from the same prostitutes among whom the serial killer begins to wreak havoc. Although her husband is not the murderer, this linkage indicates a pointed identification that indicts society at large.

The shuttling between biographical reconstruction and back projection operates on a much more intricate, intertextual level than this foregrounding of the texts' contexts might at first sight suggest. The projections of various *Sherlock Holmes* cases back onto Conan Doyle's life are not just insider jokes. Accentuating the blurring between fact and fiction from the beginning, the film opens up with a waterfall and a close-up of Holmes's trademark items (such as his hat). After a sudden cut that jumps to Conan Doyle walking towards the office of the *Strand Magazine*, newspaper criers are heard announcing Holmes's death. In the office, the camera zooms in on an illustration of Holmes and his arch-nemesis Moriarty locked in each others' arms, plunging down the waterfall. The editor places letters of complaint on top of the illustration, letters that "arrive by the sack load" to ask, "Why kill him off?" When challenged by his editor, the author enigmatically muses, "Because it was time," and this comment is followed by a cut back to the hat plunging further down the waterfall, this time with the author watching. Background violin music then introduces the main plot as an extended flashback. Young Mr. Doyle is back in the "most colorful and depraved streets" of Edinburgh, as an overvoice rather clumsily tells the viewer, and the fiddler is going to be among the serial killer's first victims. Subsequent scenes are so entirely preoccupied by the introduction of topical women's issues as to make one nearly forget that this film is going to have anything to do with the creator of Sherlock Holmes. All of the minutely detailed background, including the progress in medical science and the controversies about women being actively involved in dissecting rooms, however, also works towards the introduction of Bell, a pioneer in forensic methods, whom Doyle first considers "a bit of a performer," even a charlatan. That Bell's clinical approach to crime as a diagnosable disease corresponds to Holmes's is spelt out in one of the most extended passages projected back onto the author's life. He challenges his lecturer to prove his theory that nobody can keep "an object in daily use without leaving his personality" inscribed on it. It is the same challenge Watson poses to Holmes in *The Sign of Four*:

> "I have heard you say that it is difficult for a man to have any object in daily use without leaving the impress of his individuality upon it in such a way that a trained observer might read it. Now, I have here a watch which has recently come into my possession. Would you have the kindness to let me have an opinion upon the character or habits of the late owner?"

> I handed him over the watch with some slight feeling of amusement in my heart, for the test was, as I thought, an impossible one, and I intended it as a lesson against the somewhat dogmatic tone which he occasionally assumed. (9–10)

Despite the fact that the watch has recently been cleaned, Holmes deduces correctly that Watson has received it from his eldest brother. He adds an accurate character sketch:

> He was a man of untidy habits,—very untidy and careless. He was left with good prospects, but he threw away his chances, lived for some time in poverty with occasional short intervals of prosperity, and finally, taking to drink, he died. That is all I can gather. (10)

Understandably, Watson reacts "with considerable bitterness":

> "This is unworthy of you, Holmes," I said. "I could not have believed that you would have descended to this. You have made

> inquires into the history of my unhappy brother, and you now
> pretend to deduce this knowledge in some fanciful way. You
> cannot expect me to believe that you have read all this from
> his old watch! It is unkind, and, to speak plainly, has a touch of
> charlatanism in it." (11)

After an apology that significantly foregrounds the dangers of forgetting the "personal and painful" in considering any form of analysis "as an abstract problem" alone (11), Holmes explains his methodology: the pawnbroker as well as the owner's unsteady hands have left their marks on the watch. The entire passage is replicated in *Dr. Bell and Mr. Doyle*, or rather, it is projected back onto the author's life as if he had then later put it into his fiction. In the same manner as Holmes, Bell examines Doyle's watch and exposes the previous owner, in this case Doyle's alcoholic father. Like Watson, Doyle finds this "unworthy" of Bell, and the explanation follows the novella almost word for word. This is not the only projection of fictional passages. A number of Holmes's adventures are worked into the cases Bell and Doyle encounter. Thus, the first murder Bell solves shows striking affinities with the case of "The Speckled Band." Both involve a carefully contrived domestic murder involving a seemingly supernatural element that is then cleared up as an invisible or at least unseen agent entering from an adjacent room: in the film, it is redirected gas from a lamp; in the novella, it is an exotic snake entering through the ventilator. A tracing of similar parallelism forms a fruitful activity in class, drawing attention to different levels of intertextuality in the reworking of literary legacies.

Leading questions in the close analysis of *Dr. Bell and Mr. Doyle* (working well in the classroom as well as for the larger reassessment of Holmes's iconography to which this chapter seeks to contribute) radiate out from the ways the film functions as a multilevel projection of various aspects of Conan Doyle's fictional work. How are they used and to what effect? How is the film framed, and what is the effect of this framework? How does the love story operate as a plot catalyst? Why bring in the New Woman question? How does the film in general foreground social or cultural issues at the time, and how are these issues presented as supposedly having influenced the making of Sherlock Holmes? How does the film's approach to Arthur Conan Doyle's life, his fiction, and the cultural myth that became Sherlock Holmes retrace the classic detective story's emphasis on ratiocination to new clinical discourses at the time? How are insanity, its definition, and its diagnosis brought out? How does the film rework the Victorians' connection between insanity and criminality? How are connections between detective, narrative, and clinical (including forensic) analysis established in the original stories (e.g., *The Sign of Four*); how are they established in the film? What is the effect of bringing in Jack the Ripper? This is followed by an additional discussion of the cultural myths circulating around the Victorian serial killer, including a brief comparison with his representation in *From Hell* (2001), a Hollywood film based on the graphic novel on the Ripper by Alan Moore and Eddie Campbell (serialized between 1991 and 1996, with an appendix appearing in 1998). The latest Hollywood Sherlock Holmes film, *Sherlock Holmes* (2009), deepens this discussion through the portrayal of Holmes as a James Bond–style action hero.

But, if such changes are clearly for the sake of making Holmes "sexier"—more amenable to the action-film environment into which his unchanging popularity as an iconographical figure has been transposed—the final example of a transposed Holmes is more self-consciously engaged with the transposition process itself. "Elementary, Dear Data" shows how Holmes can be evoked in popular culture, but his reappearance within a likewise well-known science fiction series is more than just detective work in outer space. Fred and Wendy Erisman have traced what they call the "Holmesian Echoes" throughout the television series *Star Trek: The Next Generation*. What I wish to emphasize here, by contrast, is the significance of the transposition for this particular episode's thematic concerns. In an encompassing debate on rational analysis versus intuition, the television episode addresses issues of artificial intelligence through a twofold projection onto a literary character—a creation of the imagination—who has long been identified with ratiocination. In the linkage of the figure of Holmes to an android, the main theme revolves around the question of what it is that makes one human. Can an android think independently, and what does one understand by that? If this connects philosophical queries on reason as opposed to feeling, or the imagination, to the ethical dilemma of artificial intelligence, the familiar *Frankenstein* topos is simultaneously revived with a twist as artificial life gets out of control in new ways: in a doubling of two artificial creations, an android plays at being a literary figure in his leisure time, and a hologram of Holmes's arch-nemesis Moriarty becomes self-aware in the process.

Briefly, the episode is a part of the cult television series *Star Trek*, first conceived in the 1960s and then revived in numerous spin-off series and films, including *Star Trek: The Next Generation* (1987–1994). Among the crew of a spaceship in this series is an android called Data who strives to become more human, a lead character who is not surprisingly compared to Pinocchio in the pilot film. In this episode, Data plays Holmes on an interactive holodeck that serves as a regularly used (and regularly malfunctioning) recreational activity, yet he spoils the game for his human friends by having memorized all *Sherlock Holmes* adventures. He is challenged by the ship's doctor to solve an "original" Holmes adventure that is to be conceptualized by the computer. Their request for an opponent who is able to defeat Data generates a holographic recreation of Professor Moriarty that soon dangerously exceeds the initial programming. After the threat is contained, Moriarty's entity is saved in the databanks rather than deleted. The recurrent theme of the dangers of technology combines with the debated dichotomy of scientific analysis versus the powers of the imagination to connect questions of artificial intelligence both to larger philosophical problems, and at the same time, to a new engagement with the figure of Holmes.[2]

I would like to conclude with a brief description of the main assignment in the course "Film and Literature." Initially, students decided to present impromptu group classroom work based on the question of how they would transpose Sherlock Holmes into a present-day world by acting out scenes. As a fully fledged group presentation, it is now the course's main assignment. Students are required to form groups of three or four and sketch a potential transposition of a nineteenth-century text or character into a different time frame (past, present, or future) or distinct genre. They may draw on a transposed plotline or create their own. Because they can choose any text or texts, they may have recourse to the primary reading list, but they are, as always, encouraged to read more widely. Increasingly, groups have preferred producing short films or multimedia displays, but whatever their form, these performances have always been a part of a presentation that includes a critical analysis of their own transpositions as well. Whereas early ventures were often limited to a simple projection of a scene, plotline, or motif from a nineteenth-century text into a local, present-day scenario, both the choice of themes and the presentation method have become more and more complex. From transpositions of the main plotlines or retold adventures with Dr. Watson as the more astute detective or, alternatively, as a criminal figure rebelling against an overbearing Holmes, these transpositions show that students have fully engaged with the practical and theoretical difficulties of the most creative or interpretative modes of literature adaptations.

The comparison of a range of adaptations assists in a critical reviewing of literary legacies as well as of the ideological limitations of cultural mythmaking. Versions that may feel all the more dated now than even the original narratives precisely because of their emphasis on the process of updating therefore best prepare the way for a heightened alertness to any such agendas. Self-defined or frankly acknowledged propaganda pieces, such as *Sherlock Holmes: The Voice of Terror*, can be especially eye-opening in examining the appropriation of iconographic figures or recognizable, culturally marketable clichés for the war effort in films of the 1930s and 1940s. In the classroom, this deliberate defamiliarization of the concept of updating proves particularly fruitful. Students learn to see beyond the assumed dichotomies of the original text and the adaptation as well as of classic (what they perhaps consider "outdated") texts and their updates; they see the limitations of ideological mythmaking more clearly, and they are also compelled to step back and analyze later, contemporary updates from the same critical vantage point. In looking at several Sherlock Holmes adaptations, produced over half a century, they trace an iconographical figure's changing cultural significance and see how the continuous innovations that Holmes undergoes work in—and help to create—new genre experiments. Choosing such unlikely, loose adaptations helps students realize that film and television versions are never about authenticity, and it extends their understanding of the complexities and versatility of literature adaptations.

ENDNOTES

1. As Nicholas Meyer has pointedly put it, "Rathbone made an excellent Holmes, but unfortunately was paired with the worst of Watsons in Nigel Bruce. Who can for a moment believe that Bruce's dim-witted buffoon is the chronicler whose voice we hear when we read the case histories? Why does a genius hang out with an idiot? Why have the 'Rathbone' Holmes stories been removed from their proper time and place? In short, why are they so dumb?" (3).

2. This reworking of Holmes achieves additional interest in the face of a controversy it sparked off at the time. "Elementary, Dear Data" contained not just direct references to, but recycled plot elements of a number of Sherlock Holmes adventures, including "A Scandal in Bohemia" (1891), "The Red-Headed League" (1891), and "The Adventures of the Speckled Band" (1892)—stories the producers erroneously believed to be in the public domain. After the episode had been aired, the estate of Sir Arthur Conan Doyle notified Paramount Pictures about copyright issues. Partially based on a misunderstanding that involved *Young Sherlock Holmes* (1985), directed by Barry Levinson and produced by Steven Spielberg, this delayed further recourse to Holmes in subsequent episodes. The sequel, "Ship in a Bottle," was not produced until 1993, in exchange for a licensing fee. It once again presents Moriarty, the sentient hologram, attempting to take over the ship. The copyright debates give one occasion to rethink issues of intertextuality, borrowing, imitation, and also the two sides of originality, of being creative and of being true to the original text.

BIBLIOGRAPHY

Doyle, Arthur Conan. "Adventure of the Speckled Band." *The Complete Illustrated Short Stories*. London: Bounty Books, 2004. 137–156. Print.

———. *The New Annotated Sherlock Holmes*. 3 vols. Ed. Leslie S. Klinger. New York: Norton, 2005. Print.

———. *The Sign of Four*. London: Penguin, 2001. Print.

Erisman, Fred, and Wendy Erisman. "'Data! Data! Data!' Holmesian Echoes in *Star Trek: The Next Generation*." *Sherlock Holmes: Victorian Sleuth to Modern Hero*. Ed. Charles R. Putney, Joseph A. Cutshall King, and Sally Sugarman. Lanham: The Scarecrow Press, 1996. 90–101. Print.

Klinger, Leslie S. "The World of Sherlock Holmes." *The New Annotated Sherlock Holmes*. By Arthur Conan Doyle. Ed. Leslie S. Klinger. 3 vols. New York: Norton, 2005. xvii–lxvii. Print.

McFarlane, Brian. *Novel to Film: An Introduction to the Theory of Adaptation*. Oxford: Clarendon Press, 1996. Print.

Meyer, Nicholas. "Sherlock Holmes on Film: A Personal View." *Sherlock Holmes: Victorian Sleuth to Modern Hero*. Ed. Charles R. Putney, Joseph A. Cutshall King, and Sally Sugarman. Lanham and London: The Scarecrow Press, 1996. 2–14. Print.

Thomas Ronald R. *Detective Fiction and the Rise of Forensic Science*. Cambridge: Cambridge University Press, 2000. Print.

FILMOGRAPHY

Dr. Bell and Mr. Doyle: The Dark Beginnings of Sherlock Holmes. Dir. Paul Seed. Perf. Robin Laing, Ian Richardson, and Charles Dance. BBC, 2000. DVD.

"Elementary, Dear Data." *Star Trek: The Next Generation.* Season 2. Dir. Rob Bowman. Paramount Home Entertainment, 2002. DVD.

Sherlock Holmes. Dir. Guy Ritchie. Perf. Robert Downey Jr. and Jude Law. Warner Bros Pictures, 2009. Film.

Sherlock Holmes: The Voice of Terror. Dir. John Rawlins. Perf. Basil Rathbone and Nigel Bruce. Universal, 1942. Film.

Sherlock Holmes: The Definitive Collection. Optimum Releasing, 2005. DVD.

Sir Arthur Conan Doyle's Sherlock Holmes. Dir. Rachel Lee Goldenberg. Perf. Ben Syder, Gareth David-Lloyd, and Dominic Keating. The Asylum, Revolver Entertainment, 2010. DVD.

CHAPTER 11

AUSTEN'S AND MICHELL'S *PERSUASION* IN THE UNIVERSITY CLASSROOM

PEDAGOGICAL STRATEGIES

*Laura Carroll, Christopher Palmer,
Sue Thomas, and Rebecca Waese*

We shared the experience of teaching Jane Austen's *Persuasion* and Roger Michell's film adaptation of the novel in "Text, Criticism, and the Visual," a first-year undergraduate course on literature and film. The pairing of Austen and Michell, which followed pairings of more popular texts, enabled students to recognize the subtleties of the expressive and critical dimensions of cinematic adaptation. To effect that recognition, we used "triangulation" by introducing a third entity to supplement the pairing of the novel and the film, either Austen's cancelled chapter, or

Nick Dear's published screenplay of the film, to destabilize the notion that either novels or films as a broad category are fixed in their meanings or possess some sort of documentary authority. Our object was to develop critical literacies around narrative decisions, romance as a genre, and representations of gender, class, race, and empire, as well as to highlight adaptation as an act of interpretation and translation across media, which opens the primary source text and the adaptation to new readings.[1]

TEXT, CRITICISM, AND THE VISUAL

"Text, Criticism, and the Visual," a semester-long course on adaptation focused on the study of pairings of novels, plays, or historical texts with films, is offered to first-year students in the Humanities and Social Sciences Faculty at La Trobe University in Melbourne, Australia.[2] Students are invited to begin with close comparisons of scenes, sequences, and details so as to start thinking about how narrative works in written and visual forms, and what interpretive and formal decisions might be reflected in a given adaptation. Issues to do with the popular as against the canonical are highlighted, as will be seen shortly. Both students and teachers find a variety of other themes for discussion—to do, for instance, with gender or race—while continuing to examine concerns of adaptation, interpretation, and ideology.

The intention is to set a series of literary texts, the distinctive formal qualities of which can be underlined and discussed, so that the texts are not treated simply as transparent preludes to the films. In this connection, it is sometimes the students' impression that *Persuasion* is simply a realistic reflection of an early nineteenth-century society that needs refinement. The pairings of set texts, however, make it almost impossible not to think about point of view and interiority in different kinds of narrative or about matters of closure as against openness in the way endings are handled in novels, plays, and films. An approach to this latter issue is discussed later in "Uncharted Waters."

In the sequence in which set texts are studied, which begins with films that are popular and in most cases violent and sometimes controversial (the depiction of addiction in *Trainspotting*, for example, or attitudes to gender in *Blade Runner*), *Persuasion* occupies a hinge position that makes teaching both the novel and the film a challenge. For most students, the novel offers less immediate pleasures and "grabs," and the film is subtle, not expensively produced, and centers around an actress (Amanda Root) and a heroine (Anne Elliot) who make no claim to glamour. Some students remain wedded to populism and judge every film by how well it adapts the given novel to meet the perceived demands of the Hollywood popular movie, as if there were no other kinds of movies to be made. Other students welcome the shift to more contemplative material, which has usually opened an examination of the narratives of patriarchal society (e.g., *Persuasion*, *The Well*, *Washington Square*). When the shift, which hinges around *Persuasion*, is successful, then the ongoing discussion is less about the qualities of the successful movie for the presumed mass market and more about matters of historicity, a topic that is discussed later in "Reading the Complexion of a World in Transition."

INTRODUCING THIRD TEXTS

Adaptation is usually thought of as a fundamentally binary textual system, involving a book and a film pair standing in a simple and commonsensical relation of an original and a copy, a single spoke or ray in the spoke or sunburst model of intertextuality discussed by Thomas Leitch in "Jekyll, Hyde, Jekyll, Hyde, Jekyll, Hyde, Jekyll, Hyde" (p. 28). The binary model is what is advertised in the marketing of adapted movies and the books they are based on, implied by "literature and film" scholarship and pedagogy and championed by mass media and popular discourse on adaptations, all of which stress the book-film set as the basic textual unit of significance. The book and the film are yoked together in a well-worn groove that is difficult to break away from, particularly in pedagogical contexts. Observing this, yet reluctant to abandon the obviously rich field of adaptation studies, critics have suggested remedies ranging from a moratorium on comparative book/film "case studies" to the discontinuation of attention to source texts altogether. There is perhaps something slightly perverse about such proposals, seeking as they do to jump the tracks by cutting down the textual reference points from two to one. Another way of exceeding that straight and narrow conception of the original and the copy is to look at both texts by considering their relations with a third—in effect, to stabilize, divert, and redistribute the either/or, seesawing dynamic by including a third corner, producing a three-sided relational structure which is stable and balanced without being inert.

It was André Bazin who first proposed a rethinking of adaptation from linear into pyramidal form:

> All things considered, it's possible to imagine that we are moving toward a reign of the adaptation in which the notion of the unity of the work of art, if not the very notion of the author himself, will be destroyed. If the film that was made of Steinbeck's *Of Mice and Men*...had been successful (it could have been so, and far more easily than the adaptation of the same author's *Grapes of Wrath*), the (literary?) critic of the year 2050 would not find a novel out of which a play and a film had been "made," but rather a single work reflected through three art forms, an artistic pyramid with three sides, all equal in the eyes of the critic. The "work" would then be only an ideal point at the top of this figure, which itself is an ideal construct. The chronological precedence of one part over another would not be an aesthetic criterion any more than the chronological precedence of one twin over another is a genealogical one. (49)

The major obstacle that is met with in the study of literary adaptation is what might be called the illusion of inevitability. Studying literary works with film adaptations of them can exacerbate a tendency to view the source text as reified or monumental, or to fetishize period authenticity in the film. Conversely, successful and convincing adaptational gestures have the paradoxical effect of appearing to be the inevitable products of instructions gleaned from the source text, which downplays the possibility for discovering artistry in the work adaptors have done—in the selection, interpretation, commentary, and translation of adaptation. Copies create originals, and this is especially so of originals which are associated with just one highly successful film adaptation. It can be difficult for students to grasp that adaptors might have made different decisions, and that the decisions adaptors do make must be assumed to have expressive significance—we often hear or read students asserting that cuts or interpolations have "obviously" been carried out to make a film simpler and thus more commercial. What the third text does is gently complicate ideas about the naturalness of both the novel and the film as well as the simplicity and obviousness of their relationship with each other.

Persuasion is a demanding novel. Novice and confident readers alike must come to terms with Austen's realism and learn to see it as an expressive technique. Novice readers feel themselves locked out by the unfamiliar language and setting, the stream of small details, and the apparent lack of large, dramatic incidents and symbolism; they sometimes view the novel as a historical document rather than a fiction. Confident readers are drawn into the novel in an absorbingly intimate relation with character, which makes it difficult to step back and observe larger motifs and structures. Both kinds of readers have difficulty recognizing why it matters that it is his pen which Wentworth drops on overhearing Anne's conversation with Captain Harville about the storying of fidelity, and not some other piece of writing paraphernalia, as happens in the film. Similarly, they may not understand that the high incidence of spousal deaths in *Persuasion* has an expressive dimension beyond its reflection of early nineteenth-century mortality rates. The novel is neither a documentary nor a fable. Understanding its realism as artifice is a step that is necessary to readers who are invited, as they have been invited in recent years, to consider it as a war novel, an investigation of the psychology of mourning, or a romance predicated on class and gender in a state of alteration, perhaps improvement. Roger Michell's film of *Persuasion* is also vulnerable to fetishizing or ossifying reception. Film, the preeminent modernist medium, has a privileged but complicated relationship with realism. Its documentary command of the world appears to be immediate and complete: as Erwin Panofsky comments, "the medium of film is physical reality as such" (qtd. in Cavell, 16). Film opens a view onto a world which appears to be found, not made, unlike the world that is detailed in a literary work, which readers know they have played some part in fleshing out.

A third text for *Persuasion* is available in the form of the alternate ending, widely known as the "cancelled" chapters, which Austen discarded from a late draft of the novel. In this climactic passage, perfect understanding between Anne and Wentworth is reached when Wentworth enquires of Anne, ostensibly on behalf of a third party, whether she intends to marry her cousin William Elliot; her denial confirms to Wentworth that her feelings for him persist. The reconciliation of Anne and Wentworth in the cancelled passage is pleasurable for the reader, but it makes no greater contribution to the psychological scheme of the novel. The ending Austen settled upon completes the process by which the woman finds her voice and the man learns to hear it—a more satisfying conclusion in every way. Because these concluding chapters were voluntarily rejected by the novelist—and voluntarily reincorporated by the filmmaker—noticing them in the classroom is an excellent opportunity to explore the mutability of fiction and the opportunities it offers for profoundly expressive storytelling.

It is a surprise to realize how often a third text of this kind is extant in adaptation—a third text, moreover, which actively undoes what Bazin calls "the notion of the unity of the work of art" (49). Screenplays clearly come into this category, but so too do alternate cuts of movies, earlier adaptations, other texts alluded to by the book or the film, and sources used by authors of the book and the film. This undoing through attention to the "generation" of literary and film texts (Leitch, p. 44) is not a debunking activity but an animating, deepening one.

READING THE COMPLEXION OF A WORLD IN TRANSITION

The BBC "classic" brand has been characterized as engaging in "the production of a mythologized British 'history'; and 'tradition'" (Gardner and Wyver, qtd. in Kerr, 19). Raphael Samuel comments tellingly on the "fetishization of period effects" in this branding, a fetishization that is "inseparable from the claim that the film or television programme is 'intensely real'...richly detailed and authentic as possible" (409). In Michell's *Persuasion*, these effects—for some of which it won awards—include lighting and authenticity in costumes and manners.[3] Developing particular kinds of film literacies around visual signifiers of race, class, and empire in the classroom draws out fissures within *Persuasion*'s fetishizing of period effect and its creative and critical gaze at its sense of Austen's world and its pitch to different audiences.

Michell and Nick Dear read Austen's representation of naval officers as an engagement with a pivotal moment in the Long Transition, the gradual social and cultural empowerment of a middle class in Britain, which Dear characterizes as "an old order fading away into decadence, and...a meritocracy coming to the fore" (vi).[4] Philip Cohen analyses the Long Transition, brought about by the selective absorption of bourgeois values into the outlook of the aristocracy and gentry and of individuals from the middle class into the upper class, in terms of competing codes of "breeding." "There is," he writes,

> the aristocratic code, which first emerged in the late seventeenth century, linking notions of social pedigree and ancestral blood to a hierarchy of human sensibilities; and there is a bourgeois version which linked the practice of refinement to that of reason in a new way, by emphasizing hierarchies of individual achieve-ment based on inherited differences of "intelligence" or "natural aptitude." (64)

The scene at Laura Place in which Sir Walter Elliot, his daughters Elizabeth and Anne, Lady Russell, and Mrs. Clay call on Lady Dalrymple uses manners and the spatial configuration of people within the drawing room "as a metaphor for the [everyday] political inequities of a soci-ety governed by class" (Dear, vi). It suggests that the aristocratic code of breeding is ossifying into patterns of obsequious manners. Of Lady Dalrymple and Miss Carteret, the discriminating and critical Anne thinks in the novel and says to William Elliot in the film, "[N]o superiority of manner, accomplishment, or understanding" (Austen, 121; Dear, 65). Stereotypically, decadence is orientalized in the exotic room decoration and highlighted by the inertness of Lady Dalrymple flanked by black servants in a film which, Mary A. Favret nicely suggests, favors "a kind of animation that puts things in motion, releasing a restlessness, a potential for upheaval" (72). The function of the black attendants is to represent Lady Dalrymple and Miss Carteret as exemplars of extreme moribund whiteness. Their presence also reminds a modern audience that much British wealth of the period had been accumulated through the use of slave labor and that black people were "a visible minority" in Britain in the period (Innes, 11). In *White*, Richard Dyer comments on the use of images of extreme whiteness in contemporary film. He observes that the "very, very white image"—and he is not simply referring to complexion—"is functional in relation to the ordinary, is even perhaps a condition of establishing whiteness as ordinary.... An image of what whites are like is set up, but can also be held at a distance" (222–223). In his argument, that distance establishes "a space of ordinariness," a "position" that can claim "to speak for and embody the commonality of humanity" (222–223).

Sir Walter Elliot's suppositions about the complexions of navy men—that they are the color of "mahogany" (Austen, 22; Dear, 4) or a "macaroon" (Dear, 6), "as orange as the cuffs and capes of my livery" (Austen, 24)—position him in a place of extreme whiteness. The position makes ordinary the comparative ruddiness of the characters who work for a living. The extremity of Sir Walter's whiteness is played out satirically in scenes at his dining table, with, for example, the eating of sorbet from an ice-carved swan, his looking at his reflection in a knife, and the fantastic pineapple centerpiece that is circled by the camera. The pineapples are a visual reminder of Britain's place as a center of imperial trade, its trade routes being protected by the navy.

The filmmakers are savvy in their referencing of cultural theory to introduce the new; indeed, the referencing plays to academically trained viewers, a niche audience for adaptations of classic texts. Anne and Wentworth's kiss, for instance, is authorized with visual reference to

Bakhtinian theory of carnival in a manner that self-consciously ironizes this and subsequent clichés of the happy, romantic ending. The passing carnival performers are a stark contrast to the street scene in Austen's novel, with its "sauntering politicians, bustling house-keepers, flirting girls, and…nursery maids and children" (194). The satirical use of the black servants is authorized by David Dabydeen's *Hogarth's Blacks: Images of Blacks in Eighteenth Century English Art* (1987). The black servants are faceless, and perhaps deliberately so, as a sign of their relegation as "mute background figure[s]" (Dabydeen, 21), symbols of an "artificial elegance" (Dabydeen, 114). Dyer explains in *White*:

> The photographic media and *a fortiori*, movie lighting assume, privilege and construct whiteness. The apparatus was developed with white people in mind and habitual use and instruction continue in the same vein, so much so that photographing non-white people is typically constructed as a problem…. Malkiewicz (1986: 53) states that "a Caucasian face has about 35 percent reflectance but a black face reflects less than 16 percent." This creates problems if shooting very light and very dark people in the same frame. (Dyer, 89)

Michell makes telling use of visual echo. The pale, artificial whiteness of Lady Dalrymple and Miss Carteret is linked visually to the gloves, stockings, and cravats of the black servants. In a circling camera movement in the filming of a scene at Camden Place, Sir Walter's elegantly posed, white-stockinged legs are echoed in the white-stockinged legs and gloves of the silent white servants. The "mobile, circling camera," Sidney Gottlieb suggests, is often employed for purposes of "social analysis and critique" by Michell (108). The referencing of black servants to white through visual echo invites reflection on freedom, constraint, discipline, and the terms of fidelity—themes that are also taken up in the main romantic plot.

The way in which the film *Persuasion* draws out the contrast between the world of naval officers and the embarrassed baronetcy is a staple of critical work on the film; here, we draw out further examples in which extreme whiteness is a film currency. As the Elliots prepare to leave

Kellynch Hall, servants place white sheets over the furniture. As John Wiltshire points out, this "shroud[ing] in white" is not warranted by the arrival of the Crofts, who "are to have the freedom of the house they have rented," and hence, it functions as a sign of "the end of an era" (94). The desired visual effect is spelled out in the screenplay: "*The linen billows around ANNE. It's a sad picture, as if the deceased house is being wrapped in a shroud. On and on it goes: an ocean of white linen*" (10–11). The scene, in which extreme whiteness represents the material implications of Sir Walter's self-indulgence, echoes the translucent animated seascape that opens the film. Richard Dyer observes that "[t]he photographic media hold together translucence and materiality. This provides them with an extraordinary supple and subtle mode of representation.… [Translucence] allows the spiritual to be manifest in the material" (115–116). Dyer highlights the way in which translucent light is a filmic register of the ideal. The seascape is a sign of "the animation that puts things in motion," the naval officers being idealized symbols of an emerging meritocracy. As Dyer points out, a stock use of translucence is the film "glow" (122) of the white female romantic lead (122–142). The language associated with Anne's regaining of her bloom in the screenplay is glow and radiance.[5] The turning point in Anne's recovery of bloom in the film is a scene on the Cobb at Lyme; the light in the scene is relatively translucent, an effect of the refraction of light from the sea.

UNCHARTED WATERS: INTERPRETING THE MOTIF OF THE SHIP AND THE SEA

Beginnings and endings can be useful tools when studying novel-to-film adaptations in classroom situations because key motifs and images are established early and reaffirmed at the end. Michell and Dear's emphasis on the motif of the ship and the sea in their film *Persuasion* highlights fluid and transformative values that contrast with the more staid and entrenched attitudes represented by the characters who live in grand estates. Michell and Dear invoke symbols of ships and incorporate the unfixed motion of the sea in film techniques to further unsettle the grounded tradition of landed gentry in Austen's text.

In "Romancing the Ending: Adaptations in Nineteenth-Century Closure," Maryanne C. Ward observes that many of the admirable characters of nineteenth-century fiction "find themselves at the end of their adventures removed from the world of the novel into tiny enclaves" (18). Some enclaves are moral centers or places of retreat from an inveterate society that cannot be reformed in a tidy ending (Ward, 18). Enclaves provide solace and comfort and come to replace the conventional grand estates that are featured in some nineteenth-century novels. Ward rightly argues that the estates featured in Jane Austen's later novels do not reflect the values of the protagonists and can "no longer be either the moral center of the community or an enclave for the worthy characters in the novel" (21). Michell and Dear's *Persuasion* introduces new enclaves through fluid filming techniques and images of ships and the sea to mark a shift in values where the principal characters are released from the confines of grand estates and set adrift in a new and uncharted world.

Austen's novel opens in Kellynch Hall as Sir Walter Elliot rereads the Baronetage, his prized book listing the history and lineage of his class, which symbolizes tradition, authority, and male privilege. In contrast, the film begins underwater, looking at the underbelly of a ship that is the "estate" where Anne Elliot and Captain Wentworth will live together at the film's end.

An awareness of politics and war comes sooner and more overtly in the film than it does in the novel. Admiral Croft, in an opening scene that does not exist in the novel, talks about the war with his crew, and he does so once again in the party scene at the film's end. In the novel, the first mention of the outside world comes at the beginning of the third chapter after a lengthy exposition on the Elliot family and the dire financial state of Kellynch Hall.

Throughout the film, symbols of letters and books are transformed into images that signify the sea. Anne discovers an old, treasured love letter from Wentworth that is folded into a ship. In another scene, the symbol of textual tradition is set afloat when Admiral Croft makes for

Mary's young sons a paper boat that they sail in the stream. Subtly, these images begin to unsettle and displace the values of a traditional estate and anticipate the film's final image of a "house" on the sea that is free from the conventions of patriarchal lineage, tradition, and corrupted values.

Through a series of close-ups, Michell portrays private enclaves between characters. These shots detract attention from the physical surroundings of the grand estates and suggest instead deterritorialized and intimate retreats. When Anne quotes poetry to Captain Benwick, and he to Anne, there is a close-up on the speaker and the back of the other's head, followed by a reverse shot of the same. The speakers are ensconced in their own poetic enclave. Another moment of privacy and retreat from society occurs in the scene where Anne reads Wentworth's letter. The camera pulls in from a close-up on Anne to an extreme close-up as Anne becomes immersed in Wentworth's words. There is a merging of minds and hearts as Wentworth and Anne's voice-overs alternate, softly and loudly, and join in chorus. The moment is enhanced by the movement of the camera, which gives the impression of being unfixed and fluid. In "*Persuasion* and Cinematic Approaches to Jane Austen," Sidney Gottlieb suggests that the "constantly moving camera" in the film "asserts a fundamental instability" and "fluidity in a literal and metaphorical sense: as water is a key element and symbol in both the novel and film" (107). The camera's mobility contrasts with the rigidity of the traditional values exhibited by characters who are preoccupied with land.

The film depicts another personal enclave in the reunion scene, which is set, fittingly, in Union Street, where Anne and Wentworth appear alone together amidst a large crowd of circus performers, fire-eaters, gymnasts, children, dancers, and musicians. The tight focus assures viewers that nothing will penetrate the couple's solitary world, and the scene is appropriately shot outdoors, far from Camden Place, Uppercross, and Kellynch Hall.

The novel's ending leaves readers unsure as to where Anne and Wentworth will reside. Volume 2, chapter 12 opens somewhat hurriedly with Austen's ironic question, "[W]ho can be in doubt of what followed?"

(Austen, 199)—yet the novel leaves the details of the couple's future unexplored. The last chapter is not set in a specific location; the narrator speculates from an omnipotent and displaced perspective. Readers know the married couple will not live in Kellynch Hall and that the young Mr. Elliot will inherit. Though Wentworth has money, he has no estate. Are the lovers destined to remain apart indefinitely while Wentworth is at sea? In "The Radical Pessimism of *Persuasion*," Julia Prewitt Brown writes, "*Persuasion* is the only one of the novels that ends with a vague ignorance of where the hero and heroine are going to live, and even of what the years ahead will bring for them" (127). She notes, "For the first time in Jane Austen, the future is not linked to the land" (146).

In the final scene of the film, Anne appears to be at home writing to her husband at sea, but as the camera pans out and upwards, one sees the mast, crew, open seas, and Wentworth. Anne is at sea with her husband; the newly wed Wentworths emulate the older Crofts, the moral compass and ideal couple of the story, who sailed together in their day. The Crofts are depicted to be as flexible as Sir Walter is entrenched, and they are more progressive and fluid in their ideas and behaviors than Sir Walter and most of the other characters are. In both the novel and the film, Mrs. Croft says, "We none of us expect to be in smooth waters all our days" (Austen, 60; Dear, 33), and Michell and Dear's film portrays Anne taking up Mrs. Croft's challenge as she and Wentworth sail off into the glorious sunset.

Through the motif of the ship and the sea, the film presents a regenerative vision of a couple who are not heavily embedded in tradition and places little emphasis on land and property. Perhaps the image of sailing off into the sunset is as recognizable an ironic signal of love today as Austen's customary and curt closure of marriage in her later novels was to her nineteenth-century audience. Despite its saccharine resonance, the iconic image establishes a sense of "happily (enough) ever after" for contemporary film audiences.

In her primer *Adaptation and Appropriation*, Julie Sanders comments that "it is usually at the very point of infidelity that the most creative acts of adaptation and appropriation take place" (20). When teaching

Austen's *Persuasion* and the film of the novel directed by Michell, we highlight both overt and subtle points of creative fidelity and infidelity to open out critical engagement with the generation of both texts. Reading critically across three texts allows students to undo "simple" correlations of a text with history or a text with a story, and to grasp the shaping presences of artistic intention in densely realistic fictions. The material Jane Austen excised from *Persuasion* acutely underlines the provisional and nominal nature, not just of the decisions involved in adaptation, but in the making of all works of fiction. Michell's fetishizing of period effects produces an aura of faithfulness, and both the director and the screenwriter work to honor their sense of Austen's narrative interest in "a world in transition,…an organically evolving society…an undertow of political reality" (Dear, vi). Working to develop film literacies around representations of race, class, and empire authorizes students to critique heritage branding, to look past the fetishizing of period effects to the creative and critical edge of the adaptation's engagement with the original and the artifice and artfulness of the adaptation as a film and the original as literature. Highlighting the treatment of enclaves in the texts also draws attention to the expressive and critical reach of the film's *mise en scène* and camera technique. The passages of the characters from Kellynch Hall to Lyme and Bath mark a changing of the guard and of values as well as houses. Ships and the changeable and invigorating sea air in the novel and film play roles in creating a freer and more open ending in opposition to a more rigid and traditional closure. When multiple versions of *Persuasion* offer alternate and compelling futures, Austen's provocative question in the last chapter, "[W]ho can be in doubt of what followed?" invites not closure, but worlds of possibility.

ENDNOTES

1. The authors have each had primary responsibility for a section of the chapter, Christopher Palmer for "Text, Criticism, and the Visual," Laura Carroll for "Introducing Third Texts," Sue Thomas for "Reading the Complexion of a World in Transition," and Rebecca Waese for "Uncharted Waters: Interpreting the Motif of the Ship and the Sea."

2. The films selected for study in "Text, Criticism, and the Visual" are all contemporary, though *Blade Runner* (for instance) appeared first in 1982, before most of the students were born; they are not all multiplex films, however, and the syllabus has included subtitled films such as Oliver Hirschbiegel's *Downfall* and Claire Denis's *Beau Travail*. The syllabus usually begins with popular films of relatively popular novels (*Trainspotting*; *Do Androids Dream of Electric Sheep?*/*Blade Runner*; *Rum Punch*/*Jackie Brown*), then moves to canonical or high literary texts and their film adaptations (*Persuasion*; *Washington Square* with the film by Agnieszka Holland; Elizabeth Jolley's *The Well* with the film by Samantha Lang; "Billy Budd" with *Beau Travail*), and finishes with a play by Shakespeare (*Romeo and Juliet* with Baz Luhrmann's film; *Richard III* with Richard Loncraine's film; or *Hamlet* with Franco Zeffirelli's film).

3. Among the BAFTA awards won by the film in 1996 are Best Costume Design, Best Design, and Best Photography and Lighting.

4. The phrase "a world in transition" in the heading of this section is also from Dear's introduction to the screenplay (vi).

5. Dear writes in the directions of the scene on the Cobb in which William Elliot admires Anne, "*She glows*" (49). In the scene at the card party, he directs, "ANNE *looks radiant as she moves confidently through the room*" (90).

Bibliography

Austen, Jane. *Persuasion*. Ed. James Kinsley. Oxford World's Classics. Oxford: Oxford University Press, 2004. Print.

Bazin, André. "Adaptation, Or the Cinema as Digest." 1948. Trans. Alain Piette and Bert Cardullo. *Bazin at Work: Major Essays and Reviews from the Forties and Fifties*. Ed. Bert Cardullo. New York: Routledge, 1997. 41–52. Print.

Brown, Julia Prewitt. "The Radical Pessimism of *Persuasion*." *Mansfield Park and Persuasion*. Ed. Judy Simons. New York: St. Martin's, 1997. 124–136. Print.

Cavell, Stanley. *The World Viewed: Reflections on the Ontology of Film*. Enlarged ed. Cambridge: Harvard University Press, 1979. Print.

Cohen, Philip. "The Perversions of Inheritance: Studies in the Making of Multi-Racist Britain." *Multi-Racist Britain*. Ed. Philip Cohen and Harwant S. Bains. Houndmills: Macmillan Education, 1988. 9–118. Print.

Dabydeen, David. *Hogarth's Blacks: Images of Blacks in Eighteenth Century English Art*. Manchester: Manchester University Press, 1987. Print.

Dear, Nick. *Persuasion by Jane Austen: A Screenplay*. London: Methuen Film, 1996. Print.

Dyer, Richard. *White: Essays on Race and Culture*. London: Routledge, 1997. Print.

Favret, Mary A. "Being True to Jane Austen." *Victorian Afterlife: Postmodern Culture Rewrites the Nineteenth Century*. Ed. John Kucich and Dianne F. Sadoff. Minneapolis: University of Minnesota Press, 2000. Print.

Gottlieb, Sidney. "*Persuasion* and Cinematic Approaches to Jane Austen." *Literature/Film Quarterly* 30.2 (2002): 104–110. Print.

Innes, C. L. *A History of Black and Asian Writing in Britain, 1700–2000.* Cambridge: Cambridge University Press, 2002. Print.

Kerr, Paul. "Classic Serials—To Be Continued." *Screen* 23.1 (1982): 6–19. Print.

Samuel, Raphael. *Theatres of Memory. Volume 1: Past and Present in Contemporary Culture.* London: Verso, 1994. Print.

Sanders, Julie. *Adaptation and Appropriation.* London: Routledge, 2006. Print.

Ward, Maryanne C. "Romancing the Ending: Adaptations in Nineteenth-Century Closure." *Journal of the Midwest Modern Language Association* 29.1 (Spring 1996): 15–31. Print.

Wiltshire, John. *Recreating Jane Austen.* Cambridge: Cambridge University Press, 2001. Print.

FILMOGRAPHY

Persuasion. Dir. Roger Michell. Perf. Amanda Root and Ciaran Hinds. BBC Films WGBH/Mobil Masterpiece Theatre Millesime Productions, 1995. DVD.

A BIBLIOGRAPHY OF ADAPTATION AND FILM STUDY

Abigail Burnham Bloom, Thomas Leitch,
and Mary Sanders Pollock

BIBLIOGRAPHY

Albrecht-Crane, Christa, and Dennis Cutchins, eds. *Adaptation Studies: New Approaches*. Madison: Fairleigh Dickinson University Press, 2010. Print.

Altman, Rick. "Dickens, Griffith, and Film Theory Today." *South Atlantic Quarterly* 88 (1989): 321–359. Print.

Andrew, Dudley. "Adaptation." *Concepts in Film Theory*. New York: Oxford University Press, 1984. 96–106. Print.

Aragay, Mireia, ed. *Books in Motion: Adaptation, Intertextuality, Authorship*. Amsterdam: Rodopi, 2005. Print.

Balfour, Ian. "Adapting to the Image and Resisting It: On Filming Literature and a Possible World for Literary Studies." *PMLA* 125 (2010): 968–976. Print.

Bluestone, George. *Novels into Film: The Metamorphosis of Fiction into Cinema*. Baltimore: Johns Hopkins Press, 2003. Print.

Bortolotti, Gary R., and Linda Hutcheon. "On the Origin of Adaptations: Rethinking Fidelity Discourse and 'Success'—Biologically." *New Literary History* 38 (2007): 443–458. Print.

Boyum, Joy Gould. *Double Exposure: Fiction into Film*. New York: Universe Books, 1985. Print.

Cahir, Linda Costanzo. *Literature into Film: Theory and Practical Approaches*. Jefferson: McFarland, 2006. Print.

Cardwell, Sarah. *Adaptation Revisited: Television and the Classic Novel*. Manchester: Manchester University Press, 2002. Print.

Carroll, Rachel, ed. *Adaptation in Contemporary Culture: Textual Infidelities*. London: Continuum, 2009. Print.

Cartmell, Deborah, and Imelda Whelehan, eds. *Adaptations: From Text to Screen, Screen to Text*. London: Routledge, 1999. Print.

246 VICTORIAN LITERATURE AND FILM ADAPTATION

———. *The Cambridge Companion to Literature on Screen*. Cambridge: Cambridge University Press, 2007. Print.

Chanon, Michael. "The Emergence of an Industry." *British Cinema History*. Ed. James Curran and Vincent Porter. Totowa: Barnes & Noble Books, 1983. 39–58. Print.

Cohen, Keith. *Film and Fiction: The Dynamics of Exchange*. New Haven: Yale University Press, 1979. Print.

Conger, Syndy, and Janice Welsch, eds. *Narrative Strategies: Original Essays in Film and Prose Fiction*. McComb: Western Illinois University, 1980. Print.

Corrigan, Timothy. *Film and Literature: An Introduction and Reader*. New Jersey: Prentice Hall, 1999. Print.

Cutchins, Dennis, Laurence Raw, and James M. Welsh, eds. *The Pedagogy of Adaptation*. Lanham: Scarecrow Press, 2010. Print.

———. *Redefining Adaptation Studies*. Lanham: Scarecrow Press, 2010. Print.

DeBona, Guerric. *Film Adaptation in the Hollywood Studio Era*. Urbana: University of Illinois Press, 2010. Print.

Desmond, John M., and Peter Hawkes. *Studying Film and Literature*. Boston: McGraw Hill, 2006. Print.

Eisenstein, Sergei. "Dickens, Griffith, and the Film Today." *Film Form: Essays in Film Theory*. Ed. and trans. Jay Leyda. New York: Harcourt Brace & World, 1949. 195–255. Print.

Elliott, Kamilla. *Rethinking the Novel/Film Debate*. Cambridge: Cambridge University Press, 2003. Print.

Genette, Gérard. *Palimpsests: Literature in the Second Degree*. Trans. Channa Newman and Claude Doubinsky. Lincoln: University of Nebraska Press, 1997. Print.

Geraghty, Christine. *Now a Major Motion Picture: Film Adaptations of Literature and Drama*. Lanham: Rowman & Littlefield Publishers, 2008. Print.

Giddings, Robert, and Erica Sheen, eds. *The Classic Novel from Page to Screen*. Manchester: Manchester University Press, 2000. Print.

Giddings, Robert, Keith Selby, and Chris Wensley. *Screening the Novel: The Theory and Practice of Literary Dramatization*. New York: St. Martin's, 1990. Print.

Griffith, James. *Adaptations as Imitations: Films from Novels*. Newark: University of Delaware Press, 1997. Print.

Hutcheon, Linda. "In Defence of Literary Adaptation as Cultural Production." *M/C Journal* 10.2 (2007): n. pag. Web. 21 Dec. 2010. <http://journal.media-culture.org.au/0705/01-hutcheon.php>.

———. *A Theory of Adaptation*. New York: Routledge/Taylor & Francis Group, 2006. Print.

Jeffers, Jennifer M. *Britain Colonized: Hollywood's Appropriation of British Literature*. New York: Palgrave Macmillan, 2006. Print.

Klein, Michael, and Gillian Parker, eds. *The English Novel and the Movies*. New York: Ungar, 1981. Print.

Kranz, David L., and Nancy C. Mellerski, eds. *In/Fidelity: Essays on Film Adaptation*. Newcastle: Cambridge Scholars Publishing, 2008. Print.

Kucich, John, and Dianne F. Sadoff, eds. *Victorian Afterlife: Postmodern Culture Rewrites the Nineteenth Century*. Minneapolis: University of Minnesota Press, 2000. Print.

Leitch, Thomas. "Adaptation Theory at a Crossroads." *Adaptation* 1 (2008): 63–77. Print.

———. *Film Adaptation and Its Discontents: From Gone with the Wind to The Passion of the Christ*. Baltimore: Johns Hopkins University Press, 2007. Print.

———. "Twelve Fallacies in Contemporary Adaptation Theory." *Criticism* 45 (Spring 2003): 149–171. Print.

Lothe, Jakob. *Narrative in Fiction and Film: An Introduction*. New York: Oxford University Press, 2000. Print.

Lupack, Barbara Tepa. *Nineteenth-Century Women at the Movies: Adapting Classic Women's Fiction to Film*. Bowling Green: Bowling Green State University Popular Press, 1999. Print.

McDougal, Stuart Y. *Made into Movies: From Literature to Film*. New York: HBJ, 1985. Print.

McFarlane, Brian. *Novel to Film: An Introduction to the Theory of Adaptation*. Oxford: Clarendon Press, 1996. Print.

Murray, Simone. "Materializing Adaptation Theory: The Adaptation Industry." *Literature/Film Quarterly* 36 (2008): 4–20. Print.

Naremore, James, ed. *Film Adaptation*. New Brunswick: Rutgers University Press, 2000. Print.

Raw, Laurence. "Towards a Pedagogy for Teaching Adaptations." *Journal of Adaptation in Film and Performance* 2 (2009): 223–237. Print.

Reynolds, Peter, ed. *Novel Images: Literature in Performance*. London and New York: Routledge, 1993. 49–63. Print.

Richardson, Robert. *Literature and Film*. Bloomington: Indiana University Press, 1969. Print.

Sanders, Julie. *Adaptation and Appropriation*. New York: Routledge/Taylor & Francis Group, 2006. Print.

Sinyard, Neil. *Filming Literature: The Art of Screen Adaptation*. New York: St. Martin's, 1986. Print.

Stam, Robert. *Literature through Film: Realism, Magic, and the Art of Adaptation*. Malden: Blackwell, 2005. Print.

Stam, Robert, and Alessandra Raengo, eds. *A Companion to Literature and Film*. Malden: Blackwell, 2004. Print.

———. *Literature and Film: A Guide to the Theory and Practice of Film Adaptation*. Malden: Blackwell, 2005. Print.

Stewart, Garrett. "Film's Victorian Retrofit." *Victorian Studies* 38 (Winter 1995): 153–198. Print.

Vincendeau, Ginette, ed. *Film/Literature/Heritage: A Sight and Sound Reader*. London: British Film Institute, 2001. Print.

Welsh, James M., and Peter Lev, eds. *The Literature/Film Reader: Issues of Adaptation*. Lanham: Scarecrow Press, 2007. Print.

FILM STUDY

Bazin, André. *What is Cinema?* Berkeley, University of California Press, 1971. Print.

Braudy, Leo, and Marshall Cohen, eds. *Film Theory and Criticism: Introductory Readings*. 7th ed. New York: Oxford University Press, 2009. Print.

British Film Institute. "Teaching Film and Media Studies." Web. 10 July 2010. <www.bfi.org.uk/education/teaching/tfms>.

Chatman, Seymour. *Coming to Terms: The Rhetoric of Narrative in Fiction and Film*. Ithaca: Cornell University Press, 1990. Print.

Craddock, Jim, ed. *VideoHound's Golden Movie Retriever 2010*. New York: Gale, 2010. Print. [Editors' note: The encyclopedic (around 2,000-page) *VideoHound* is updated annually.]

Dudley, Andrew. *What Cinema Is!* Malden: Wiley-Blackwell, 2010. Print.

Giannetti, Louis. *Understanding Movies*. 12th ed. Needham Heights: Allyn & Bacon, 2010. Print.

Internet Movie Database. Web. 10 July 2010. <www.imdb.com>.

Katz, Ephraim. *The Film Encyclopedia: The Complete Guide to Film and the Film Industry*. 6th ed. New York: HarperCollins, 2008. Print.

Kracauer, Siegfried. *Theory of Film: The Redemption of Physical Reality*. Princeton: Princeton University Press, 1997. Print.

Library of Congress. National Film Preservation Board. Web. 10 July 2010. <www.loc.gov/film>.

Metz, Christian. *Film Language: A Semiotics of the Cinema*. Chicago: University of Chicago, 1991. Print.

Monaco, James. *How to Read a Film*. 30th anniversary ed. New York: Oxford University Press, 2009. Print.

Villarejo, Amy. *Film Studies: The Basics*. London: Routledge, 2007. Print.

Wollen, Peter. *Signs and Meaning in the Cinema*. 4th ed. London: bfi, 1998. Print.

INDEX

ABOUT THE CONTRIBUTORS

Laura Carroll lectures in the English program at La Trobe University, Melbourne. Her main research project investigates ways that films adapted from novels accommodate and reconcile readers' competing experiences of the source works. Her other research interests include the afterlife of Jane Austen and post-Romantic fiction about animals. She has published essays on Austen adaptations, James Thurber, Shakespearean tragedy, and Australian cinema.

Michael Eberle-Sinatra is an associate professor of English at the Université de Montréal. Prior to this appointment, he served as a research associate at the Northrop Frye Centre, University of Toronto. He holds a DPhil at Oxford. Dr. Eberle-Sinatra is the author of *Leigh Hunt and London Literary Scene*, the founding editor of *Romanticism on the Net*, and the editor of *Mary Shelley's Fictions: From Frankenstein to Faulkner*. He is working on a project titled *Queering Adaptations of Nineteenth-Century Novels*.

Sarah J. Heidt is an associate professor of English at Kenyon College, where she teaches nineteenth-century British literature and culture, life-writing and autobiography, and film. She is working on two book projects, *Composite Beings: Writing Victorian Lives* and *Reel Lives: Autobiography and Memoir on Screen*. She has published articles on Thomas and Jane Carlyle, John Addington Symonds, and the written and filmed versions of *The Diving Bell and the Butterfly*.

Jean-Marie Lecomte is an associate professor at the University of Nancy, France. He specializes in the study of filmic speech and audio-visual semiotics. He has published essays on King Vidor's cinema, the birth of the talking film, women's speech in early movies, and discourse in horror movies. His research centers on the interaction between verbal language and film language in silent and early talking movies. He is working on a collection of essays on King Vidor.

Thomas Leitch is professor of English and director of film studies at the University of Delaware. His most recent books include *Film Adaptation and Its Discontents: From Gone with the Wind to The Passion of the Christ and A Companion to Alfred Hitchcock,* coedited with Leland Poague.

Louise McDonald is a senior lecturer in English and film studies at Newman University College in the West Midlands. Her teaching and research areas include American literature as well as Victorian and early twentieth-century literature, and she also leads courses in film theory and adaptation studies. She is researching the interwar work of English novelist, playwright, and screenwriter, Clemence Dane.

Ellen Moody teaches at George Mason University. Dr. Moody has produced etext editions of works by Isabelle de Montolieu and Sophie Cottin. In addition to her book, *Trollope on the 'Net* (1999), which combines research with her experiences leading discussions about Trollope in a listserv community, she also created a website dedicated to Austen and Trollope and is working a book project that focuses on film adaptations of Austen.

Gene M. Moore is a comparatist by training and teaches English and American literature at the Universiteit van Amsterdam. His publications as author or editor include *Proust and Musil: The Novel as Research Instrument, Conrad's Cities, Conrad on Film, The Oxford Reader's Companion to Conrad, Faulkner's Indians*, and a casebook on Conrad's *Heart of Darkness*. He coedited the final two volumes of *The Collected Letters of Joseph Conrad*, and his edition of Conrad's last novel, *Suspense*, appeared in 2011.

Natalie Neill teaches in the English department at York University. Her teaching and research areas include Romantic and Victorian literature, the gothic, and film adaptation. Neill has published on Jane Austen's *Northanger Abbey*, among other topics, and is editor of *Love and Horror*, a rare 1812 gothic parody. In addition to a second edition, she is working on William Harrison Ainsworth's *Rookwood*.

Christopher Palmer has taught English literature and served as head of the English department at La Trobe University in Melbourne since 1977, with exchanges at Warwick University and the State University of California at Chico. He has published on Shakespeare, Umberto Eco, the practice of adaptation, and science fiction.

Sue Thomas is a professor of English at La Trobe University, Melbourne. She is the author of *The Worlding of Jean Rhys* and *Imperialism, Reform and the Making of Englishness in Jane Eyre*, co-author with Ann Blake and Leela Gandhi of *England through Colonial Eyes in Twentieth-Century Fiction*, and compiler of *Elizabeth Robins (1862-1952): A Bibliography*. She has published extensively on nineteenth- and twentieth-century women writers, decolonizing literatures, and nineteenth-century periodicals.

Rebecca Waese is an honorary associate, lecturer and tutor at La Trobe University in Melbourne and has instructed drama to young people at The National Drama School in St. Kilda. She holds a PhD from York University. Dr. Waese has also lectured at the University of Toronto and York University, and she has published on Allison Muri.

Tamara S. Wagner is associate professor at Nanyang Technological University in Singapore and obtained her PhD from Cambridge University. Her books include *Financial Speculation in Victorian Fiction, Longing: Narratives of Nostalgia in the British Novel, 1740–1890*, and *Occidentalism in Novels of Malaysia and Singapore, 1819–2004*, as well as edited collections on *Consuming Culture in the Long Nineteenth-Century, Antifeminism and the Victorian Novel: Rereading Nineteenth-Century Women Writers*, and *Victorian Settler Narratives: Emigrants, Cosmopolitans and Returnees in Nineteenth-Century Literature*.

Lightning Source UK Ltd.
Milton Keynes UK
UKOW04n0608221115

263265UK00003B/9/P